AF328717

innovation-ish

innovation-ish

RICH BRADEN · TESSA FORSHAW

How Anyone Can
Create Breakthrough Solutions
to Real Problems in the Real World

WILEY

Library of Congress Cataloging-in-Publication Data is Available:

ISBN 9781394318902 (Cloth)
ISBN 9781394318940 (ePub)
ISBN 9781394318957 (ePDF)

Cover Design: Wiley
Cover Image: Design by Andrew Merit.
© People Rocket
Author Photos: Courtesy of Tessa Forshaw, Courtesy of Richard Braden

Printed and bound by CPI Group (UK) Ltd, Croydon, CR0 4YY

C9781394318902_150725

To the many students and clients who have shared their stories, curiosity, and generosity in shaping Innovation-ish and our own practices. Your wisdom fills these pages. Your willingness to challenge innovation hesitation and dive in by taking small steps and learning along the way has shown us what it means to be truly Innovation-ish.

Contents

Contents

Contents

Contents

This is nothing like other books and methodologies you might find on innovation. You know, the ones that spell out a checklist for innovation.

Except the steps don't stick and frequently lack resilience against existing corporate cultures, at least from what we've experienced from speaking with thousands of people over the years teaching creative problem-solving at the Stanford University d.school and Graduate School of Business, Harvard University Innovation Labs, the Harvard Division of Continuing Education, the London Business School, Aalto University, and in innovation consulting at People Rocket.

Far too many of these talented people, each with unique backgrounds, believed that they couldn't innovate. Hearing their stories, we started to see why they believed it. They shared an unattainable view of what innovation was and who innovators were. Then we watched these same people show creative skills and create truly innovative solutions.

We could see that the problem wasn't the people. It was innovation itself.

The solution was to make innovation more accessible. More approachable. More, well Innovation-*ish*.

So, we decided to look at creative problem-solving and innovation through a new lens and focused on the underlying cognitive science that explains *why* certain methods work and why others fail to stick. Understanding how our brains function makes it easier to recognize what helps us move forward.

Creative problem-solving methods, like Innovation, Design Thinking, Human-Centered Design, and others, aren't exclusive mystical processes reserved for a select few that require innate talents. They're messy, evolving, and accessible to anyone willing to engage with curiosity and adaptability.

To illustrate these principles, we share real-world stories from organizations small and large. One example comes from Dermalogica, a premium skincare company whose CEO, Aurelian Lis, believes that Innovation-ish must be embedded in every function and department.

In the 1980s, Dermalogica's founder, Jane Wurwand, set an explicit cultural norm and rule that the company would focus on skincare products, and would not make hardware devices. When Aurelian Lis took over as CEO, he had been continuing to uphold the rule. Until something innovative-ish changed his mind.

Aurelian believes that everyone in the business needs to be able to engage in innovation, and has himself taught many employees what it means to prototype and gather data to inform product decisions. A team within the company took this learning on board, and prototyped handheld appliances to skincare spas. The results were so convincing that Dermalogica pivoted its position, opening new markets in small beauty appliances, despite the 30 year old rule.

Another example comes from the Native American Community Clinic in Minnesota that was providing healthcare support to an encampment of nearly 500 housing-insecure people. Their initial approach to supporting this community was to add more staff, mobile clinics, and a shuttle service to their main clinic. However, these actions failed to address the underlying issue.

Using Innovation-ish mindsets they reframed the problem to see what the real problem was; they realized that the root cause was housing. Instead of simply treating the symptoms of homelessness, they designed a new facility with on-site housing, a far more effective solution to the health crisis.

Both stories show how small shifts can lead to bigger outcomes. Dermalogica challenged an old rule and opened a new market. The clinic stopped treating symptoms and addressed the real problem.

Neither needed a formal process or outside experts. Innovations came from real people inside the system willing to test, adapt, and act. That's Innovation-ish.

How to Use This Book

As you read this book, it will be like you're right there in one of our Innovation-ish workshops. We wrote this book in the same way we teach Innovation-ish in a classroom. We use plain language to present concepts, share research, and tell stories to make the information accessible to everyone.

We provide exercises designed to build your understanding step by step, so we encourage you to pause and try them as you go along. After all, the journey is usually more interesting than the destination! Whenever a concept or story resonates with a challenge you're facing, we invite you to pause to apply it to your situation and experiment in real-time.

We draw on each of our unique backgrounds and expertise to bring this to life for you. This book is a practical guide to building your own Innovation-ish practice paired with an immense amount of academic research by leading cognitive scientists, psychologists, organizational behaviorists, and neuroscientists into practical insights.

We also reference sources of our research and stories in the Endnotes section broken up by chapter. More detailed information can also be found on our website, www.innovationish.com.

What You'll Learn

This book unfolds in clear, manageable stages:

Part I explores the concept of Innovation Hesitation, introduces the Innovation-ish Compass, and proposes Innovation Dynamics as a practical three part framework to take action.

Part II breaks down the Mindsets component of the Innovation-ish Compass, explaining how they serve as cognitive frameworks to guide your approach.

Part III introduces the Moves component of the Innovation-ish Compass, which are small, deliberate actions that help you test, refine, and build on your ideas.

Part IV focuses on introducing the Metacognition component of the Innovation-ish Compass, helping you reflect on and continuously improve your creative problem-solving approach.

Part V shifts to activating innovation, showing you how harnessing ambiguity, embracing failure, and curiously learning can drive progress and increase your Innovation-ish-ness.

Together, these sections create a straightforward path from insight to implementation, proving that anyone can innovate in the real world.

Who This Book Is For

We wrote this book for you. It's not just for designers, innovators, or researchers, it's for *anyone* looking to apply creative problem-solving to real-world challenges.

- **If you're new to innovation,** you'll find it easy to begin.
- **If you've attempted innovative projects before and struggled,** you'll learn how to overcome barriers that used to hold you back.
- **If you struggle with imposter syndrome and wonder,** "Who am I to be an innovator?" you'll see that you already have the skills, tools, and creativity to succeed.
- **If you're an experienced innovator,** you'll learn ways to accelerate and build on your successes through a new lens.

You can create breakthrough solutions to real-world problems, no matter your experience or background. The tools and concepts themselves aren't complicated. Like with any practice, the effort lies in applying them consistently. As we often say, "Innovation is not hard; it's hard work."

We are thankful for the collective intelligence that has shaped this book. First and foremost, we want to acknowledge our co-teachers who helped develop this material over the years – especially Jake Hale, Emily Meland, Sergio Rosas, Erika Woolsey, and Meredith Caldwell, who personify Innovation-ish. Many of the concepts in this book emerged through our collaborations. And a special thanks to Andrew Merrit, improviser, graphic capture artist, and true Innovation-ish partner who embodies the Iterations Mindset for developing the visual concepts for Innovation-ish, and Michael Gray, who developed and patiently revised and revised the final images for the book.

Our students continue to amaze us. Their willingness to embrace becoming Innovation-ish and apply these principles in their lives has made a real impact. Both our classes and this content have evolved thanks to their feedback. We particularly want to thank Smrithi Sukumar and Steve Gardner for their input during the writing process.

Our time at these institutions has been significant. We're grateful to the team at the Stanford d.school – Carissa Carter, David Kelley, Kathryn Velcich, Bernie Roth, Justin Ferrell, Leticia Britos Cavagnaro, Maureen Carrol, Seamus Yu Harte, Jeremy Utley, Perry Klebahn, and Charlotte Burgess-Auborn. As well as Lynn Larsen, Laura Wilcox, Jorge Cortell-Albert, and Leo Guyshan, who have helped bring these ideas to life for Harvard Extension School students at the Harvard Innovation Lab.

We thank Rich's colleagues at the Stanford GSB and Graduate School of Engineering Tina Seelig, Alberto Savoia, Stefanos Zennios, Dan Klein, and to his BATS colleagues William Hall, Rebecca Stokley, Kat Koppett, Rafe Chase, Tim Orr, Regina Saisi, and hundreds of colleagues, students, and friends in that amazing community in San Francisco. We also thank Tessa's mentors and leaders at the Stanford Graduate School of Education and Harvard Graduate School of Education who sparked and fostered her interest in cognitive science and creativity in adults – particularly Dr. Tina Grotzer, Dr. Chris Dede, Dr. Roy Pea, Dr. Daniel Schwartz, and Dr. Megan Cuzzolino.

We've seen People Rocket's clients bring Innovation-ish to life, achieving "roof-shots" that solve real problems. To everyone whose stories appear here – and to all we've worked with – thank you for being great partners.

This book exists thanks to Leah Spiro, our agent and guiding light. We're grateful to the late Ken Norwick for seeing the potential and making the introduction. For their feedback, we thank our colleagues and friends Tiffany, Andy, James, Holly, Chet, Mark, Dave, Megan, Maddie, Emily, Rhea, and Jake, and our family members Cher, Phill, Davida, Cameron, and Juno. Since it is 2025, we also acknowledge and thank our editing and writing assistance tools such as Hemingway App and Grammarly.

Becoming Innovation-ish

Innovation Hesitation

"Hands up if you're an innovator – if you think you're creative."

After 15 years of teaching creativity and innovation, we have asked this question to hundreds of groups all over the world. In this instance, we were in front of a roomful of managers and top employees of a global quick-service restaurant, the superstars of their business. They were agile, used to adjusting quickly to changing market conditions and solving complex problems, week after week. They had decades of experience and had won many industry awards because of it.

Despite their achievements, not a single hand went up. These were high-performing professionals actively seeking new ideas to tackle persistent supply-chain challenges, yet they didn't see themselves as innovators. The hesitation in the room was striking. How could this be?

We have encountered the same response in nearly every one of the organizations we've worked with or classes we have taught. Even our students at leading universities around the world are often reluctant to call themselves innovators. A few hands may go up, although never more than 10 percent of the class.

Yet, when we visit elementary school classrooms nearly every eight- and nine-year-old eagerly raises their hand. They are delighted to share their ideas, bursting with confidence in their ability to be creative.

How is it that elementary school kids display more creative confidence than top business leaders and university students? Why don't we see that same energy and boldness in high-achieving professionals? The reality is that years of doubt, scrutiny, cultural norms, and rigid structures have chipped away at their belief in their own creative abilities. The confidence they once had as children has eroded. They've become paralyzed by doubt.

We regularly work with major global organizations, from Coca-Cola Company to the Australian Department of Foreign Affairs and Trade. Again and again, we see that this loss of confidence holds back even the most capable and successful of teams.

Holding Ourselves Back

This reluctance isn't just an individual experience, it's part of a larger pattern we call Innovation Hesitation. Across industries, we've seen hesitation show up in predictable ways that block creative potential, no matter how capable someone is. It takes three primary forms: the Creativity Gap, Innovation Mythology, and Cognitive Caution.

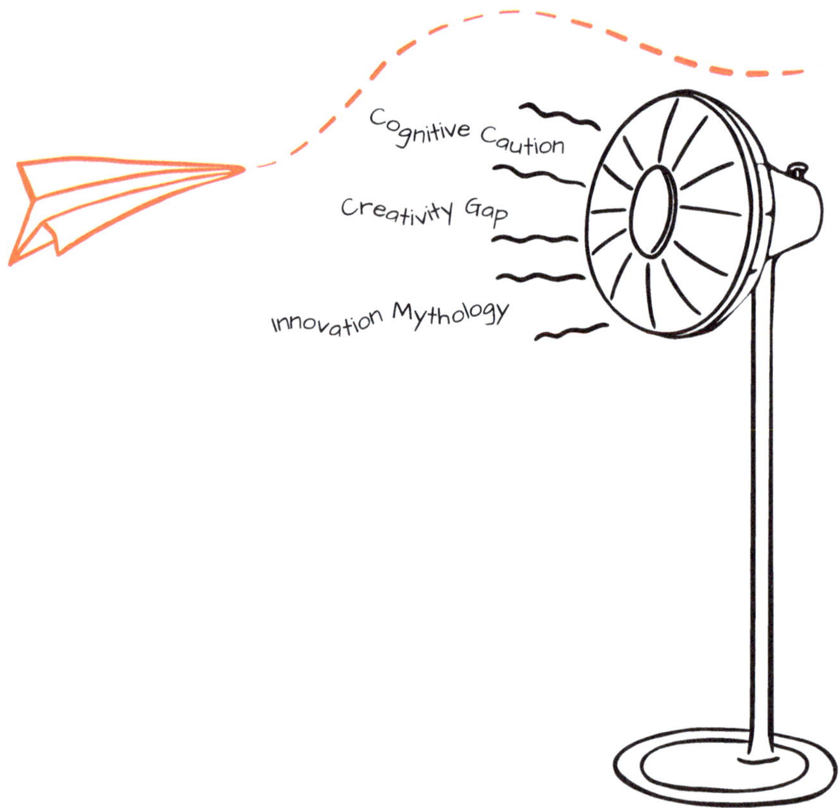

Innovation Hesitation is the Creativity Gap, Innovation Mythology, and Cognitive Caution.

Innovation-ish

The *first* source of this hesitation is the Creativity Gap that our students and clients feel about their creative capacity, which we described above. They often hold the belief that innovation is reserved for a select few. Iconic innovators are celebrated in books, movies, and news stories, reinforcing the idea that only a select few are truly creative.

This leads people to question themselves:

Who am I to be an innovator?

Often, it's grounded in self-doubt and imposter syndrome. People feel like they're not creative enough or not allowed to participate in real innovation, and this prevents them from engaging in creative problem-solving, further reinforcing their own self-doubt and self-perception as non-creatives.

The Creativity Gap can look like a junior employee hesitating to share a new process improvement idea because they assume only senior leaders drive innovation, or a team defaulting to the "way we've always done it" rather than experimenting with a new approach.

We also see it when a student tells us that they want to start a small business or side project and doubts their ability to come up with original ideas, or when they suggest an out-of-the-box idea, that is quickly shut down because it was "silly."

The Creativity Gap is fueled by the headlines of books, movies, and articles that tell us stories about what innovation should look like. But, it shows up in small moments for people. Hesitation, self-doubt, imposter syndrome, and the implicit assumption that it is for someone else.

Faced with this hesitation, many people look for inspiration from those they perceive as "real" innovators. They turn to places like Silicon Valley, where innovation is portrayed as larger-than-life. New ideas, new disruptions, new products, and new dreams ignite everywhere. Circular glass and steel buildings rise like sentinels across the landscape, while bright colors, open spaces, and modular furniture serve as the backdrop to where the future is invented. It is the big idea capital.

In these designated "innovation centers," you find 3D printers, laser cutters, walls covered with sticky notes, and racks of craft supplies ready to be turned into prototypes at 3 p.m. or 3 a.m., whenever the "Eureka!" moment strikes. Posters on the wall explain the "recipe" of innovation; the creative process is diagrammed and documented so that all the technicians and thinkers can align with the magic that produces the next great thing.

It's easy to believe that if you just had the right environment filled with 3D printers, sticky notes, and late-night brainstorming sessions, that you could innovate like the best.

Sure, it's an intoxicating image. There's just one problem. It's not true!

While these images are loosely based on high-level facts, they don't reflect the common-day reality. As former residents ourselves, we love Silicon Valley, the people, and the vibe – but true innovation rarely happens like this. Strip away that image to its foundation: one genius, by themself, follows a secret process and has a revolutionary idea in a moment of epiphany because they are using sticky notes in a brightly colored room.

The belief in these mythical innovation stories can make real innovation feel unreachable, and that is why Innovation Mythology is our *second* Innovation Hesitation.

Within the Innovation Mythology there are many common mythical tales and characters. For instance, the Special Places myth is the notion of innovation hubs filled with special buildings and sticky notes that makes people believe innovation only happens in high-tech labs, incubators, or trendy coworking spaces. In reality, true innovation happens anywhere. Wherever people are willing to test ideas, adapt, and engage with real-world problems innovation can happen.

The myth of the Lone Genius tells us that breakthroughs come from a single, brilliant mind working in isolation. History shows that the best ideas emerge through collaboration, iteration, and shared knowledge. The famous stories of "lightbulb moments" – the Eureka myth – convinces us that great ideas strike like lightning, when in fact, they evolve over time through trial, failure, and refinement.

These stories might sound harmless, but they shape behavior. For instance, we have often seen schools or companies spending millions of dollars to build special innovation buildings so that they can do innovation. Or a product management team waiting for a "big idea" to strike before getting started on a new product feature, rather than testing small, imperfect concepts and iterating. Innovation Mythology isn't just misleading, it delays progress, and reinforces a deeper, more instinctive apprehension.

When individuals hesitate to innovate, entire organizations stagnate. It spreads through teams and organizations, and entire businesses miss opportunities and fail to adapt. They hold back from taking risks, and in today's world, where change happens faster than ever before, that hesitation can have serious consequences.

The *third* form of Innovation Hesitation isn't external; instead, Cognitive Caution is deeply ingrained in how our brains function. Our minds are wired to avoid uncertainty, ambiguity, and risk in order to protect us from harm. However, these same instincts can hold us back from taking the necessary risks that drive innovation.

For more than 100 years since its founding in 1888, the Eastman Kodak Company dominated the photography industry. They transformed photography and placed portable cameras in the hands of everyday people. Families, for the first time, could capture those spontaneous moments in their lives, such as their children's first steps. Their iconic "Kodak Moments" became part of everyday language, making photography a staple of modern life.

Then, in 1975, Kodak engineer Steven Sasson invented the world's first digital camera. Kodak's response was something like: "That's a nice idea, but don't tell anyone about it. That's how you shoot yourself in the foot!" Kodak was focused on protecting its dominance in the film market. They dismissed digital photography, fearing it would disrupt their core business. Meanwhile, competitors asked a different question: How can photography evolve in a digital world? By the time Kodak recognized the shift, it was too late. In 2012, Kodak filed for bankruptcy.

Kodak's hesitation wasn't due to a lack of talent or knowledge; it was a perfect example of Cognitive Caution at work. Cognitive Caution is the cognitive instinct to cling to safety and the known world. That means sometimes protecting the familiar at the expense of progress. This natural instinct can work against us, preventing us from taking the very leaps necessary for innovation.

People often prefer predictability and have a tendency to favor the status quo, meaning that they typically prefer to maintain the current state rather than risk change. One reason for this is that people tend to fear losses more than they value equivalent gains. Another reason is that people are social beings, and our brain is a social organ. It is wired to seek acceptance, and risking a new idea means risking potential criticism. This means that even if an innovative idea has great potential, people may avoid it because the risk of failure feels disproportionately significant and so does the risk of criticism.

This can look like a teacher who wants to introduce a new, hands-on approach to teaching math but worries that deviating from the traditional curriculum might invite criticism from parents. Or a researcher working on a novel drug delivery system discovers an unexpected and promising side effect. Instead of pursuing it, they hesitate to bring it up in team discussions since it might distract from the main project focus.

Any one of these three Innovation Hesitations can be enough to stop you before you even begin. In our fast-paced lives, it can feel overwhelming to take on something new and dynamically scale hurdles in an ever-changing world. And if that weren't enough, the ever-changing world around us keeps adding even more obstacles. It's no surprise that so many people convince themselves that they simply aren't capable of innovating.

These widespread Innovation Hesitations keep good ideas from surfacing and a more efficient process, a new product, or a transformative technology from coming to life. And that means organizations struggle to keep pace with a changing world, or that time, money, and energy are spent on inefficient systems and processes.

The problem isn't that innovation is rare. The problem is that too many people have convinced themselves it's not for them.

Creativity Isn't Optional

You might notice, we talk about creativity and innovation as one thing because, in practice, they are inseparable. Creativity is the ability to generate new ideas, while innovation is the process of turning those ideas into real-world impact. What connects them is creative problem-solving: the ability to approach challenges with fresh thinking, adapt to uncertainty, and experiment with new possibilities.

When people hesitate to engage in creative problem-solving, it stalls innovation. Creativity is not just a "nice-to-have,"it's essential for success in today's world. It is a key ingredient in driving meaningful change and innovation in systems and organizations.

That's why innovation skills such as creative thinking, problem-solving, resilience, comfort with ambiguity, iteration, and prototyping are increasingly in demand. According to the World Economic Forum's 2025 Jobs Report, nearly three-quarters of employers today consider creative thinking an essential skill.

Employers are embracing creative thinking as an essential skill right now because businesses with strong internal innovation strategies tend to be more resilient in the face of disruption. They also often outperform industry benchmarks in revenue growth.

Employees should also embrace creative thinking because creative thinking is a competitive advantage in the job market; it enhances career development by making individuals more adaptable and resourceful; and it is a distinctly human skill that AI can enhance or augment but not replace (although it might try).

Beyond the workplace, creativity enhances well-being. Research shows that creative thinking can increase empathy, support emotional processing, boost energy, and improve intellectual flexibility. It helps people see opportunities for improvement in their surroundings.

The ability to engage in creative problem-solving is important.

You may be concerned if you don't think of yourself as creative. You are not alone, however, and we believe in your creativity.

Anybody Can Do It

Remember when we asked our students and professionals, "Hands up if you're an innovator, if you think you're creative?" The number of hands that went up was routinely small. More than 90 percent of adults in the United States believe that some people have an innate gift for innovation and that some are simply born creative while others, unfortunately, are not. This belief is a myth. It perpetuates Innovation Hesitation by reinforcing the false idea that creativity is exclusive to a select few.

We ask this question in our classes not because we expect every hand to go up but because we know that the lack of response has nothing to do with ability. The reluctance we see is often the result of social conditioning, a reflection of how environments can unintentionally stifle confidence in creativity.

For example:

- When students are rewarded only for coloring inside the lines or reprimanded for wearing their school uniforms in unconventional ways, it sends the message that individual expression and creativity don't matter. This erodes motivation to think creatively.

- When workplaces demand perfection and discourage risk-taking, they instill fear of failure in their employees, teaching them to avoid the very experimentation that fuels innovation.

- When children are over-scheduled with structured activities, leaving little room for free play, it inadvertently suppresses cognitive flexibility, which is the very skill that nurtures creative thinking.

Most leaders, whether in education, business, or parenting, say they value creativity. They claim they want people to be innovative. Yet when people stop engaging in creative thinking, those skills atrophy. Pressure to conform, fear of failure, lack of autonomy, time constraints, cognitive overload, and limited resources all serve as social signals that suppress creativity.

Here's the good news: just as creativity can be suppressed, it can also be enabled. It can be practiced, nurtured, and strengthened.

No matter what background, discipline, or education you have, everyone has the potential to be creative. One example is a preschool with one class that happened to have a much higher than normal number of children who loved to scream. Working together, they came up with a solution. They set a specific time when the whole school, staff included, screamed for 10 minutes. They called it "Scream O'clock." This creative solution sets boundaries for the children to enjoy themselves. It also taught appropriate and inappropriate times for screaming. They didn't need to hire designers; the staff already had the creativity they needed.

Regardless of your background, you have Innovation-ish moves.

Another example is a biotech firm with a large campus. People walked from building to building, sometimes taking 10–15 minutes. They wondered if a shuttle service would solve the problem but didn't know if the staff would use it. They already communicated using Slack for group discussions. They posted a schedule to all employees and scheduled by letting them reply to the message. They rented shuttles to provide the rides for that one week. This moment of creativity gave them the information they needed to test their idea.

These were not designers or "creatives." They were successful professionals in several different fields who came together to solve

Innovation Hesitation

problems. In all our years of teaching, consulting, and working with individuals from every background, we have never met a single person who couldn't do it.

We also see a transformation in our students. By the end of our courses, they not only viewed themselves differently, they also redefined what innovation means to them. When we ask the same question, "Who here is an innovator?" in the final class or at the end of a workshop, hands shoot up confidently.

Creativity isn't a rare gift; it's a skill that can be developed. We can learn to overcome the common hesitations that hold us back. This is how anyone can become Innovation-ish.

Key Takeaways

Innovation Hesitation Is Real

Many people don't see themselves as creative or as innovators. Years of doubt, rigid structures, and myths about creativity have chipped away at their confidence.

There Are Three Forms of Innovation Hesitation

The three key areas of Innovation Hesitation:

- The Creativity Gap
- Innovation Mythology
- Cognitive Caution

You Can Be and Need to Be Creative

Creativity is no longer optional. It is essential for navigating change, driving innovation, and staying relevant in the modern world. Thankfully, everyone has the potential to be creative, and it's a skill that can be practiced, supported, and grown.

Chapter 2

Innovation-ish Dynamics

What does it actually mean to be innovative?

If you open an issue of the *Harvard Business Review*, chances are you'll find an article about innovation. Attend a corporate training retreat or leadership development program, and innovation will likely be on the agenda. The word itself has become ubiquitous, in business, sports, the arts, science, politics, technology, and education, and for good reason.

In today's fast-changing and hypercompetitive world, both big and small innovations are essential for maintaining relevance. While we celebrate innovation in theory, too many people still don't see themselves as innovators in practice. So, what does innovation actually look like in practice?

One of our favorite examples of small and impactful innovation is the Post-it Note. Originally, 3M was attempting to create a strong aerospace adhesive; instead, they accidentally developed a weak adhesive that could be peeled off surfaces without leaving residue. Eventually the company proposed that its practical use was bookmarking pages in church hymnals. While marketing it at a conference, the technicians were using them at the booth in a new and different way; stick up comments on the call and annotate poster boards. This led the 3M team to experience a new use case themselves, and to take the product a step further. Thus, the Post-it Note was born. While the technical innovation from hymnals to sticky notes was minimal, its real-world impact was significant.

On the other hand, Apple's introduction of the iPhone was a much larger-scale innovation. It wasn't just about launching a new gadget;

it reshaped communication entirely. The iPhone merged a phone, an internet communicator, and a media player into one device, featuring an intuitive touchscreen interface that made technology more accessible. This single innovation spurred entirely new industries, from app development to mobile entertainment, and transformed how people interact with technology.

While innovation is essential in the business world, it also plays a transformative role in tackling societal challenges, from food security and education quality to mental health, housing, and disaster response.

A powerful example of this is microfinance. In the 1970s, Muhammad Yunus, an economics professor at the University of Chittagong in Bangladesh, conducted a research project to explore how small loans, sometimes as little as $25, could help impoverished entrepreneurs, many of them women, build sustainable businesses. The idea was simple yet profound: with even a small amount of capital, micro-businesses could break cycles of poverty, access raw materials, and maintain inventories.

The results were so promising that in 1983, Yunus founded the Grameen Bank, a financial institution specializing in microloans. What started as an experimental lending program became a global movement, lifting millions out of poverty. Yunus was awarded the Nobel Peace Prize in 2006, and the United Nations designated 2005 as the Year of Microfinance.

When we say anyone can be Innovation-ish, we mean anyone.

Take a kindergartener that we met in San Rafael, California, as part of a workshop we facilitated where children were asking their teachers about their morning routines. One teacher described the daily challenge of rushing out the door in time for school. The students were then asked to come up with ideas to help her. The kindergartener's solution? A clock with 13 hours instead of 12, giving her teacher an "extra" hour to get ready. While imaginary, it was a creative way of reframing the problem!

(Kindergarteners tend to not suffer from Innovation Hesitation).

The ability to challenge assumptions and rethink everyday problems isn't just isolated to kindergarteners. Adults can do it too.

Take, for example, Smrithi, a corporate counsel at SmugMug. Smrithi doesn't have a background in design or engineering. She is a corporate lawyer, and yet she's leading an Innovation-ish movement within her company.

A year after taking our class, excited by the impact of her own Innovation-ish practice, she decided to bring it to her company by actively teaching it herself. She developed a workshop on Innovation-ish, guiding her colleagues through exercises to rethink innovation, based on the idea that it is built from assets you already have.

Smrithi received overwhelming positive feedback and stories from her colleagues about how they were applying it every day, proving that anyone can be Innovation-ish.

Focusing on People, Not Steps

Creative problem-solving is often thought of as a kind of process or methodology. There are several variations of course, although most approaches frame creativity as a step-by-step method for generating ideas. It's like climbing a conceptual ladder methodically moving rung by rung until you reach "The Solution."

In an analysis we did of over 80 of the most famous approaches to creative problem-solving, this structured approach was without doubt the dominant model. These frameworks share many common traits, and include intentional steps that help force divergent and convergent cognitive processes. They are great "on average" representations of what the typical steps of creative problem-solving are. But, the reality is that breakthrough innovations to real-world problems, like avant-garde art, are not created by paint-by-numbers.

The origins of this approach date back to the real life of *Mad Men*. You might remember that in the TV show, ad executive Don Draper famously told employee Peggy Olson, "It's your job. I give you money. You give me ideas," reflecting the show's nod to the real-life ad agency Batten, Barton, Durstine & Osborn (now BBDO). Back in the 1940s, BBDO partner Alex Osborn introduced brainstorming sessions to spark fresh thinking by suspending judgment and prioritizing quantity over quality.

Innovation-ish Dynamics

By the 1970s, Osborn, alongside Dr. Sidney J. Parnes, Nobel Laureate Herbert A. Simon, and cognitive psychologist Allen Newell, had each developed their own structured problem-solving methodologies. By the 1990s, thinkers like Don Norman and firms like IDEO popularized Human Centered Design and Design Thinking; processes that took the business and social impact worlds by storm.

Given the success of these methodologies, universities rushed to create programs teaching the process. Companies established entire innovation departments, and consulting firms offered million-dollar programs to guide their implementation.

For a time, this approach seemed like a magic formula for creativity. Countless new innovation frameworks, books, and proprietary methods emerged.

Yet, somewhere along the way, we lost sight of the bigger picture.

Ironically, Innovation became a series of checkboxes rather than an organic, evolving, human-driven process.

We saw this firsthand when we met a very frustrated student in one of our courses. She had followed a popular five-step innovation process to the letter, completing each phase exactly as outlined. Yet, her project wasn't working.

Why?

Because she was so focused on following the "rules" that she never paused to ask if she was solving the right problem in the first place.

According to our own research, more than three-quarters of adults in the US believe that innovation, creativity, and design follow a structured process. This belief isn't surprising, as it's how the innovation story is commonly packaged, reinforcing the Mythology of Innovation. Many assume that just as following a cake recipe leads to a perfect dessert, following a predefined innovation model will automatically generate breakthrough ideas.

Methodical and disciplined approaches have value. Processes help organize efforts, structure thinking, and ensure progress. However, human creativity isn't just about following steps; it thrives on conceptual leaps and iterative learning. Sometimes, these leaps are bold and game-changing; other times, they are small yet transformative.

Innovation-ish

Imagine a dancer performing a perfectly rehearsed routine, while the orchestra is playing at a different tempo, and the other dancers miss their cue. The performance, though technically flawless, falls apart because the dancer failed to adjust to the reality unfolding around them. This is what happens when process takes precedence over people, and such rigid adherence to a formula can stifle adaptability and, ultimately, innovation.

As design thinking gained popularity, organizations sought to make it more repeatable, teachable, and scalable. We get that – from a business perspective, a structured process feels safer, as it eliminates ambiguity and provides a clear path to follow.

Over time, however, the process itself became more important than the people executing it.

This false sense of security removed the human elements such as insights, and critical thinking from innovation. These well-intentioned efforts to simplify innovation and methodically avoid Innovation Hesitation unintentionally weakened its core strength: the human beings involved.

In reality, it wasn't "the process" alone that made Steve Jobs, Muhammad Yunus, or 3M successful, and it won't be what makes your innovation successful either.

Innovation isn't just about the process; it's about people. True breakthroughs require human curiosity, and adaptability. Processes can guide us, but creativity thrives when people, not checklists, are at the center.

You don't have to look far to see this in action; it is all around us. A great example is watching how young children naturally engage in creativity every day. They see the world not just for what it is, but for what it could be.

Thinking Creatively Is Human Nature

Every night in my (Tessa's) house, my pre-school-aged daughter picks out a book for us to read together before bedtime. One of her favorites is a story about all the different things a box can be besides a box. In the tale, a box becomes a rocket ship, then a fire engine, and several other props that the child in the story uses in this game of make-believe.

Recently, she decided that the "Not a Box" imagination game applies to more than just boxes. So last week, when I came downstairs and found her busy in the living room, I asked, "Darling, what are you doing with the couch cushions?" With emphatic attitude, she replied, "Mama, these are not couch cushions! This is a flying saucer going to Mars."

The transformations had just begun. Later that day, I found her again, deeply engaged. "Darling, what have you made?" I asked, pointing to a pile of cushions assembled on the floor. "That is my fort to keep out the dragon," she said matter-of-factly. Minutes later, the fort was gone. The cushions had now become a bouncy castle for a princess.

Then, about a month later, she grew afraid that monsters were lurking in her bedroom at night. One afternoon, she came to me and said, "Mama, I found a pink lamp and some wheels. If we put the lamp on the wheels and make it into a robot, it can drive around my room and check for monsters, so I won't be scared." That was a playful innovation. She came up with something novel to solve a real pain point she was facing.

As people who research or teach creativity in adults, we are constantly awed by the wonderfully flexible and divergent thinking we see in children. They fully engage with their ideas, imagining freely, without constraints. Yet, somewhere along the way, often by early adulthood, our relationship with creativity changes, and not always for the better.

Surprisingly, this shift isn't generally due to cognitive decline. In fact, studies suggest that adults often outperform children on some types of creative tasks. The issue is practice. As we grow older, we engage in these kinds of imaginative exercises less frequently. However, adults also have an advantage: we know more about how the world works, allowing us to apply our creativity more effectively. The key is being able to tap into that innate cognitive and imaginative power.

Innovation-ish

This kind of creativity is innate. We all possess it. It's a widely held "neuro-myth" that we are either "left-brained" (analytical) or "right-brained" (creative). Often when we say this in workshops, at first a lot of people are shocked. After all, it is a belief that many of our parents and grandparents had too and taught us. Except the thing is, very reliable and replicated science, including brain imaging, tells us that one side of the brain isn't more dominant than the other in healthy individuals.

Yes, each side of the brain is different in some respects; however, the two hemispheres work together to do most things – including being analytical and creative. Both sides of the brain collaborate, complementing each other to help us navigate creative problem-solving. Being creative requires a dynamic interaction between several different brain regions and networks. It truly is whole brained.

It's also true that some cognitive abilities, like general intelligence, musical talent, or language skills, are partially attributed to genetics. However, psychologists and cognitive scientists overwhelmingly agree that creative problem-solving involves skills that are developed. And just like any skill, they can be improved through practice and experience.

So what does this mean for you?

It means creativity isn't just for a select few, especially since there is no such thing as a "creative" or "non-creative" brain. It also means that creativity is a skill. The more you practice, the better you get.

Unlocking Your Innovative Brain

To better understand how creativity actually works, let's consider an analogy from aviation, an industry that relies on balancing competing forces to stay in motion. We find it useful to think of creative problem-solving as analogous to an airplane in flight. Or rather, the cognitive processes involved in creative problem-solving are a lot like the forces acting upon an airplane in flight. Growing up with parents who are both airline pilots, I (Tessa) have learned a thing

Innovation-ish Dynamics

or two about aircraft aerodynamics over the years. This is Innovation Dynamics:

Divergent Thinking processes are the lift. Lift is the force that enables an airplane to rise up into the air. Divergent thinking processes allow you to zoom out, generate wild ideas, adopt different perspectives, and break free from constraints. They help you diverge from the thing that is concrete and grounded and let your imagination take flight. There is, of course, some inherent risk with lift, and it makes some people anxious. It's both exhilarating and uncertain, like flying through the sky with nothing but air beneath you.

Convergent Thinking processes are like weight. They ground your ideas, forcing you to focus and make practical decisions about where and when to land. They help bring your specific problem sharply into focus. While flight can be thrilling, many people find comfort in being back on solid ground.

Executive Function is thrust. This is the force that propels your airplane forward. Executive Function keeps you on track and ensures your ideas gain momentum. Without it, you may have a great idea that you never get off the ground. If you are in the air already and have some momentum and the thrust shuts down, you might glide a short way. Although, you are unlikely to arrive at the destination.

Innovation Hesitation is drag. Just as air resistance opposes the motion of an aircraft, drag, in this sense, opposes your creativity. Innovation Hesitation – the Creativity Gap, Innovation Mythology, and Cognitive Caution – are the internal and external forces that slow down or obstruct creativity, like fear of failure, risk aversion, self-doubt, belief in innovation mythology, or a sense of not being creative enough. Overcoming drag requires executive function (thrust) to push past hesitation and execute your ideas.

No analogy is perfect, but it is useful to imagine these as the elements of successful creative problem-solving.

Innovation-ish

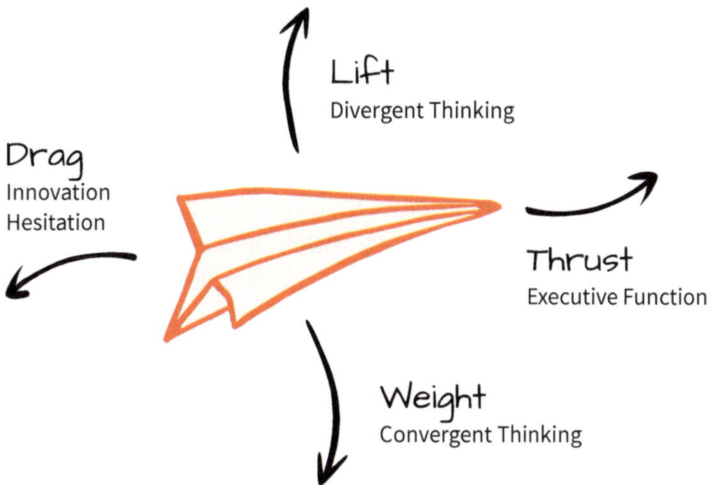

The forces of Innovation Dynamics that overcome Innovation Hesitation.

Divergent thinking is perhaps the best-known element of creativity. It's the skill of "thinking outside the box," generating fresh ideas and exploring multiple possibilities. Several parts of the brain, including the prefrontal cortex, default mode network, and hippocampus, play a role in this process, helping individuals interpret new information, recall past knowledge, form connections, and shift perspectives. It involves opening up our attention and broadening our perceptions. Divergent thinking also requires stepping into ambiguity and uncertainty, embracing a space where multiple possibilities coexist.

By contrast, convergent thinking isn't often linked to creativity and innovation, yet it is just as essential. It relies on logical and analytical thinking to focus, evaluate, and make decisions. It engages many of the same brain regions as divergent thinking. Although likely it does not involve the default mode network, which is responsible for daydreaming and expansive thinking. This distinction is a key factor in understanding the differences between the two processes, as convergent thinking is controlled and focused. Convergent thinking feels more comfortable for most people because it is rooted in concrete realities and is a process we use constantly in daily problem-solving.

Innovation-ish Dynamics

Creativity also depends on fundamental executive function processes, which are critical for goal-directed problem-solving and determining when to apply divergent or convergent thinking. Executive function plays a crucial role in planning, executing, and sustaining the actions required to move ideas forward and overcome obstacles. It engages working memory to hold, sort, connect, and process information; enables cognitive flexibility to switch between different concepts or hold multiple ideas at once; and applies self-control to resist distractions and follow tasks through to completion. Without executive function, creative ideas risk stalling, making it difficult to transition from inspiration to meaningful action. Too much executive function is just like too much thrust. Instead you want to find the right amount of thrust (executive function) to move forward at optimal speed.

These three things all work together to overcome Innovation Hesitation. Just as there is an entire field of study dedicated to overcoming drag for flight – aerodynamics. Innovation Dynamics is how we overcome drag for innovation.

In *Innovation-ish*, we use the analogy of a series of flights to illustrate the cognitive processes involved in creative problem-solving. As the airplane lifts off the ground, divergent thinking is required to explore new ideas and expand possibilities. When it's time to land, convergent thinking comes into play, helping to refine and focus those ideas into actionable solutions. However, to keep the airplane moving forward through the problem space, thrust is needed. Thrust is executive function, the driving force that sustains momentum and ensures progress.

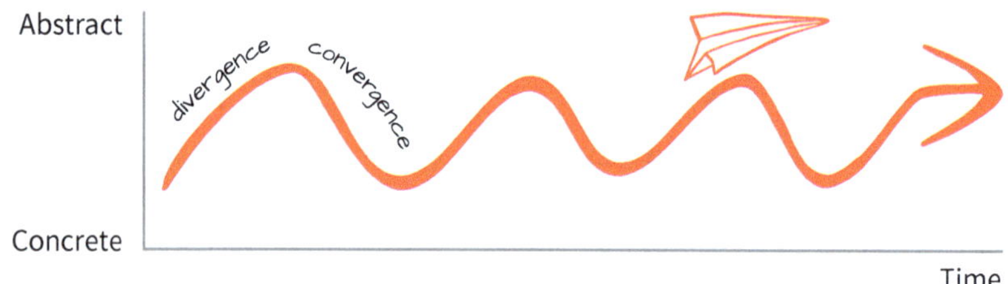

Innovation happens in a series of divergent and convergent moments.

In the world of creativity and innovation, the interplay between divergent and convergent thinking is often visualized as a series of diamond shapes; most notably by the British Design Council's Double Diamond. Every project begins at a concrete starting point, where the designer has a clear understanding of the process and objectives. From there, they must push their thinking outward into the more abstract, uncertain space of exploration, engaging their divergent thinking skills to generate fresh perspectives.

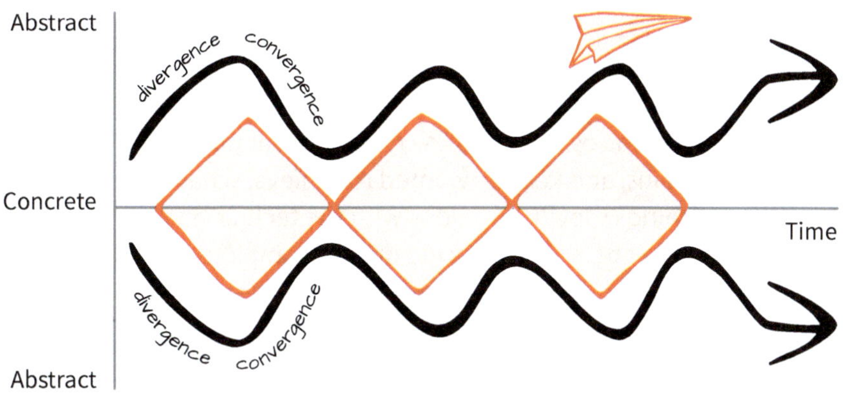

Often represented as a series of diamonds, Executive Function guides the inflection points.

When they discern that they have explored widely enough and it's time to bring their ideas back to a practical resolution, executive function guides the transition to convergent thinking, allowing them to focus, evaluate, and land the airplane with a well-defined solution.

Innovation Dynamics example at work

Cognitive Process	What It Does	Example: Revisiting the Plumbing Business Owner
Divergent Thinking (Lift)	Generates multiple ideas and possibilities. Think outside the box.	The plumbing business owner steps out and gathers a wide range of insights from technicians and customers, embracing various experiences to understand the full scope of emergency call delays.

(continued)

Innovation-ish Dynamics

(continued)

Cognitive Process	What It Does	Example: Revisiting the Plumbing Business Owner
Convergent Thinking (Weight)	Narrows options, makes logical decisions, and focuses on feasibility.	She analyzes the data methodically to spot recurring issues, finding that poor communication and outdated scheduling are the primary factors behind the delays.
Executive Function (Thrust)	Organizes, plans, and keeps things moving forward.	She created a clear plan for what she wanted to achieve, scheduled sessions with the technicians, and set aside time to complete a detailed analysis, moving steadily toward a solution.
Innovation Hesitation (Drag)	The Creativity Gap, Innovation Mythology, and Cognitive Caution.	Despite pushing for change, she struggles with feelings of inadequacy and questions her creativity, experiencing imposter syndrome as she attempts to implement innovative solutions.

The relationship between these four forces is the thread that ties the entire creative problem-solving process together. In our classes as well as in our consulting work with organizations, we emphasize their importance. Roughly half of the activities rely primarily on divergent thinking, while the other half focuses on convergent thinking. Executive function is what helps teams progress. Recognizing and addressing Innovation Hesitation allows us to make intentional choices to overcome drag.

Let's take another example from the business world. Imagine you're an accountant looking to integrate AI into your monthly close process. First, you generate ideas for automation tools, such as those that classify invoices or detect anomalies. This is divergent thinking, providing the lift that propels new possibilities.

Next, you evaluate the costs, consider compliance requirements, and narrow your choices. This is convergent thinking, acting as the weight to bring your ideas back to a focused, grounded decision.

Along the way, you may encounter resistance from colleagues concerned about errors or job security, or you might experience imposter syndrome, questioning whether you have the expertise to implement AI. This is Innovation Hesitation, creating drag that slows progress.

However, your executive function provides the thrust to push through obstacles. It helps you take those promising ideas and turn them into a structured plan. You establish timelines, assign responsibilities, and drive the initiative forward to execution.

Understanding Innovation Dynamics helps us make sense of the mechanics behind creative problem-solving. While these cognitive processes provide the foundation, they work best in the right environment with other people. They come to life through collaboration, shared insights, and the exchange of diverse perspectives.

Innovating as a Team Sport

The cognitive processes of creativity might happen inside our minds, but in truth creativity and innovation are a social practice. It takes place in real-world contexts, shaped by culture, collaboration, and shared experiences. Nearly all breakthrough ideas emerge through collective engagement, where the whole becomes greater than the sum of its parts.

While Steve Jobs was a visionary, many of Apple's most iconic innovations were the result of deep collaboration involving Steve Wozniak, Jony Ive, and other talented team members. Apple also drew inspiration from research centers like Xerox PARC and Pixar, exchanging ideas that reshaped the tech industry. Don't just take our word for it; Steve Jobs himself said:

> "Great things in business are never done by one person.
> They are done by a team of people."

Yet, when we asked adults in the US, "Who or what comes to mind when you think of an innovator?" nearly every answer identified a lone man. When we followed up with, "Where do you believe innovation typically happens?" the overwhelming response was "in the mind." Shockingly, less than a third of a percent (0.33 percent) identified a team, partnership, or group setting as a place where innovation happens.

This persistent belief that brilliant individuals create world-changing ideas in isolation is a classic example of Innovation Mythology. In reality, creativity thrives through interaction, iteration, and shared insight.

Many people view creativity and soccer as pure individual talents – you either have it or you don't. That view misses the bigger picture. Creativity isn't just something you have; it's something you develop, and often through collaboration with others. Just like soccer, it is a skill best honed through continuous practice with other players. In fact, we often tell our students that creativity is a social practice, just like soccer is a social practice.

Both are deeply social practices that thrive on interaction. Sure, you can practice penalty kicks alone or sketch ideas in your notebook. That builds a foundation. The real growth happens when you're engaged with others.

Think about playing soccer. My (Tessa's) daughter plays soccer and I watch her each week improving by reading the game, anticipating passes, and aligning with her teammates' movements. Creative problem-solving follows the same pattern. Every project, brainstorming session, or problem-solving challenge is unique because of the different skills, perspectives, and ideas each person brings. The more you collaborate, adapt, and engage, the stronger your creative abilities become. Without practice, these abilities can atrophy, just like a soccer player's skills decline without regular play.

Innovation Is About People

Frameworks and step-by-step methods can help, yet true innovation isn't a rigid formula. Creativity thrives when people are at the center.

Everyone Has Creativity Capacity

Everyone has the potential to be creative. Creativity is a skill everyone can improve with practice. Adults may have lost touch with their creative practice, but the ability is still there. It's a myth that some people are creative and others are not.

Innovation Dynamics: The Forces of Creative Problem-Solving

Innovation works like flight:

- Divergent Thinking (Lift) – Expands possibilities and generates new ideas.

- Convergent Thinking (Weight) – Narrows focus and turns ideas into action.

- Executive Function (Thrust) – Drives momentum and keeps ideas moving forward.

- Innovation Hesitation (Drag) – The Creativity Gap, Innovation Mythology, Cognitive Caution.

Innovation Is a Social Practice

Innovation is a team sport and is improved through collaboration, iteration, and shared insights. The lone innovator is a myth, because innovation thrives on interaction, diversity of thought, and shared experiences.

Chapter 3

The Innovation-ish Compass

We have started many workshops over the years with executives encouraging them to focus on the high-level landscape or "30,000-feet" view. But, until recently, we had never kicked off a workshop mid-flight, over the in-flight PA system, literally at 30,000 feet above NEOM.

NEOM is Saudi Arabia's vision for a futuristic, sustainable city. It is one of the most ambitious innovation projects in modern history. We were leading a workshop with CEOs from around the world to engage with the vision and spark some inspiration for the NEOM team.

NEOM is often described as a moon-shot; that is, an audacious, paradigm-shifting idea. However, when you're on the ground, you see it differently. For the vision to become reality, thousands of smaller, incremental innovations are required across technology, construction, sustainable power, water management, and more.

We often imagine innovations as giant leaps or "moon-shots," yet in reality, they emerge through a series of small, deliberate advances. These steady, incremental – Innovation-*ish* – improvements may not grab headlines. Instead they expand the boundaries of what's possible, one step at a time. The challenge, then, is knowing when to zoom in on these small moves and when to step back and see the bigger picture.

Choosing Roof-Shots Over Moon-Shots

We break down these types of incremental innovations into jump-shot, roof-shot, cloud-shot, orbit shot, and ending of course with moon-shot.

In NEOM:

They require **jump-shots** – simple improvements in construction techniques and materials.

As well as **roof-shots,** like developing more efficient solar panels or water systems.

And **cloud-shots,** like smart infrastructure networks or advanced energy management systems.

Orbit-shots emerge through revolutionary breakthroughs in urban sustainability and AI integration.

That build toward NEOM's ultimate **moon-shot** vision.

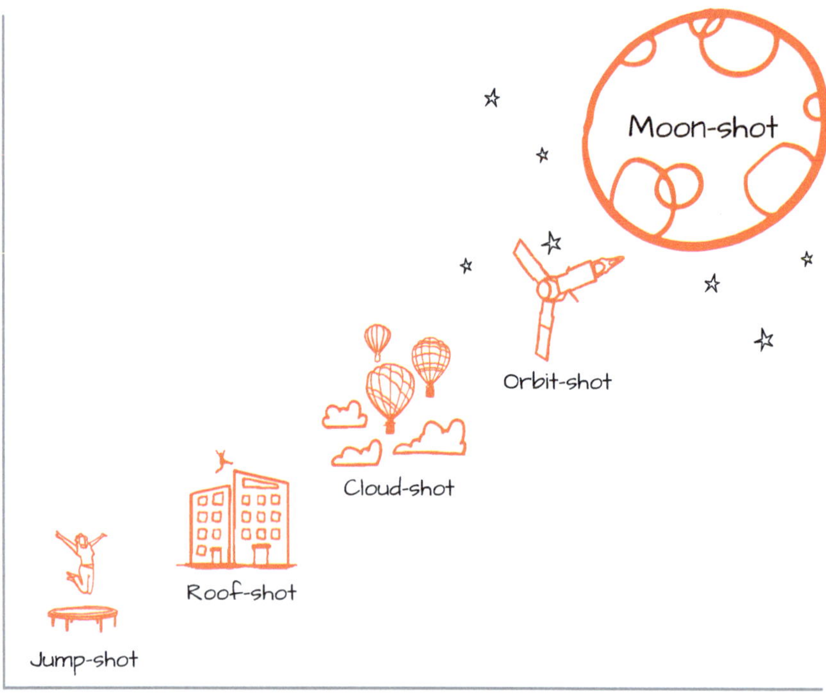

The spectrum of innovation impact – it's not only moon-shots.

Innovation-ish

For the vision to become reality, thousands of smaller, incremental innovations are required across technology, construction, sustainable power, water management, and more. This pattern holds true everywhere. Most innovation doesn't come from radical leaps forward; it comes from steady, strategic improvements. Whether you're making a "jump-shot," or aiming for the roof or the clouds, it is this type of everyday, incremental innovations that drive meaningful progress towards reaching orbit or the moon.

During our workshop with CEOs from around the globe, we learnt that NEOM knows this deeply, and has dedicated an entire team, the Design and Construction Sector, to champion these roof-shot innovations. Their mission isn't to launch the next big idea; it's to reduce costs, increase safety, and mitigate risks by taking small, crucial steps that ensure large-scale success.

People often only think about NEOM – the moon-shot – and not the many hundreds of smaller breakthrough solutions to real-world problems. When we ask students and clients to name the most significant innovations they can think of, they typically list the printing press, the lightbulb, the airplane, television, the internet, the iPhone, and, more recently, AI. What we don't often hear about are the smaller, everyday innovations that shape our lives, such as a new scheduling method at a daycare center, Cherry Coke, or Netflix's "Are you still watching?"

In fact, our research shows that 84 percent of US adults believe an idea must be groundbreaking or revolutionary to be considered "innovative." The common assumption is that innovation only happens in moon-shots or orbit-shots that transform industries overnight. These may be the most famous, but smaller-scale innovations are the most common and, often, the most impactful.

While moon-shots attract attention, they are rare. Roof-shots, jump-shots, and cloud-shots are by far the bulk of innovation efforts and often have a greater cumulative impact. To paraphrase renowned psychologists Karl Weick and Robert Quinn – small changes often accumulate into large impacts.

So ask yourself what kind of innovation are you aiming for? Not every problem requires a groundbreaking solution. Some challenges call for small, practical improvements, while others demand big, system-changing shifts. The real skill is in knowing what kind of innovation fits the moment and how to get there.

Each scale of innovation requires different ways of thinking, decision-making, and problem-solving. Without a way to navigate, even the most ambitious ideas can stall.

Navigating with Innovation-ish

Once you know the scale of the innovation you're working toward, the next challenge is navigation to reach your goal. Big or small, every innovation effort faces uncertainty. What matters is having a way to move forward, that helps you decide on the innovation dynamics that gives you thrust to move forward and decide the amount of Lift and Drag.

That's where the Innovation-ish Compass comes in. It is our antidote for navigating beyond Innovation Hesitation and the movement of putting process over people. A traditional compass always points north, helping set your course, adjust your direction, and keep you on track to your desired destination.

Similarly, the Innovation-ish Compass doesn't decide your destination for you the way a process or checklist sets out every step. Instead, it provides a clear, practical framework to help you determine your path forward. It helps you navigate innovation dynamics choosing the right next step based on the current conditions, ensuring that you take the essential next steps toward achieving breakthrough solutions to real problems in the real world.

Our approach uses three key elements: mindsets, moves, and metacognition. These elements guide how you think about and solve your creative problems, whether you're making an incremental improvement or preparing for a transformational leap.

> **Mindsets:** The ability to engage different perspectives or ways of thinking while solving problems. These are cognitive frameworks, or lenses, that shape how we approach challenges and opportunities.

Moves: The problem-solving methods and activities you already use, whether at work or in your personal life. These are cognitive strategies, actions you take to make progress, drawn from your existing and ever expanding toolkit.

Metacognition: The capacity to reflect on your actions, assess whether they are yielding the desired outcomes, and determine what adjustments are needed. This self-awareness helps refine your thought process and continuously improve your approach.

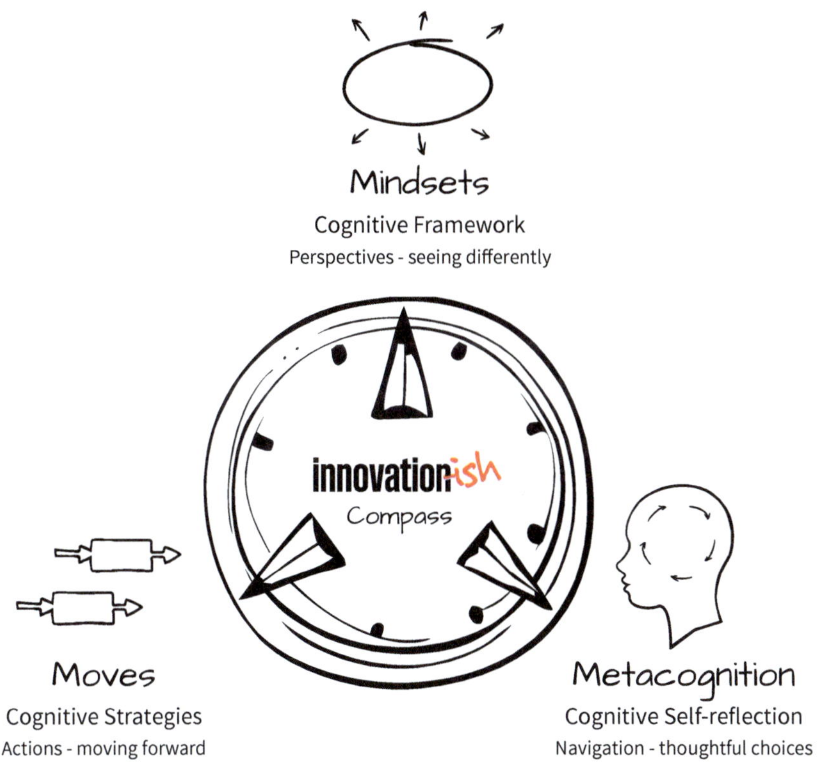

Navigating with the Innovation-ish Compass requires mindsets, moves, and metacognition.

The Innovation-ish Compass

Mindsets

Mindsets are lenses through which we make sense of our challenges and opportunities; they shape what we notice, the choices we make, and how we engage with the world. The Innovation-ish Compass introduces six core mindsets: Interactions, Insights, Ideas, Iterations, Inspirations, and Implications.

Each mindset doesn't follow a sequence as part of a rigid process. They're not a linear checklist; instead, the key is figuring out which Mindset you need at any given moment to take one step closer to solving real-world problems.

Imagine the owner of a local plumbing business facing delays in emergency calls. She wants to learn more about what is going wrong and decides to get out of her office and talk to the technicians about the situation. She engaged in an Interaction Mindset by listening closely to her technicians' firsthand experiences, thoughts, and perspectives.

Next, she reviewed the notes she took in those conversations, and by engaging an Insights Mindset she noticed that poor communication and outdated scheduling tools were likely the main culprits. Seeking further clarity, she re-engages with an Interactions Mindset to see what else she can learn from both technicians and customers.

Finally, intent on considering how a revamped system might have cascading impacts and unintended consequences, she adopts an Implications Mindset.

The Innovation-ish Compass helps you move flexibly between these mindsets to take concrete actions in the world: moves.

Moves

Moves are the small, concrete actions that help tackle your creative problem-solving challenge through the lens of the Mindset you are engaging in. Rather than succumbing to Innovation Hesitation, moves lets you take small, immediate steps to tackle problems.

A move creates a small plan of action, when to start and stop and what you will do. It explains what the goal is and what information you will collect to share with others.

Consider the plumbing business owner who wants to improve how her team handles emergency calls. Instead of overhauling the entire scheduling system, she builds a rough, low-cost prototype of a new communication tool that reorders and prioritizes service requests.

She tests it with her technicians, gathers feedback, and refines the process based on real-world insights. This move – prototyping – driven by an Iterations Mindset, lets her quickly test assumptions and make small, practical adjustments before fully committing to change.

Metacognition

While moves are about taking action, metacognition is the process of assessing your actions, emotions, and thought patterns to refine your approach. It's the process of reviewing what you've done, considering what you learned, and thinking about how you showed up – so that you can adjust your approach as needed. It helps you choose the right mindset and move at the right time.

After testing her prototype for reordering emergency calls, the plumbing business owner sets aside time to reflect on her process. She asks herself questions like: "What did I expect to happen? What surprised me? How did my assumptions influence the outcome?" She realized that she assumed every technician would find the new tool as intuitive as she did, yet several team members struggled with the interface during peak hours. This reflection prompts her to invite the technicians to a design workshop where they collaboratively refine the interface.

The foundation of Innovation-ish is simple. Mindsets shift perspectives, moves drive action, and metacognition ensures you take an intentional approach.

By following these principles, you'll strip away the mystique surrounding innovation and adopt a pragmatic, learnable approach to creative problem-solving. The Innovation-ish Compass gives you agency and autonomy over your creative problem-solving process, which ultimately will enhance it.

The Innovation-ish Compass

Starting Is Easier Than You Think

By now, you've probably recognized some places Innovation Hesitation has slowed or stopped your progress, and you can see how the Innovation Compass gives you the ability to navigate to achieve your own goal from jump-shot to moon-shot.

If there's a voice in your head expressing doubt, tell it to pipe down. We have taught this on six continents to everyone from enthusiastic five-year-olds to startup CEOs to eighty-five-year-olds. They all succeeded simply by taking the first step.

We're going to break through your Innovation Hesitation *right now* by showing you that you *can* do this.

Consider a problem you're facing today, preferably one that you've wanted to solve for a while and might have put off because it feels too big to start.

Start-Somewhere Activity

Take one to two minutes and answer the following questions, listing as many specific actions as you can.

- How can you better understand the problem you are trying to solve?
- How can you get other people involved to help you?
- How can you generate ideas to solve your problem?
- How can you learn from other people?
- How can you experiment with your ideas to try them out?
- If you could eliminate your problem today, how would you know it was solved?

Now, review your responses and reflect:

1. How did you feel before the questions, and how has that changed?
2. What has changed in the way you think about this problem?

Innovation-ish

We use this exercise regularly to introduce our approach, and we often hear similar responses. Many people report feeling a sense of relief, newfound clarity, or inspiration for their next step. They say things like, *"The problem looks smaller now."* or *"It's not as big as I thought."* or simply, *"I know where to start."*

Congratulations! You are now Innovation-ish! No, really, we mean it. By completing this exercise, you've taken your first steps toward building your Innovation-ish practice.

Every breakthrough starts with the simple act of starting somewhere. The Innovation-ish Compass reminds us that by shifting our mindset, taking small, deliberate moves, and reflecting on our process through metacognition, we can bridge the creativity gap, dismantle innovation mythology, and overcome our natural cognitive caution.

Key Takeaways

Roof-Shots Over Moon-Shots

Innovation isn't about giant, industry-shaking moon-shots. It's about practical, incremental "roof-shots" that lead to meaningful progress. Small, steady improvements drive real innovation. Innovation is a spectrum:

Jump-shots → Roof-shots → Cloud-shots → Orbit-shots → Moon-shots

Navigate Innovation with the Innovation-ish Compass

The Innovation-ish Compass helps guide your own Innovation-ish journey using three interrelated elements:

- **Mindsets:** Six distinct ways of thinking.
- **Moves:** Small, concrete actions.
- **Metacognition:** Choices from ongoing self-reflection.

(continued)

The Innovation-ish Compass

(continued)

The Innovation-ish Compass Will Guide You

By using mindsets, moves, and metacognition, you can overcome hesitation, navigate challenges, and turn ideas into impact. These start-somewhere questions can help you get started right away:

- How can you better understand the problem you are trying to solve?
- How can you get other people involved to help you?
- How can you generate ideas to solve your problem?
- How can you learn from other people?
- How can you experiment with your ideas to try them out?
- If you could eliminate your problem today, how would you know it was solved?

Mindsets

Your Mindset Matters

Innovation begins with mindsets.

Mindsets shape how we understand and react to the world around us. They filter what information we pay attention to or ignore. They are cognitive frameworks that influence how we interpret and respond to situations, acting as lenses we can choose to put on and take off.

Academics have studied many different mindsets over the years. A mindset is any set of beliefs, attitudes, or mental shortcuts that shape how we perceive, interpret, and respond to the world. The key feature of a mindset is that it acts as a mental filter, influencing our thoughts, emotions, and behaviors.

Our brains like to seek patterns and consistency. When we enter new situations, we rely on mental shortcuts built through past experiences to help us navigate what's in front of us. These shortcuts or *mental models*, create the foundation for mindsets. They serve as learned and practiced tools that shape how we process situations and determine how we respond.

We also are more likely to notice things that match what we're focused on. A chosen mindset effectively "tunes" us to certain cues. As one team of behavioral scientists at Stanford SPARQ (Social Psychological Answers to Real-world Questions Lab) put it, "what we believe will happen can have surprisingly strong effects on what does happen" because mindsets shape what we pay attention to and how we interpret events.

Since mindsets influence our cognitive processing, different mindsets lead to different results. Expressed another way, imagine two identical versions of yourself approaching the same situation with different mindsets. Your interpretations, decisions, and outcomes would all be different.

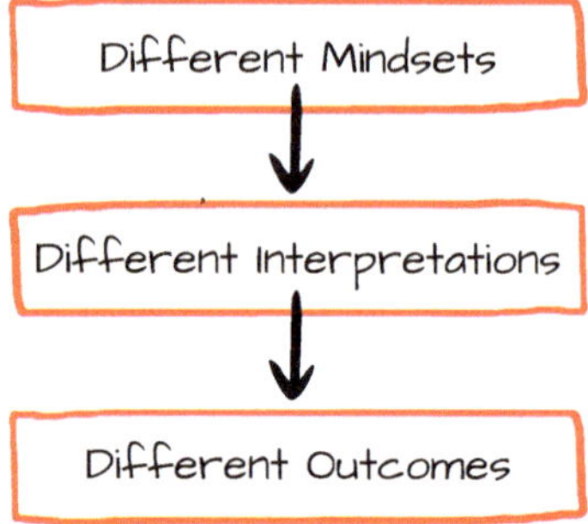

Mindsets change interpretations leading to varied outcomes.

One of the most well-known mindsets is the Growth Mindset, popularized by Stanford psychologist Carol Dweck. A Growth Mindset is the belief that talents and skills can be developed through effort and persistence. Although, it's certainly not the only one.

For instance, the behavioral psychologists at Stanford SPARQ showed that people with a stress-is-enhancing mindset actually responded better to stress, than those who have a stress-is-debilitating mindset.

Outside of academics mindsets are also popular – consider the phrase "seeing the world through rose-colored glasses." This refers to a mindset that romanticizes reality and focuses only on the positive aspects of a situation.

When I (Tessa) was visiting potential schools for my daughter, I approached each one with an evaluative mindset. I focused on assessing the information presented to me, identifying strengths and weaknesses, and determining which school would be the best fit for her. If I had approached the visits with a "tick-the-box" mindset, my experience would have been entirely different. I might have checked off a list (e.g., touring all the facilities, speaking to every representative), but missed the subtle interactions that revealed the heart of

Innovation-ish

the school. For instance, a teacher explaining how they encourage creative thinking or a student excitedly sharing a project might have gone unnoticed.

Similarly, imagine two chefs walking into the same unfamiliar kitchen. The first chef, trained in high-end restaurants, immediately scans for premium ingredients, expensive knives, and sous-vide machines. The second chef, experienced in resourceful home cooking, looks for leftovers, simple spices, and ways to repurpose scraps into something delicious. The tools at their disposal are identical and their mindsets shape how they interpret the space and what they create. The first chef might struggle without gourmet supplies, while the second thrives by adapting.

These are mindsets. They are lenses that we, with practice, can intentionally choose to put on, take off, or adjust as needed.

Choosing Your Mindset

I (Tessa) experienced firsthand the impact of choosing a mindset during the global CrowdStrike outage, which disrupted online services worldwide. I was traveling for work in Europe when I found myself stranded, flights delayed, people locked out of Microsoft tools, businesses struggling to function.

At first, I was frustrated by the inconvenience, checking flight updates obsessively and feeling irritated by the situation. Then my husband reminded me of the power of mindsets. I consciously shifted into a flexible mindset, which shaped how I interpreted what was happening, how I perceived peoples' actions, and, most importantly, how I responded to the situation.

That shift changed everything. Instead of anxiously refreshing the airline app, I embraced the uncertainty and rescheduled my flight for the next day. I decided to make the most of the extra time by exploring the city. If I had stayed in my rigid mindset, I would have spent the entire day complaining and waiting. Instead, I discovered local spots, met new people, and turned a frustrating delay into an opportunity.

Mindsets don't just shape how we think, they determine how we see the world, which influences our decisions, the problems we notice, and the solutions we create. Every time we discuss mindsets in class, at least one student raises their hand and asks:

"But isn't it hard to change someone's mindset as an adult?"

That's a great question. Our answer: no one can be forced to change their mindset; they have to choose to do it. Mindsets are deeply ingrained mental shortcuts, and our default responses often happen automatically. However, with practice, we can develop the ability to engage different mindsets intentionally.

In fact, one of the biggest benefits of practicing mindset shifts is that it makes us more self-aware when a particular mindset becomes too rigid or unhelpful. Over time, we learn to recognize when a different mindset might serve us better.

Even better? Mindsets are contagious.

When you intentionally engage a mindset you inspire those around you to do the same. Just like culture, mindsets spread through teams and organizations, shaping how people approach challenges together.

Because mindsets shape how we interpret and tackle problems, they are essential for innovation. Creative problem-solving isn't just about having good ideas, it's about knowing when and how to apply the right mindset to the right challenge.

By understanding how our brains work, we can intentionally shape our thinking to foster breakthrough solutions in the real-world. And that's where Innovation-ish begins.

Exploring the Six Innovation-ish Mindsets

If you look up Innovation Frameworks, Design Thinking Frameworks, or Creative Problem-Solving Frameworks, you'll find dozens of results. And, if you were to dissect the most popular ones, you'd notice they all teach the same core principles, just communicated in different ways.

After analyzing over 80 frameworks from design schools, nonprofits, think tanks, consulting firms, tech companies, and governments, we made a surprising discovery: the core of every effective innovation process isn't a rigid sequence of steps, it's about the mindsets they unintentionally ask you to engage with. We boiled it down to six core mindsets.

Not every mindset appeared in every framework we studied. Some were more common than others, some were repeated, and some were skipped entirely. We also noticed that they didn't always appear in the same order or a fixed sequence. We arranged the mindsets in this book in a conventional order for ease of reading and to align with the most common order we saw represented.

The six mindsets we noticed are Interactions, Insights, Ideas, Iterations, Inspirations, and Implications.

(Call it a happy accident, call it fate, call it what you will. The universe clearly wanted these to start with "I," just like innovation. And yes, feel free to roll your eyes – our students do!)

They aren't about following a formula, because they aren't linear. It's more like a messy, fluid, dynamic scribble. You can begin with any mindset and use just one or a few in any order. Sometimes you revisit a mindset multiple times, and sometimes you skip one entirely. The key is knowing which mindset to activate and when, depending on where you are in your project and what you need.

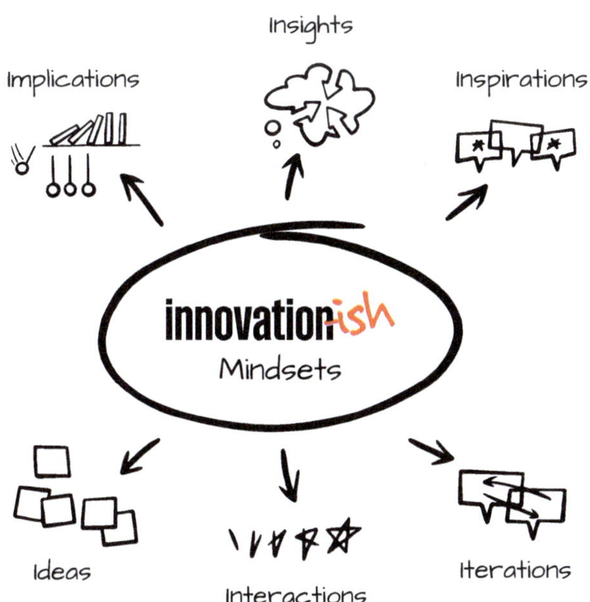

To innovate there are six mindsets to choose from, in any order.

Your Mindset Matters

The Interactions Mindset (Chapter 5) encourages genuine curiosity about how people live, work, and play. It involves seeing the world with a curiosity to get out into the world and learn from others. It sets you up to seek out learning from, interacting with, and immersing yourself in the human experience to uncover real needs.

How this mindset often appears in frameworks:

- Empathy and observation.

- User interviews and research.

- Discovery and need-finding.

Start here when you're unsure about the real issues or want to understand the landscape before diving in deep. Getting out into the real-world and talking to real people can reveal overlooked perspectives, grounding your approach in real experiences.

The Insights Mindset (Chapter 6) is a lens for seeking out interesting patterns, contradictions, and surprises that might help you generate new inferences and questions. It prompts you to look beneath the obvious. It's about noticing what others overlook and making meaning from the unexpected.

How this mindset often appears in frameworks:

- Clarifying the problem space.

- Reframing challenges.

- Developing a unique point of view.

Start here if you already have data or observations, or feedback and test data from your prototypes. The Insights Mindset helps you sift through information to identify patterns and contradictions that might otherwise be missed. If you are really looking to make sense of what is going on based on the data you already have, begin here.

The Ideas Mindset (Chapter 7) fosters expansive, abundant, and unconventional thinking. In Chapter 7 we will discuss how it is about generating bold, wild, and unexpected possibilities before selecting and refining the best ones. This mindset embraces an "anything can happen" perspective.

How this mindset often appears in frameworks:

- Brainstorming and ideation.

- Opportunity identification.

- Expanding beyond safe, incremental ideas.

Start here if you need to inject some wild ideas into your project and push the boundaries of possible and acceptable solutions to achieve a breakthrough.

The Iterations Mindset (Chapter 8) invites you to learn by doing, and see everything as an opportunity to improve. This means testing, refining, and evolving ideas based on real-world feedback. It encourages holding ideas loosely, sharing unfinished work, and letting data guide the process.

How this mindset often appears in frameworks:

- Prototyping and experimentation.

- Building Minimum Viable Products (MVPs).

- User testing and iterative refinement.

Start here if you have an idea, or a few of them, and want to test or prototype them. This can help you get some real-life feedback on what you are doing to help inform your way forward.

The Inspirations Mindset (Chapter 9) is the perspective that emotional and human connections can help you to connect with others, gain support, and validate ideas. It embraces empathy, shared experience, and genuine engagement as essentials for making concepts resonate beyond logic or data.

Your Mindset Matters

How this mindset often appears in frameworks:

- Crafting compelling narratives.
- Storyboarding and storytelling frameworks.
- Developing value propositions and pitch decks.

Start here when you need to communicate your vision or inspire others to join in. Doing so will help you compel others through narrative, emotion, and passion.

The Implications Mindset (Chapter 10) takes the view that real-world impact matters. It encourages us to evaluate whether ideas are viable, feasible, and scalable, while also watching for unintended consequences and long-term sustainability.

How this mindset often appears in frameworks:

- Business model design.
- Financial projections and feasibility analysis.
- Implementation and deployment strategies.

Start here when you need to pause and think about the long-term impact of an idea and possible unintended consequences. You may want to consider its feasibility and viability as a real-life concept.

Together, these six mindsets transform innovation from a rigid process into a flexible, adaptable way of thinking. There is no right order or starting place; instead the order that suits your project at any given moment is the one you should follow. Start with the one that resonates with where you are on your Innovation-ish journey.

Key Takeaways

Mindsets Are Powerful Filters That Can Be Chosen

Mindsets shape how you see, interpret, and respond to the world. They are not fixed and we can choose to intentionally engage a particular mindset, much like looking through a lens. Engaging a particular mindset can inspire the same in people around you. Different Mindsets lead to Different Interpretations, which lead to Different Outcomes.

Six Key Mindsets Underpin Most Innovation Frameworks

Interactions, Insights, Ideas, Iterations, Inspirations, and Implications mindsets capture the essence of most popular innovation frameworks and their different phases or activities.

There's No One Right Order. Just Start

Innovation isn't linear. There is no order or pattern to choosing the right mindset. Use the mindset that fits your current challenge, whether it's understanding the problem, generating ideas, testing solutions, or communicating impact. Innovation is about knowing when and how to apply the right mindset.

Your Mindset Matters

Chapter 5

The Interactions Mindset

We were standing in an industrial parking lot filled with semi-trucks with a team of executives from several companies, each of which plays a key role in getting products from manufacturers to restaurants. As the door to one of the tractor trailers rattled open, we could see inside rows of stainless steel tanks, which held the ingredients for a popular soft drink, destined for local restaurants.

These executives, representing the soft drink manufacturer, distribution and logistics partners, and the fast-food restaurant where the drinks would be served, were responsible for ensuring the on-time delivery of these tanks. From their perspective, the process looked smooth, efficient, and compliant with company policies.

Then, something shocking happened.

The receiving manager casually snapped off the security tags and carried them inside the office. A collective gasp rippled through the executives. This was a violation of the policy. Those tags were supposed to stay in the tanks until they reached their final destination. In the event of contamination, the entire supply chain theoretically depended on these security measures.

When we asked the receiving manager about it, it turns out that the official process required employees to manually write down tag numbers on clipboards and later enter them into the computer system. This double-handling introduced lots of errors, causing costly inventory mismatches and delays, and so to avoid these issues, the warehouse staff had developed a faster and more accurate workaround.

The warehouse staff were not trying to violate or break the process; they were adjusting it to make it more reliable and faster. They were aiming to produce better performance metrics, even if the safety rules stated that the tags ought to be left on the tanks at all times.

This moment revealed a fundamental truth: the executives had designed policies without fully understanding frontline operations or interacting with the stakeholders at the distribution center loading docks.

Had they engaged with the Interactions Mindset earlier, they could have witnessed the problem firsthand before creating a solution. Instead of creating the procedures in a conference room, they could have designed a system that balanced security with efficiency, ensuring compliance while supporting the realities of day-to-day operations.

Going into the Real World

The Interactions Mindset is built on the idea that to truly understand any challenge, you need to engage with the real world. It requires stepping outside your home or workplace and interacting with people in their environment: listening, observing, and picking up on their constraints and needs.

This sounds simple in theory, yet it's surprisingly difficult in practice. In our introductory courses, we give students a problem to solve during the first class and the entire session to start working on it. The problem is often quite big and undefined, such as improving the sustainability of the local strip mall, or improving the experiences of students on campus. Out of eight groups, sometimes only one (often none) leaves the classroom to talk to real people experiencing the problem. Yet, the group that does always ends up in a better position than those who remain at their desks; knowledge is context-dependent, and real insights come from direct engagement in the real world.

At its core, the Interactions Mindset is about recognizing the value of learning from other people at every opportunity. To truly put on an Interactions Mindset, we must:

- Suspend our assumptions.

- Engage empathetically.

- Show deep respect and care.

Suspending our assumptions means approaching problems with beginner's eyes or acting as if you know little or nothing about the issue.

Imagine watching a magician perform a trick. The first time, you're completely fooled. You have no idea how it works. Until, after learning the secret, the trick is obvious. Now, imagine trying to reverse the process and to forget how the trick is done so you can experience it with fresh wonder.

That's the challenge of engaging with beginner's eyes. The more experience we have, the harder it is to see problems the way a true outsider would. Our knowledge creates blind spots. To truly adopt the Interactions Mindset, we need to ask basic questions, listen without assumptions, and step into unfamiliar perspectives. We're not there to prove anything; we're there to learn.

By engaging with the world through beginner's eyes, we activate our ability to recognize that others have different perspectives, experiences, and emotions. It's not just about intellectually understanding that people think differently; it's about emotionally connecting to their experiences. This is the foundation of empathy.

Engaging empathetically is about looking beyond our own perspectives to understand why people think and act as they do. It's built through direct engagement with others while maintaining beginner's eyes. Empathy is important because it quite literally makes you think differently.

A key part of empathy is being open to transformation or allowing ourselves to be affected by others' experiences, challenges, and needs.

For example, we worked with a philanthropic funding organization on a youth mental health project. Our goal was to understand how students accessed mental health services. During our fieldwork, we interviewed a school superintendent who shared a major challenge.

In her county, a law required that students receiving counseling be in a room separated from the rest of the school by another room. This meant that a student couldn't simply meet with a counselor in an empty classroom; rather, they needed a "buffer" space. At her

The Interactions Mindset

school, the only place that met this requirement was a small broom closet, too small for a person to sit in. As a result, there was no regulation approved space for counseling to happen.

This superintendent had worked tirelessly to expand counseling services. She secured funding, hired providers, and built new support systems. However, this law meant students still weren't getting the help they needed.

Although we originally set out to learn about students' experiences, her story highlighted systemic barriers. Empathy meant listening closely, holding space for her concerns, and letting ourselves be affected by her frustration.

Before this interview, we had assumed the issue was access to mental health providers, not access to legally compliant rooms. Empathy requires flexibility or a willingness to shift perspectives as we learn. It allows us to move beyond our own viewpoints and uncover hidden obstacles that might otherwise go unnoticed.

Engaging with a community is a privilege. It's important to approach these interactions by **showing deep respect and care,** treating people as co-teachers, honoring their ways of being, and building trust and rapport.

For instance, we saw this firsthand while working with a Native American health clinic on an Innovation-ish project. Part of our work involved engaging with the community and learning from their elders.

In this community, when seeking guidance from an elder, it is customary to offer tobacco as a sign of respect. However, because this was during the COVID-19 pandemic, meeting in person was unsafe. Instead of ignoring the tradition, we worked with a younger community member who helped us send tobacco ahead of our Zoom meeting. They also facilitated the online conversation.

This step wasn't just a formality. It showed that we respected their customs and valued their knowledge. By honoring their traditions, we built trust and created a genuine partnership. Respect means adapting our methods to align with the needs and values of the communities we engage with in the process of learning.

Respect also means checking our own biases and recognizing how our backgrounds influence what we see. Both the superintendent's story and our work with the Native American clinic highlight the importance of self-reflection.

In the case of the superintendent, we initially focused only on students' experiences. Until, by questioning our assumptions, we uncovered systemic barriers we hadn't considered. We reflected on our assumptions and adjusted our inquiry to include the impact of regulations on mental health access.

Similarly, as we discussed the Native American clinic, we didn't assume our usual meeting format would be appropriate, we asked questions and adapted our approach to fit their cultural context.

Examining your own beliefs, values and biases involves recognizing when reality challenges your expectations allowing you to rethink your approach. It's not just about collecting data, it's about actively reflecting on your role and adjusting to truly learn from the community.

That is precisely what the Interactions Mindset is about. It means stepping into the real-world and seeking perspectives different from your own. If you rely too much on your expertise and stop asking fundamental questions, as those executives did, you risk overlooking key insights that could fundamentally reshape your approach.

Adopting this mindset requires humility, a willingness to challenge your own assumptions and an openness to learning from others as co-teachers. Through honest conversations and unexpected discoveries, you gain a deeper understanding, uncover real challenges, and design solutions that truly work.

Collecting Different Types of Data

The world is full of data. When you step into the real-world, you have the opportunity to gather many types of information. Quantitative data is collected by measuring and counting events or characteristics in a structured way. For example, in our youth mental health project, we could have counted the number of times students canceled mental health meetings or measured the percentage of students affected by the buffer room regulation. We could have also analyzed existing data sources, such as public records, databases, or statistical reports from government agencies. However, the Interactions Mindset is about engaging with the real-world, not just downloading a pre-existing data set.

Typically, quantitative data provides clear, numerical insights that reveal trends and patterns. Organizations and policymakers value this information because it offers objective, replicable metrics.

At the same time, you can also collect qualitative data, the kind of information that tells the story behind the numbers. In our work with the school superintendent, her detailed account of not being able to use a closet to meet strict room separation rules revealed the true impact of the law on student care, something that numbers alone would not have captured.

Similarly, with the supply chain executives, qualitative data uncovered what the numbers missed. The executives already had extensive performance metrics and analytics, but they had never observed the real work happening on the ground. By watching the receiving manager in action and listening to his explanation, they discovered an informal workaround that staff had created to deal with inefficiencies in the system. This firsthand insight exposed a gap between policy and reality. Without qualitative details, the executives would have missed the opportunity to collaborate with staff and design a better solution.

Qualitative and quantitative data require collection methods.

Innovation-ish

Qualitative data captures emotions, personal experiences, and unexpected details that add depth and context. It doesn't just tell you what happened; it helps you understand why it happened and how people felt about it. This is why qualitative research is so powerful, as it allows you to see the world through others' experiences. It forces you to step outside of your comfort zones and adopt the standpoint of people unlike yourself.

In practice, both types of data complement each other. Each serves its own purpose and plays an important role in understanding a problem.

However, qualitative research is essential for creative problem-solving and innovation. It reveals hidden needs and opportunities that might otherwise go unnoticed. By understanding how people feel and the challenges they face, you can develop human-centered solutions that truly resonate and work in the real world.

Why not give it a try?

The Dinner Experiment Activity

You can try a small experiment to practice learning from others and applying the Interactions Mindset. The next time you are having a conversation with a friend, explore their thoughts and feelings about meals.

1. Without announcing the questions or your intent, navigate the conversation toward eating dinner. *Perhaps comment on a recent dinner, or ask for recommendations for a future event.*

2. Try asking questions like these in your own style:

   o "What are the most important qualities you look for in a great dinner?"

   o "What makes a dinner great for you?"

   o "What ruins a meal for you?"

(continued)

The Interactions Mindset

> *(continued)*
>
> **3.** As you listen, pay attention to responses that surprise you or feel particularly meaningful.
>
> **4.** After the conversation, think about their responses and what you learned about your friend.
>
> **5.** Based on what you learned, try making an educated guess about what kind of dinner they would truly enjoy.
>
> This educated guess is based on a small and meaningful data set. It may lead to an even more enjoyable dinner experience, all from a simple experiment in qualitative information gathering. Not bad for just one thoughtful interaction!

Preparing for Interactions

Getting ready for interactions, like the dinner experiment, can be challenging, even when you have a great reason to do it. Remember, those executives didn't step into the field and engage with the Interactions Mindset until they were supported.

In our experience, this gut feeling of interactions being too hard or uncomfortable is Cognitive Caution – the third form of Innovation Hesitation. Cognitive Caution happens because putting yourself out there means stepping outside your comfort zone and making yourself vulnerable. Many of our students describe their minds racing with questions like:

- What if I get shut down?
- What if the person says no when I ask to talk to them?
- What if others judge me?
- What if… what if… what if…

This is partly a survival response, as our brains have evolved to detect social threats as potential dangers. It's important to remind yourself that this hesitation is normal. It's an Innovation Hesitation, and like any Innovation Hesitation, it can be overcome by being Innovation-ish.

Innovation-ish

Remember that the Interactions Mindset involves seeing the value of learning from other people at every opportunity. In our work, we've found a valuable way to overcome the Cognitive Caution, is to prepare.

When we worked with a Clean Tech Start-up Incubator, we set out to understand workforce development programs in that sector. We needed to speak with students in these programs, their educators, hiring managers, and others. Before we jumped into those conversations, we had to prepare ourselves.

Step 1: Acknowledging Our Own Biases and Assumptions

First, we had an honest conversation with ourselves about what we already knew or thought we knew about clean tech and green energy workforce development. We wrote down our assumptions about how it worked, what it involved, and any biases we might have about the sector.

For example, we have worked extensively with workforce development clients. This step was particularly important for us to avoid bringing in a "this is how it's supposed to work" mentality, just like the executives at the distribution center who assumed their processes were being followed.

We also forced our team to articulate our initial thoughts on what the problem might be and what solutions might fix it. Later, when we gathered real insights or brainstormed ideas, we could compare them to these initial thoughts. This allowed us to check for confirmation bias and ask ourselves "were we only noticing evidence that reinforced our existing beliefs?"

Step 2: Foundational Learning and Desktop Research

Next, we conducted foundational learning and desktop research to grasp the terminology and landscape of clean tech and green jobs.

- This helped us engage in meaningful conversations with our participants.

- It gave us the language of the field, making our discussions more productive.

- It helped us build a mental model of the broader environment surrounding the problem.

We read articles, reports, and data sets, all materials created by others that were incredibly valuable for understanding the context before we stepped into the field.

Step 3: Designing the Interactions

After building a foundational understanding, we designed our interactions to collect just the right amount of data, not too little and not too much.

We brainstormed many possible interactions we could have and identified who we needed to speak with across the Clean Tech Start-ups ecosystem. We then decided on interviewing as our primary method. To guide these interactions, we created a field guide, which outlined:

- Our goal for the conversation.

- Our opening question to ease into the discussion.

- Key topics we wanted to explore.

With these steps in place, we were finally ready to immerse ourselves in the world of the Clean Tech Start-up and learn from the real people in it.

Interacting with People

In any challenge you take on, a range of people influence, implement, or are impacted by it.

Take the Clean Tech Start-up Incubator project. We started by recognizing we needed to talk to a wide variety of people including the students in these programs, their educators, and their hiring managers.

However, the list of people affected by our project was much longer than that. It includes administrators, accreditation organizations, relevant referral organizations such as one-stop-job programs, and government workforce boards. It could also involve workers unions, and their future managers and teammates.

Each of these groups has a different relationship to the problem, a different level of involvement, and likely a different perspective. For instance, a potential manager might be concerned about whether the new curriculum aligns with what they need in their future team members, while a program administrator might focus on how the change affects accreditation requirements and paperwork.

Mapping out all the relevant stakeholders makes it easier to figure out where to start. Who do you already know or have easy access to? Who could you reach out to right now?

Another reason to consider all the different perspectives is that it encourages an honest conversation about what perspectives you already understand well and where your insights are lacking. Being open about your assumptions is key to gaining genuinely new information, rather than just confirming what you already believe.

In cognitive science, this tendency is known as confirmation bias. It is a mental shortcut that leads us to seek and favor information that supports our pre-existing beliefs. Research has shown that this happens across age groups, cultures, countries, and levels of expertise.

People are constantly processing enormous amounts of information. When we encounter something new, we instinctively compare it with what we already believe. If the new information fits our existing worldview, it feels good, and we naturally reinforce that belief.

If it contradicts our assumptions, we experience cognitive dissonance, which is the discomfort of holding conflicting ideas at once. Often we are not even conscious that the dissonance is the cause of our discomfort. It requires extra mental effort to resolve, and as a result we often lean into confirmation bias, ignoring or downplaying information that doesn't align with our prior beliefs. Sometimes, we even avoid perspectives that challenge our assumptions altogether. It's natural to seek out people who affirm our ideas, as it makes us feel confident and connected. However, if

The Interactions Mindset

you only engage with perspectives that reinforce what you already think, you stop learning.

If the executives at the distribution center had only talked to manufacturers or distributors at similar restaurants, they might have learned about more efficient product tracking systems that were already improving productivity and profitability elsewhere. Missing these interactions could have meant overlooking the pitfalls in their existing process, such as profits leaking out due to cumbersome inventory recording procedures.

Only by directly engaging with different parts of your system and its stakeholders can you truly understand the problem and identify the most effective starting points for solutions. Expanding your interactions beyond your immediate circle challenges your assumptions, uncovers blind spots, and ensures that your approach is informed by real-world complexities, not just what feels comfortable or familiar.

Exploring Types of Interactions

When the COVID-19 pandemic broke out across the United States, we were in the middle of teaching a class. It was a tough moment for our students, not only because of the uncertainty surrounding the crisis but also because they were working on projects that required engaging with people and the world around them. Suddenly, they could no longer interact face-to-face.

So, they got creative. Some students engaged with dynamic online communities and discussion forums, others conducted "virtual" site visits, and some even hosted Facebook Live focus groups.

The goal of the Interactions Mindset is to learn directly from people about a problem and how they experience it while also building a broader understanding of the systems, tools, rules, and organizations that shape their world.

As it turns out, there are many ways to achieve this. From the online interactions our students explored to casual conversations at a coffee shop, formal interviews, online messaging, open-ended surveys, or site visits to distribution centers (like the restaurant executives we discussed earlier), every interaction adds valuable structure to how you engage with a problem.

Innovation-ish

There are countless ways to interact with people, and you already have some effective methods in your toolkit. Here are a few helpful approaches:

Expert Interviews: When working on problems in highly specialized or technical areas or when you need insight into an emerging facet of your challenge, expert interviews offer fast access to the knowledge you need. These interviews are best used when the subject's complexity is difficult to grasp without direct input from someone with deep expertise.

Interviews: Interviews are conversations designed to gather in-depth, open-ended insights about your problem landscape and the experiences of the people involved. Unlike surveys or structured questionnaires, semi-structured interviews allow for spontaneity, giving space for the conversation to wander and reveal unexpected insights.

Observations: Observing a person in their typical environment, whether at home, work, or in a public space, can reveal more candid insights than dialogue alone. Watching how people naturally interact with their surroundings allows you to notice patterns, behaviors, or pain points that they might not explicitly mention in an interview. After observing, you can ask clarifying questions, such as:

- "I noticed you paused before using that tool; what was going through your mind?"
- "I saw you took a different route today; was that intentional?"

Activities: We love using activities to make interactions more engaging, especially when someone might feel reluctant or shy in a typical interview setting. Asking people to draw, write, or use props like cards or sticky notes encourages them to create artifacts that offer direct insights into their thought processes. This method is handy for abstract or sensitive topics where verbalizing an experience may be difficult.

The Interactions Mindset

Online Communities: Sometimes, "going into the field" means just logging on. For many challenges, the digital world is the primary gathering space. While the logistics may differ from in-person interactions, the core principles remain the same: listening, observing, and engaging. You can:

- Join online forums and social media groups to learn from discussions already happening.
- Participate in virtual community events or Q&A sessions to hear diverse perspectives.

Qualitative Surveys: While two-way dialogue produces rich qualitative data, qualitative surveys can also be effective in certain cases. They allow access to a larger number of participants and provide self-reported insights. However, to avoid collecting only surface-level responses, make sure to include open-ended questions alongside multiple-choice or numerical ones. This ensures that you gather real human insights.

Key Takeaways

Go out into the Real World

The Interactions Mindset shows that stepping into the real-world by observing and talking with those on the front lines can reveal hidden challenges and spark fresh solutions.

Suspend Assumptions, Engage with Empathy, and Show Respect

The best insights come when you approach problems with beginner's eyes, listen deeply to others' experiences, and treat people as co-teachers. True understanding requires curiosity, humility, and a willingness to be shaped by what you learn.

Conversations Reveal What Data Misses

People's stories, behaviors, and unexpected workarounds often uncover the biggest opportunities for innovation. Respect, curiosity, and thoughtful interactions lead to solutions that actually work in the real world.

Chapter 6

The Insights Mindset

The day after watching the operations manager at the distribution center tracking inventory by pulling the security tags from the containers in the parking lot, we held a workshop to discuss the fieldwork. During the session, participants listed surprising observations and quotes from their day in the field. As they filled a whiteboard and identified recurring themes, their long-held beliefs about product distribution shifted.

As the discussion unfolded, one participant, Tom, suddenly stood up and exclaimed, "I have a problem in my company that we need this approach to solve!" His excitement caught us off guard, but we weren't surprised. Many of our students feel the same elation when they realize that tackling challenges through a new mindset can lead to fresh insights.

Tom's enthusiasm came from seeing a new approach to his biggest challenge. He led the supply chain for one of the largest fast-food chains in the United States, overseeing the movement of half a billion boxes annually to thousands of restaurants. As the final stop in the supply chain, his team spent significant time in the "back room" ordering, tracking, organizing, and inventorying supplies. His directive was simple: "Never break supply."

However, there was a problem. Restaurant labor costs were already high and getting higher, so his challenge was to reduce each restaurant's costs by reducing the amount of labor required to manage the back room. As Tom absorbed the workshop discussion, he felt the same relief many students do when they shed old, rigid assumptions and begin to see problems with fresh eyes.

To tackle the problem, we followed a similar approach to the distribution center. We engaged 50 people across the supply chain, splitting them into six cross-company teams. They adopted the Interactions Mindset and conducted dozens of interviews with stakeholders at all levels.

After gathering in a large conference room, the participants brought their interview and observation data and covered the walls with sticky notes, capturing moments of tension, surprise, and contradiction. Over three days, the group discussed, questioned, and clustered these insights.

Then, something unexpected happened.

The data did not support the original problem of labor reduction. This was not a matter of opinion. It was an objective fact revealed through hundreds of interviews. The reality was apparent: the core issue wasn't about cutting labor costs in the restaurants, it was about something entirely different.

Looking at the data, there was no way to ignore what they now knew to be true. As the reality set in, the group made a bold decision: the entire project had to pivot.

The new insights revealed that focusing on productivity gains and efficiencies across the supply chain far outweighed only focusing on restaurant labor reduction. This realization triggered a brief moment of crisis so we assured them that reframing the problem was the entire point of the Insights Mindset.

At the start of the project, there were six teams, each aligned with one facet of the original problem. That afternoon, they reorganized into new teams based on the emerging themes. The mood revealed a newfound confidence in this new direction.

Instead of eliminating labor, the teams shifted their focus to reallocating the same labor to improve productivity and the customer experience.

Radically changing direction mid-project, especially with 50 people involved, sounds like a high-risk decision. And it would be if it were based on a gut feeling. But, consider the risk of not changing direction and spending time and resources solving the wrong problem.

When insights clearly point in a new direction, the real risk isn't in pivoting; it's in ignoring the data and sticking to old assumptions. The Insights Mindset is about standing in a perspective of sensemaking and learning – that is interpreting ambiguous, often incomplete data, and revising your mental model of the problem as you go.

Seeing Insights

The Insights Mindset shapes how you view the world by helping you look past the obvious and probe deeper into the layers beneath everyday information. It means spending time with a problem, and being attuned to noticing inconsistencies, considering alternative angles, and exploring contradictions and unexpected patterns. Even when these factors complicate the picture, they ultimately enrich our understanding and lead to more thoughtful decisions.

Using the Insights Mindset allows you to move beyond assumptions and obvious interpretations to uncover the real problems worth solving. Like Tom, who initially focused on restaurant labor reduction until he discovered that the real benefits were within the supply chain, we must be willing to challenge our initial perspectives.

Through discussions with clients and students, we've observed that adopting an Insights Mindset can be difficult. It requires stepping away from familiar thinking patterns and questioning long-held assumptions. This mindset demands that we confront uncertainties and accept that our first interpretations might be incomplete or wrong. It's mentally taxing to constantly question what we believe we know, especially when our default is to rely on tried-and-true ways of thinking. The cognitive load, the mental energy needed to process information this way, can feel heavy.

Yet, despite the effort required, the Insights Mindset is worth it. It opens up new ways to tackle problems and uncover hidden solutions. I experience the value of the Insights Mindset myself (Tessa) frequently in my own research.

Let me give you a quick example of what I mean.

As part of my work at the Next Level Lab – a Harvard Graduate School of Education initiative that brings together perspectives from

67

cognitive science, neuroscience, and the learning sciences to study learning in the flow of work – I research how to enhance adults' cognitive and creative capabilities in the workplace.

One aspect of this research is looking at how people transfer existing knowledge, skills, and abilities to novel roles or tasks without further formal learning. Take for example the story of how Ventec Life Systems and the General Motors Plant in Kokomo, Indiana, helped address the global ventilator shortage in the COVID-19 pandemic.

Ventec Life Systems was a small biotech start up that was manufacturing a few thousand multifunction devices, that included ventilators for ALS patients, per year. The COVID-19 pandemic was rapidly emerging and the company pivoted to aiming to produce small, single-function critical care ventilators, about 200,000 of them in just a few months. However, they didn't have the infrastructure yet to manage the scale and pace of production required.

At the same time the GM plant in Kokomo had recently closed down. These two organizations partnered together, and began re-hiring the factory floor auto workers to build the critical care ventilators at scale.

Aside from the incredible bravery and ingenuity of these organizations and the people within them, the truly amazing part of this story, to me, is that these GM auto workers were not medical professionals or experts in medical device manufacturing. In fact, most (if not all) hadn't taken a community college course, completed a registered apprenticeship, or even taken a Massive Open Online Course and earned a digital badge in anything remotely related to medical device manufacturing when they were being rehired.

And yet, the 1,000 GM auto workers successfully translated their existing knowledge of process, operating procedures, quality assurance testing, and auto manufacturing to the novel context of critical care ventilators. They closed any gaps by using each other as resources and leveraging the expertise of the Ventec Life Systems experts.

All of this resulted in the delivery of 200,000 ventilators for critical care settings, and the saving of lives across the United States.

This is learning transfer in action. These workers were able to successfully transfer existing knowledge, skills and abilities, to a novel problem without excessive formal learning. They were able to adapt.

When I first started researching how adult workers do this, I initially believed that success depended solely on individual effort. Decades of research beforehand had focused on it being an individual cognitive skill, and so it made sense that this was my assumption walking into the research. The prevailing perspective was that learning transfer is something that happens in a person's mind as a result of their prior education.

However, as I gathered data and listened to workers' experiences at two major consulting firms through our projects at the Next Level Lab, I had to set aside my assumptions and dive deeper.

What emerged was a surprising truth: learning transfer in workplace contexts isn't just about individual ability or what happens in someone's mind. It's shaped by the task, the environment, and the more experienced people around them. It is a social process. The environment, context, and task itself can all help bring forward existing things we know into our working memory. Then through specific types of interactions with peers, managers, mentors and leaders, workers consider what is similar and different about the novel task, applying what is going to be helpful and also leaving behind what isn't.

In both my experience and Tom's, we had to collect a significant amount of data before making these shifts in thinking. When we began working on our respective challenges, we only had a small amount of information and needed to gather more. As we sifted through the data, we uncovered surprising insights.

In both cases, we never had complete information. Imagine trying to interview every person in every role within a large supply chain or every person who has ever transferred learning; it would be nearly impossible. That's okay, you don't need complete information.

The first data collected helps shape your understanding of the problem landscape. As you continue exploring, early insights and recurring themes start to emerge.

69

The Insights Mindset

Over time, if no new themes or insights appear, you reach a point called "thematic saturation," where the key ideas have surfaced, and additional data does not meaningfully change your understanding.

At this stage, durable insights begin to separate themselves from the noise. Examining them collectively allows you to make inferences and frame problems in a way that leads to breakthrough solutions.

Revisiting the Dinner Experiment

Remember the dinner experiment from Chapter 5? You had a conversation with a friend, asking qualitative questions about their experiences and perspectives on dinner. From that single interaction, you were able to make an educated guess about where to go for dinner next time, but you didn't have enough data to draw larger insights.

Now, imagine you expanded the experiment by conducting dozens of similar interviews within your community. As patterns emerged, you could infer broader insights. For example, if multiple people expressed concerns about food costs, health, and time constraints, you might conclude:

"People in our town want alternatives to restaurant delivery. While convenience and quality are important, the cost of delivery apps often leads to less healthy choices."

Now that you've gotten your feet wet with our small experiment let's explore a more structured approach to making sense of your fieldwork using the Interactions Mindset. This will help you turn observations into insights and insights into action.

Developing a Synthesizing Mind

As we learned through the Interactions Mindset, robust research is necessary to understand a problem, its stakeholders, and their needs. However, gathering data is just the first step. Once you've conducted

Innovation-ish

your interactions, you must make sense of the information to frame your understanding of the problem properly. This process follows two essential steps:

Analyze: Break the information down into smaller, more manageable pieces. This involves reading, reviewing, and scrutinizing the data to extract key elements.

Synthesize: Integrate the different pieces of related information to generate new insights. This step helps you make sense of the data and develop a deeper, more nuanced perspective.

If analysis involves breaking data down into small parts and finding their relationships, then synthesis involves combining those parts meaningfully to construct a coherent story. In Tom's supply chain challenge, his team analyzed their data by covering the walls with clusters of sticky notes filled with observations and insights. Their synthesis came when they distilled key themes and used those insights to reframe their understanding of the problem.

Synthesis is a kind of alchemy. It requires transforming raw insights into actionable knowledge, and is essential to finding the most effective solutions. In fact, Nobel Laureate Murray Gell-Mann once said:

> "In the twenty-first century, the most important kind of mind will be the synthesizing mind."

Despite its importance, synthesis is often undervalued and undertaught. Howard Gardner, a leader at Project Zero at Harvard's Graduate School of Education, wrote a book about his own synthesizing mind in which he highlights how little formal education focuses on teaching synthesis skills despite their critical importance in problem-solving and innovation. Traditional education environments tend to emphasize memorization and specialization, rather than emphasizing the core elements of sythesis: making connections across disciplines, identifying patterns, and forming coherent insights.

Synthesis is consistently the most challenging part of the courses we teach. It requires significant mental effort, and students often struggle with feeling lost at times. This is because we encourage them

The Insights Mindset

to go beyond simple synthesis and explore more complex, creative connections between ideas towards the kind of synthesis Howard and Murray were referencing. The higher level of synthesis we ask for involves more nuance. It requires weaving information together into new propositions, insights, and knowledge.

Cognitive Biases in Synthesis

Synthesis can be hindered by cognitive biases, which are unconscious thinking errors that distort our reasoning. Our brains seek efficiency, and they often take shortcuts to conserve mental energy and cognitive load.

One well-known bias people personally fall for all the time is hindsight bias, or the belief that past events were predictable all along. For example, after the Super Bowl our team discussed how they had known all along that the Philadelphia Eagles would beat the Kansas City Chiefs in their annual football game. We even pointed to "clear signs" that should have made it obvious. In reality, we were simply engaging in hindsight bias by convincing ourselves that an unpredictable event was actually foreseeable.

There are more than 150 known cognitive biases that are well documented and researched. Through years of teaching and consulting, we've observed six common cognitive biases that often interfere with synthesis in innovation work.

Common cognitive bias that can interfere with synthesis

Cognitive Bias	Description	Example
Jumping to Conclusion Bias	Making rapid judgments based on limited information. If you tend to decide quickly without all the facts, you might fail to distinguish between data-driven conclusions and personal assumptions.	A team sees a decline in sales and immediately blames social media marketing without investigating other potential causes like product quality or customer service issues.

Innovation-ish

Cognitive Bias	Description	Example
The Illusion of Validity	Overconfidence in the accuracy of your synthesis, leading you to skip the necessary follow-up work to validate your conclusions. If your synthesis is rushed and not deeply analyzed, you may overlook critical evidence, forcing you to redo your work multiple times.	A company runs a single focus group and assumes the feedback represents the entire customer base, without cross-checking with larger data sources.
Confirmation Bias	Seeking and using only data that supports your existing ideas, while ignoring or dismissing information that challenges them. This leads to false certainty and prevents truly innovative solutions from emerging.	A researcher studying remote work only looks for articles that support its benefits, ignoring studies that highlight productivity challenges.
Bandwagon Effect	A form of groupthink where the team seizes too quickly on a single idea, letting peer pressure override critical thinking. This places undue weight on an idea's popularity rather than its actual merits.	A startup shifts its business model after seeing competitors succeed with a new trend, without validating if the trend actually aligns with their customers' needs.
Anchoring Effect	Fixating on the first piece of data or insight and failing to reevaluate it in light of new evidence. This bias locks thinking onto initial assumptions, even when better information emerges.	A product team gets early feedback that one feature is essential and continues to prioritize it, even when later data suggests users prefer a different feature.

(continued)

The Insights Mindset

(continued)

Cognitive Bias	Description	Example
Bias Blind Spot	Believing that you are free from bias while easily recognizing bias in others. This leads to skipping necessary reflection jumping from data collection straight to solution mode because you assume you already know the answer.	A manager insists that their hiring process is fair and objective, while overlooking how personal preferences influence hiring decisions.

The critical problem behind these common biases is that they can prevent us from doing the essential original synthesis that will open us to fresh approaches to your problem at a big cost to innovation. We will end up with solutions that don't test well, won't connect with or satisfy users, and won't completely solve the problem that we set out to resolve. Put simply, these are bad strategies.

On the other hand, if we dive deeply into the data, engage in critical analysis, and approach synthesis with an open mind, we can make bigger conceptual leaps and generate breakthrough solutions, with less effort.

Over time, we've observed a clear pattern:

- Students who don't engage intentionally with synthesis tend to produce weaker solutions that lack depth and originality.
- Students who really work at synthesis go on to develop genuinely innovative ideas that work in the real world.

By breaking the synthesis process into clear steps and actively working against bias, we can train ourselves to think in ways that consistently generate better results.

Using Different Types of Reasoning

Imagine you are a business analyst tasked with understanding why people don't submit their expense forms on time and devising a better system. Your research shows that employees frequently open the expense form tab during downtime, like when they're having coffee or a snack, but rarely finish it, often leaving the tab open for days.

A deductive thinker would say: "If core work tasks are handled during dedicated work time, then opening the expense form only during downtime indicates that expense submission isn't considered a core responsibility."

An inductive thinker would say: "Based on this recurring pattern, employees seem to view expense submission as a low-priority task."

An abductive thinker would say: "The most likely explanation, based on the incomplete data I have, is that the expense form is too complex or time-consuming to complete in short breaks, suggesting that its design may not fit well with employees' natural workflow."

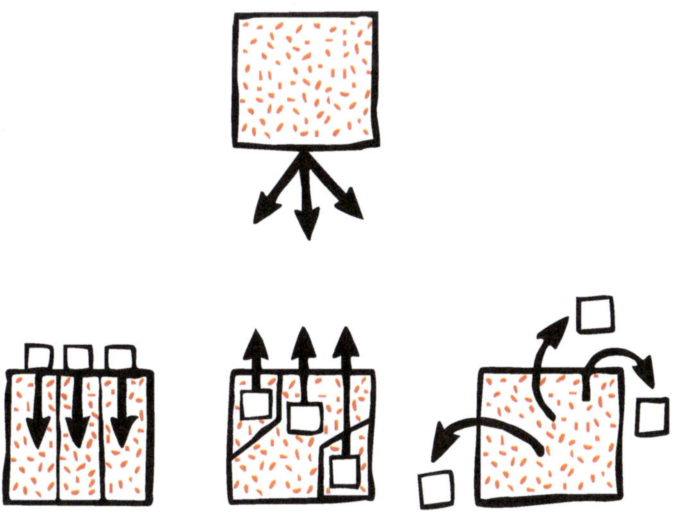

The same collected data can be synthesized deductively, inductively, and abductively.

Abductive reasoning takes incomplete data and makes an educated leap toward a new understanding. This is exactly what great innovators do. Instead of jumping to obvious conclusions, they sit with contradictions, searching for hidden patterns that shift their perspective on the real problem.

Synthesis involves thoughtful reasoning. As humans, our most powerful tool is our unique ability to reason through complex problems and make sense of diverse data. Whether we're creating new products or refining services, the type and quality of reasoning we use can significantly influence our outcomes.

As we saw with our business analyst example, there are three key types of reasoning: deductive, inductive, and abductive reasoning. While deductive and inductive reasoning are more familiar to most people, abductive reasoning is often less understood, yet it's critical for high-quality synthesis and innovation. Understanding their differences and how to apply them is essential for making informed decisions.

Deductive Reasoning

Deductive reasoning moves from a general principle to a specific conclusion. It's the kind of logic used in beginning algebra like the transitive property: if $A = B$ and $B = C$ then $A = C$. This structured, top-down approach exemplifies deductive reasoning.

In the expense form scenario, if we assume that core work tasks are handled during dedicated work time, then noticing that employees open the expense form only during downtime leads us to conclude that expense submission isn't seen as a core responsibility.

Deductive reasoning is powerful when working with clearly defined categories. Yet, its effectiveness depends on the accuracy of those categories. In dynamic, complex problems, the rigid structure of deductive reasoning can sometimes be limiting.

Inductive Reasoning

Inductive reasoning takes the opposite approach. It starts with specific observations and then zooms out to build broader theories based on those details. This bottom-up approach often leads to new insights or patterns that weren't immediately obvious. Instead of applying a predefined set of categories, inductive reasoning allows patterns to emerge organically from the data.

In the expense form scenario, observations show that employees frequently open the expense form tab during breaks yet rarely complete it. Using inductive reasoning, you might collect more detailed data through interviews or further observation and start identifying recurring themes. Employees might say that:

- The form is too complex.

- It takes too long to complete in a short break.

- They feel pressured to do it quickly and make errors.

From these specific observations, you might conclude that the expense form is perceived as a low-priority task within their workflow. Inductive reasoning is especially useful when tackling messy, open-ended problems, allowing solutions to develop naturally rather than forcing a predetermined conclusion.

Abductive Reasoning

Abductive reasoning is the most essential for innovation. It asks: *Based on the data in front of me, what is the most likely explanation for this issue?*

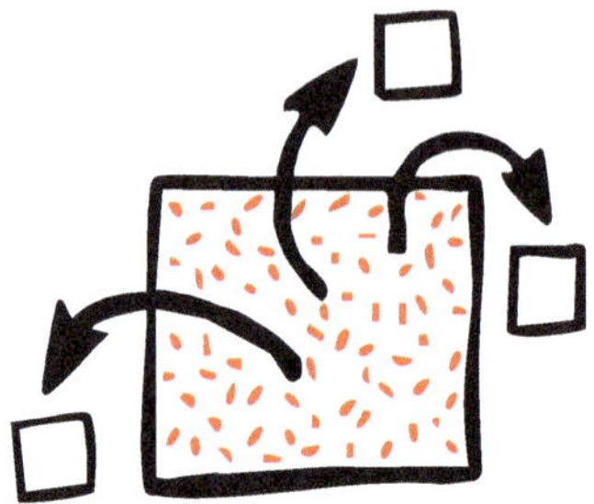

You truly get to exercise your creative muscles when applying abductive reasoning. It requires making educated guesses based on incomplete information, like fitting together the elements of a story when some parts are missing. You need to embody becoming a real life Sherlock Holmes (a famous abductive reasoner).

This form of reasoning lies at the heart of innovation because it allows us to propose new and untested solutions when faced with gaps in our understanding. It is a leap into the unknown, informed by our best interpretations of available data.

For example if we revisit the expense sanction. While we recognize this behavior, the *exact* reason remains unclear.

- Deductive reasoning tells us employees don't view it as a core task.

- Inductive reasoning suggests that complexity or time constraints might be an issue.

- *Abductive reasoning leads us to hypothesize that: The form may not be well-designed for quick completion, meaning employees get frustrated or abandon it halfway through.*

This hypothesis, drawn from partial data, prompts us to explore ways to simplify the expense form and better align it with employees' workflow.

The bottom line?

Each type of reasoning offers a different lens through which we interpret the world. When used together, they provide a powerful framework for problem-solving.

Our journey through deductive, inductive, and abductive reasoning isn't just about problem-solving; it's about storytelling, innovation, and understanding the human experience. When blended effectively, these approaches help us move beyond surface-level answers to uncover deeper, more transformative insights.

When to use each reasoning type

Reasoning Type	How It Works	When To Use It
Deductive Reasoning	Starts with general principles and applies them to specific cases.	When working with clear, well-defined categories or established principles.
Inductive Reasoning	Starts with specific observations and builds broader conclusions.	When identifying patterns in data without preconceived assumptions.
Abductive Reasoning	Uses incomplete data to make an educated guess about the most likely explanation.	When facing uncertainty and needing to formulate testable hypotheses.

Solving the Right Problem

Abductive reasoning is how you ensure you're solving the right problem. It prompts you to challenge assumptions and reframe the question you are asking. This shift in perspective can lead to breakthrough solutions, as exemplified by Doug Dietz's work at GE Healthcare.

Doug Dietz, an industrial designer at GE Healthcare, was responsible for designing Magnetic Resonance Imaging (MRI) machines for hospitals. These powerful machines can peer deep inside the human body, generating images that help doctors diagnose illnesses and determine treatments.

For patients, the MRI experience is far from comfortable. The machines are massive. Metal coils vibrate and produce loud, jarring bangs when electricity passes through them. Patients must lie perfectly still inside a narrow, tunnel-like space while enduring this noise. While the procedure is painless and non-invasive, the experience itself can be deeply unsettling, often causing anxiety.

One day, while observing an MRI scan, Doug saw a little girl approaching the machine. She was sobbing, clinging to her parents, and begging them to take her home.

At that moment, Doug saw the machine through her eyes. She was being rolled inside a large, noisy, and scary machine, told to stay perfectly still, all while the loud bangs echoed around her.

Staying motionless is difficult for any patient, so understandably it is an enormous challenge for a young child, even in the friendliest of circumstances. When Doug voiced his concern, the hospital staff reassured him: they sedate most children under the age of nine before scans.

Doug realized that he missed the bigger picture by focusing on technical features. His life-saving technology had an unintended consequence. Children were being sedated out of fear.

Reframing the Problem

Doug realized he needed to make the experience less traumatic. But what exactly was the problem that he needed to solve?

The obvious questions might be:

- How might we create an MRI that is quieter?
- How might we design an MRI that is much faster?

Both are reasonable questions; however, they assume the machine itself has to change. Redesigning the MRI machine itself would take years of development and regulatory approval. Plus, the physics wouldn't change and the coils would still make loud banging sounds.

With these constraints, the problem appears nearly impossible to solve. But what if that assumption was wrong?

Searching for inspiration, Doug sought out human-centered design, an innovation approach that prioritizes empathy and user experience. What if the problem wasn't the MRI, but how children experienced it?

The new perspective led to a new question: How might we reduce fear and anxiety for children undergoing an MRI scan?

Doug's users were children. He studied childhood experiences from many perspectives. He collaborated with child psychology specialists, daycare workers, museum staff, GE volunteers, doctors, and hospital staff to design a new solution. They tested a new approach with the Children's Hospital of Pittsburgh.

Now, when a child arrives for an MRI, they are greeted by an "adventure guide" dressed in costume who sets the scene for their journey. The once intimidating MRI room has been transformed with paint and props to look like a pirate ship or a jungle expedition.

Before the scan, children are given a storyline and props to bring the experience to life. If the MRI room is a pirate ship, they are sneaking below deck. The loud banging noises? Cannon blasts from enemy ships! Their mission? Stay perfectly still to avoid being discovered and win the treasure at the end.

What child wouldn't want to go on that adventure?

The experience now mirrors familiar storytelling formats found in museums, theme parks, or classrooms. This engages children's natural imagination and play, turning fear into excitement.

The results of this reframed approach were remarkable:

- 90 percent patient satisfaction rate.

- Less than 27 percent of children required sedation.

- Hospitals could perform more scans per day.

By reframing the problem, Doug and his team found a simple, low-cost solution that worked. They dramatically improved the MRI experience, without redesigning the machine itself. It transforms a frightening medical procedure into a creative, immersive adventure. Today it's offered as the GE Adventure Series MRI.

Doug's story proves a timeless truth: finding the right problem makes all the difference. Seemingly impossible problems often have simple solutions. Innovation is about reimagining, not reinventing.

Doug's story serves as a powerful reminder:

- **Always question assumptions:** Don't assume the "obvious" problem is the real one.
- **Reframe the problem:** Shifting perspectives can unlock unexpected solutions.
- **Prioritize user experience:** Great innovation often comes from empathy, not just technology.

Framing Problems

Abductive reasoning challenges our assumptions and pushes us to ask deeper questions. By synthesizing insights and making an inductive leap, Doug redefined the problem, reminding us that the issue we begin with is rarely the real problem that needs solving.

We often reference a famous quote (often mistakenly attributed to Albert Einstein):

> "If I had an hour to solve a problem, and my life depended on it, I would spend 55 minutes thinking about the problem and 5 minutes thinking about the solution."

Another version of this wisdom comes from Charles Kettering, an engineer and inventor who helped shape modern automotive technologies:

> "A problem well stated is a problem half solved."

Framing the problem correctly changes the solutions you generate. As our colleague Tina Seelig, a Stanford professor and longtime director of the Stanford Technology Ventures Program, says:

> "The solutions you get are baked into the frame of the problem."

This idea aligns with what cognitive scientists call the Framing Effect: the way we phrase a problem or present data changes how we interpret it.

To illustrate this, consider a common life event: a high school graduation.

- If you ask: "How do we plan a graduation **dinner**?" Quickly you likely imagine a familiar set of ideas: You might think about fancy dishes, family gatherings, and favorite recipes.

- You might include speeches, stories, or advice for the graduate.

If you ask: "How do we plan a graduation **celebration**?" Now, there are a new set of ideas:

- You might think of decorations, a cake, gifts, or even hiring a band.

- A celebration could be a party, a gathering at a venue, or an experience like a road trip.

If you ask: "How do we **mark the occasion** of a graduation?" Again, a whole new set of ideas emerges:

- You could plant a tree, write a song, plan a gap-year trip.

- You might even hire the graduate into a family business.

The question determines the type of solutions you'll generate. If you frame the problem incorrectly, it doesn't matter how many solutions you try. You won't solve the right problem.

This is exactly what happened in the supply chain case (where the original goal was reducing labor costs) and the MRI case (where making the machine quieter was years away or impossible).

Both of these frames are solving the wrong problem. Reframing based on insights transformed their approach, turning an impossible problem into an inspired solution.

When starting out, it's hard to know if you're solving the right problem. Even before collecting data, you can frame the problem based on your existing knowledge. Spending time refining the problem statement can narrow your focus and help plan your research. It's worth getting some clarity before investing time in interactions. However, once you start gathering real-world data using the Interactions Mindset, it's important to let go of your initial framing and allow insights to shape your understanding.

Most people are familiar with brainstorming, a creative process that involves generating a large number of ideas and then filtering for the best ones. Few have heard of framestorming; a process that involves generating multiple ways to frame a problem before deciding how to approach it.

Framestorming helps in three ways:

- It forces you to make your abstract understanding concrete by putting it into words.

- It makes your thinking visible to yourself and others.

- It reveals biases and assumptions that might otherwise go unnoticed.

Imagine you're on the student council at a university. A recent article in the school newspaper highlights an increase in pedestrian–bicycle accidents on campus. The publicity creates urgency, and your team is asked to address the problem.

At first glance, the problem seems clear: "How might we reduce pedestrian–bicycle accidents on campus?"

Seems like a reasonable question, right? If you're already questioning whether this is the real problem, you're demonstrating an Insights Mindset. Well done!

Instead of jumping to solutions, your team spends a few weeks observing students on campus and interviewing them. Here's what you hear:

> "I have to bike because my class schedule only gives me 10 minutes to get from one end of campus to the other."
>
> "If I don't make it to class on time, I get marked late and might lose my spot on the basketball team."
>
> "I rearranged my schedule so all my classes are near the engineering quad. I need to pick up my kids by 3:30 p.m."

Innovation-ish

"The traffic circle near the law school, mechanical engineering, and the library gets flooded when class gets out. I avoid it."

"I almost hit someone last quarter three times. I'm lucky nobody got hurt."

"My schedule is packed. I spend all day running from one building to another."

When reading these responses, you probably already see multiple overlapping issues. Each problem intersects with the idea of pedestrian–bicycle accidents, while also pointing to deeper challenges related to scheduling, infrastructure, and transit patterns.

Based on these insights, your team generates alternative problem frames:

- How might we schedule class transitions to allow students to get between classrooms on time?

- How might we reduce traffic congestion during class transitions?

- How might we ensure all students arrive at class on time without rushing?

- How might we provide supplemental services that integrate into students' schedules?

Each of these questions frames the problem differently, leading to entirely different solutions. And all of them are grounded in real insights, not just assumptions.

It's possible, even likely, that more than one problem needs to be addressed, and now, you have evidence to support your framing.

At this stage, your team has multiple possible problem frames. How do you decide where to focus?

- If you don't have enough insights yet → Use the Interactions Mindset to collect more data from a wider range of people.

- If a frame aligns with your data but has variations → Back to the Interactions Mindset to refine your questions and collect more focused data.

The Insights Mindset

- If a clear winner emerges → Shift to the Ideas Mindset and begin generating solutions.

- If you haven't learned anything substantial → Go back to the beginning and start over with the Insights Mindset to reframe your problem again. (This happens more often than you might think.)

Key Takeaways

Push Past the Obvious
True insights come from challenging assumptions, exploring contradictions, and looking for patterns that aren't immediately visible. The best solutions emerge when you take the time to see the deeper story behind the data.

From Insight to Inference
Abductive reasoning allows you to make logical and grounded inferences from the insights you have. This helps refine your understanding of the problem and point toward better solutions.

Frame the Right Problem Before Jumping to Solutions
The way you define the problem determines the solutions you'll generate. Reframing your challenge based on insights, rather than assumptions, ensures you're solving the problem that actually matters.

Chapter 7

The Ideas Mindset

"That's all we have for class today. Your homework is to generate 100 different ideas to solve your problem before class next week," we announce. It takes a few seconds for the words to sink in as the students collect their things, grab their bags, and then stop. Half of them look up with confusion, while the other half show a hint of fear in their eyes. After several questions about specifics, parameters, and the "definition" of an idea, they realize that we are indeed serious about the 100-ideas assignment.

In the next class, they return energized, bringing whiteboards or poster boards filled with ideas. Most go well beyond 100 and are eager for more. They learn that once they exhaust the first dozen obvious ideas, they can break through a mental barrier. Beyond that point, real idea generation begins.

Breaking past conventional thinking requires overcoming cognitive biases that limit creativity. The availability heuristic leads people to favor ideas that come easily to mind, often based on recent experience. Anchoring bias further constrains thinking by making the first idea unduly influence all subsequent ones. This is especially evident when people are given examples.

Research suggests that only after about 10–15 conventional ideas per person, do truly novel ones emerge. That's why we ask our students to push to 100, as we know that breakthrough solutions require a large "generative" phase before narrowing down.

The Ideas Mindset is about generating many ideas to explore a wide range of possibilities. In our classes, we challenge students to generate 100 ideas to break free from conventional thinking.

Each class we have taught for the past ten years has started with a new challenge. Sometimes, we give a broad topic described in a single word, such as "Memory," "Death," or "Lines." Sometimes, the challenges are much more specific, such as "How might we reduce fast-food companies' impact on marine life?" or "How can we make campus study areas better suit the needs of all students?" Regardless of the topic, the student team spends a few weeks defining their own unique problem within the original challenge. We ask them to suspend their natural tendency to solve the problem during that time.

In business, we need results and clear solutions to problems. That creates tension between coming up with many divergent ideas and producing practical ideas that can be implemented. Ultimately, we need an idea we can implement if we are going to succeed in achieving our goals. However, before we reach implementation, we benefit far more from generating a large volume of ideas. To quote our colleagues at the Stanford d.school, Jeremy Utley and Perry Klebahn, "Ideaflow – the number of ideas you or your team can produce – is the only business metric that matters."

Generating Ideas

Two common innovation mythology stories lead us to think that an individual genius has a magic eureka moment and comes up with a game-changing innovation or idea that launches a huge company. However, the truth is that generating a large volume of diverse ideas increases the chance of finding the ones that solve the problem more effectively and robustly.

Improv acting is a pure form of creative collaboration and idea generation, both of which are essential to the Ideas Mindset. Improv is theater that starts with nothing and creates everything. The team generates characters, dialogue, scenery, plot, and music. Each scene starts with total ambiguity and requires jumping into a state of flow with others. That's a high bar to reach.

What makes improv so powerful, and so daunting, is that it demands presence and mutual commitment. Performers must listen

Innovation-ish

deeply, then accept and build on everything others share. It also means that no one controls the evolving narrative.

In this heightened state of co-creation, psychological safety and adaptability are essential. To achieve this feat of performing in this environment, teams practice a specific set of skills. Many of these skills, like being present in the moment, perspective taking, and open-mindedness, are essential to generating ideas.

Improv and idea generation require humility to give freely, accept others, and let go of attachment to your own ideas. Will taking an improv class make you a better brainstormer? Perhaps. It will help you to build the skills you need to generate more ideas.

Young children are natural improvisers. My (Rich) son Sequoia is fully committed to the stories he creates with cars and figurines. When I join his play, he smoothly adapts, accepting my offers no matter how silly they are. Together, we build outlandish and wild stories and ideas. His flexibility and naturally playful way of engaging inspire me to be a better brainstormer when we work together. You spark that same creativity and inspiration working with your own teams to generate ideas.

The Ideas Mindset is about removing the barriers of divergent thinking and collaborating with people who think differently than you – it is about intentionally seeing the world as generative and abundant full of possibilities. When we've seen teams engage divergent thinking in their idea generation, they enter a state of flow and skillfully integrate the following factors:

Avoid judgment: Judgment of yourself and others.

Build on other ideas: Say Yes, And! to ideas.

Broaden your perspectives: Include diverse perspectives.

Focus on generation: Avoid the decision trap.

We can find inspiration for adopting this mindset in improvisational theater – a form of pure, collaborative idea generation. It requires a team that chooses to adopt these factors intensively in short bursts of scenes or performances.

Avoid Judgment

Let's try an experiment. For the rest of your day, try to suspend judgment in all the ways you might normally apply it. Are you ready? It doesn't sound so easy, does it? In fact, many people spend years practicing a variety of techniques to try to avoid judgment of themselves and others.

When I (Rich) walked into my first improv class years ago, I had no idea that my first hurdle would be overcoming my own self-judgment. Allowing unedited thoughts to come out is being vulnerable and risks others judging you harshly. Internally you may think, "What will everyone think if I say THAT?"

A lack of trust of this kind in idea generation can undermine the whole effort. Shutting down one person with critical judgments sends a signal to the others that it's not safe to try out new ideas. That removes an essential ingredient to a successful ideation session.

Years later, after teaching improv classes to thousands of beginning improvisers myself, I developed a deeper appreciation for creating a safe environment. I realized that if I failed at my first job of creating a sense of safety, nothing else truly mattered. The same principle applies to leading an ideation session. Your primary job is to foster trust. When people feel safe enough to set aside judgment, creative ideas flourish.

One powerful way to cultivate trust and minimize judgment is to build on other ideas.

Build on Other Ideas

One of the fundamental rules in improvisation is simply saying "Yes, And" as you respond to people, then building whatever they last said. The opposite of "Yes, And" is "No" or another slightly nicer way of saying no with "Yes, but." Imagine if someone asked you for ideas, and the first thing they said after each one you offered was No. Unfortunately, far too many people have experienced this; for some, this might be a daily occurrence. Now imagine how it might feel if every time you suggest an idea to your friends, partner, or co-worker, they say yes! It is energizing and encouraging.

An Experiment in "Yes, And!" Activity

1. Pick a time and person where you are reasonably safe from the consequences of saying yes – *perhaps a close friend, colleague, or family member.*

2. Try to say **"Yes, And"** to everything for five minutes with them – *and enjoy the experience.*

3. After five minutes, ask them how they feel before you reveal your secret.

In the improv world, it's common to hear people say, "Yes, And take you on adventures. And No keeps you safe."

In my (Rich) experience teaching improv for several decades, I noticed that beginning improvisers tend to say "no" a lot. When presented with an imagined offer to perhaps "ride a camel through the city streets with cars everywhere," it might be prudent in real life to say no to keep yourself safe. However, in an improvisation scene, there is no real camel, traffic, or danger. It takes time for them to learn that the most interesting option is to say yes! What an exciting opportunity in an imagined world. When they add *And,* it becomes even more exciting – "Yes, And let's make it a race!" – now they have built on the original idea with added adventure.

Saying "Yes, And!" is a powerful way to encourage idea-sharing. It validates others' contributions, making them feel valued and reinforcing their willingness to share more.

Broaden Your Perspectives

While there is no perfect formula for an ideal ideation team, certain qualities can help you assemble an effective group with a broad perspective. Prioritizing diverse backgrounds and viewpoints fosters richer idea generation. Hierarchy can sometimes hinder open sharing, so creating an environment where all voices are valued is crucial. Additionally, larger teams bring more perspectives, increasing the potential for breakthrough ideas.

First, *include people who see the world very differently from each other*. Teams of people with broad perspectives and backgrounds tend to generate more and better ideas than teams that are too homogeneous. Each new perspective brings a new set of experiences, and associations create a larger pool of potential ideas.

Second, *ensure that all perspectives are shared*. To help achieve that, it is essential to avoid adding layers of hierarchy in ideation teams. A hierarchy can cause people to defer to those who outrank them and increase the tendency to judge ideas. It's human nature to want to have the respect and approval of people who stand in a position of authority, and that can lead to self-suppression of perspectives.

Third, *include many perspectives*. The number of people you select for the team is another factor that can impact the quality and quantity of ideas from your team. Research consistently shows that collaborative teams come up with better and more varied ideas than individuals working alone or independently alongside others. Larger groups are more likely than small ones to generate rare ideas. One reason for this is that, as a group, you have access to the collective intelligence of the group, as it emerges from the collaboration efforts of the group.

Collective intelligence is more than just the sum of the individual group members' intelligence; it is the product of working together with other people. Since you all notice, perceive, and think differently from each other, your collaborative effort can amplify the landscape of possibilities.

Focus on Generation

As a great ideation session approaches its final minutes, the organizer often stumbles into a common trap. After thanking people for their great work and summarizing a few key points, they ask the group to decide the way forward. *That is the decision trap*!

Everything has gone well up to this point. The well-chosen team trusts each other, avoids judging ideas, and then builds upon them, adding their own unique perspectives. They all see the world from very different perspectives and it shows in the ideas. These are great results! So what's the problem?

We tend to include the people who generated the ideas in the decision-making because moving back to the concrete by picking one idea feels safe and satisfying. Asking them to seek consensus on a single decision would involve reversing all those positive habits you just experienced. The risk is that they would judge themselves and others, mindlessly fall in love with their favorite idea, and exclude rather than include the possibilities. That's the trap.

Decision-making is about converging on a choice aligned with a vision for the future. It takes time and work to align a team to a shared understanding of what success looks like. Brainstorming, however, is about divergence, not convergence. Asking that same team to turn around, judge ideas, and converge is almost always a mistake. Even if they had the right frame of mind to engage in evaluation, research indicates that deferring evaluation promotes more daring suggestions. Knowing evaluation is coming at the end of a brainstorming session actually can hinder the goal of wild ideas.

One of the most common conversations at my (Tessa's) house is what to do on the weekend. I often ask my kiddos to help me come up with ideas. We get everything from having a friend over, going to Hawaii, playing in the sandpit at the local park, and having a movie night. Right now my nearly two-year-old says either the pool, plane, or park, but ultimately she loves to follow her sisters wild ideas so, if I let my generative brainstorming team (a.k.a kiddos) decide, we would definitely end up with Hawaii.

Rather than having them make all the decisions, I thank them and let them know I'll think about it momentarily and consider all the elements, including the problem we are solving and real-life constraints such as cost and time. Once I have decided, I communicate and connect it to their effort. For example, I might say, "Hey, you guys came up with the idea we should go to Hawaii for the weekend. Oh my, wouldn't that be fun! So I took from that that you want to have some fun in the water, so we're going to go to the YMCA this afternoon and have water play."

The Ideas Mindset

Both my kiddos are excellent brainstorming partners, but just like your brainstorming team, they should not be the decision-makers. I find that the best way to avoid the decision trap is to conclude a brainstorming session with gratitude. Doing that means I always end up with a team that is excited and ready to return for another session when needed.

Over time you can identify and encourage individuals to embrace the Ideas Mindset – avoiding judgment, building on others' ideas, broadening their perspectives, and focusing on generation. At first, shifting mindsets may feel awkward or forced. With persistence, you will soon experience the energy of creative flow – sparking a wealth of ideas, including some that are delightfully wild!

Embracing Wild Ideas

When you are solving a problem, it seems like common sense that you want to find practical ideas. If you aim only for practical ideas, you'll end up with predictable solutions that are safe, incremental changes. Yet, if you push yourself toward wild, seemingly impossible ideas, you uncover unexpected possibilities. Every transformative innovation starts as an idea that seems, at first, impractical. The key is knowing when to take an outlandish idea and sculpt it into something usable.

We want wild ideas that go beyond our limitations. These are the kinds of ideas that, at first, don't feel safe. Ideas that may be too big or ambiguous make us unsure if we can accomplish them. Ideas that involve a touch of magic, even science fiction.

The world of innovation is filled with stories of people who have had ideas that did not seem safe.

Orville and Wilbur Wright dreamed of building a powered flying machine that could transport a person with controlled, sustained, powered flight – a truly bold idea for human civilization. On a cold December morning in 1903, Orville Wright climbed into the cockpit of the Flyer. Wilbur held his breath. The airplane lurched forward, its fragile wooden wings slicing through the air. And then, for 12 exhilarating seconds, it flew. The Wright brothers didn't magically come up with the perfect design one day. In July of 1899, they began a journey of building gliders. They built, failed, refined, and iterated dozens of times. Each attempt, each seemingly absurd experiment, brought them closer to their famous flight.

Henry Ford was a farm boy who dreamed of helping farmers get their crops to market. In 1903, he revealed his idea to revolutionize the automobile industry, which only produced a few expensive, unreliable cars. He said,

> "I will build a motor car for the great multitude. It will be large enough for the family but small enough for the individual to run and care for. It will be constructed of the best materials, by the best men to be hired, after the simplest designs that modern engineering can devise. But it will be so low in price that no man making a good salary will be unable to own one…"

On September 27, 1908, the first Model T left the factory, fulfilling one of the 15,000 orders placed in the first few days of its announcement. Nineteen years later, Henry Ford watched the 15 millionth Model T roll off the assembly line. During that time, the price dropped from about $800 to $300. Adjusted to today, almost 100 years later, it's equivalent to a drop of about $25,000 to $5,000.

United States Navy Rear Admiral Grace Hopper was one of the first programmers on the Harvard University Mark I computers in 1944. The Mark I was programmed by punching holes in paper tape 24 channels wide. Later, as computers evolved, she dreamed of programming them using English instead of symbols or mathematics. In 1953, while working at Remington Rand, she was told that she couldn't do this because computers didn't understand English. Two years later, she developed a working prototype of the first programming language, FLOW-MATIC, that understood 20 English statements. It was the foundation of another language called COBOL, which, in 1997, Gartner reported that 80 percent of the world's business ran on COBOL and is still used today globally by governments and businesses.

95

The Ideas Mindset

Each of these innovators was dismissed and even ridiculed for their outlandish ideas. They saw the world for what it could be, not what it was in their times. You don't invent ideas like the airplane, the car, and a programming language by taking existing technologies and simply adding some incremental features.

By daring to dream big, these innovators pursued all the steps required to translate their wild ideas into reality. With small steps, big ideas are made possible. When you generate a wild idea, you break the barriers of convention, practicality, and even feasibility. You reach beyond what we can do today and imagine a new magical idea that solves the problem.

Imagining ideas that reach beyond today's reality opens the door to new technologies, processes, chemicals, or materials. The idea is not to inspire large research and development investments. Instead it's taking that wild idea and pulling it back just enough to make it reality.

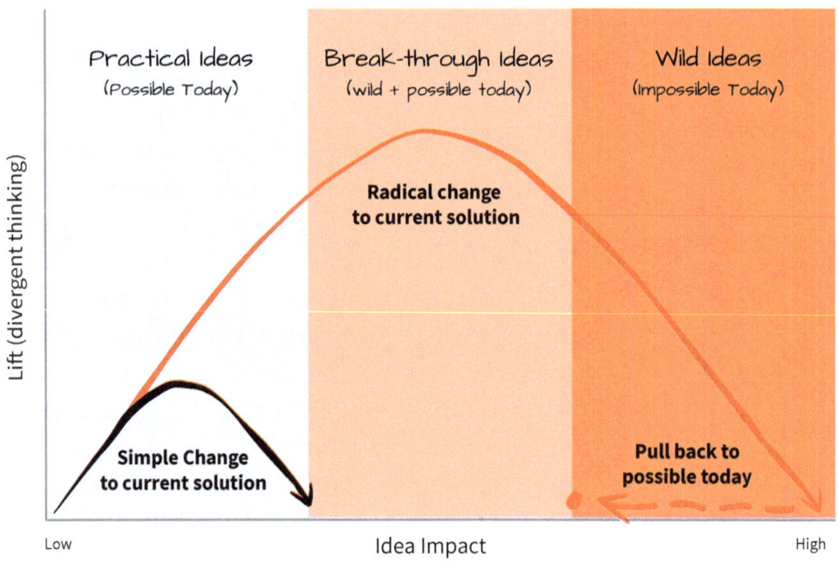

Wild ideas lead to a bigger impact in the real world.

For example, recall our story about a Native American clinic. A community clinic becoming a low-income housing developer might appear like a pretty wild idea. However, after getting a critical

Innovation-ish

insight into the population they served they were able to add this critical missing piece to the local community and further their mission with the resources they already had.

Or recall the kindergarten student who invented the 13-hour clock for their teacher to have an extra hour to get ready in the morning? While adorable and sweet, it's also a pretty wild idea. However, if we use the same lens of pulling things back to practicality, it isn't beyond possibility that people could agree to split things into 26 even segments as opposed to 24. It might work just as well. Sure a minute and second would be shorter now, and a one hour meeting would end a little earlier – would that be so bad?

Practical and doable ideas make us feel safe. However, they can also limit our potential impact and prevent us from creating real innovations that solve complex problems.

To get wild ideas, we need to brainstorm.

Brainstorming

It's not difficult to find articles on "Why brainstorming works." There are many thoughtful articles that reference academic studies and detailed examples of innovation. Conversely, it's equally easy to find thoughtful articles on "Why brainstorming doesn't work." Often both articles are from the same source like the *Harvard Business Review*. This contrast reveals that some people experience brainstorming as a flow of ideas and collaborative energy, while others feel pressured to be brilliant and perform on the spot.

What's behind these different experiences?

First, the research shows that people use different definitions of the same word.

Second, just because you know the "rules" for brainstorming doesn't mean you can use them with expertise.

Third, beyond the mechanics, your team or group's culture must be capable of humility and vulnerability to reach the creative, collaborative state that brainstorming indeed requires.

For several years, there has been an expansion in the terms people use to talk about generating ideas. In fact, according to Google Trends, published books since 2000 show that the term "ideation" is used twice the rate of brainstorming. Many words now refer to the process – generative, exploring divergence, creative exploration. In our work with experienced brainstormers, it is actually the collaboration and flow state that make it incredible. It's fun, productive, and often leads to surprising results that let you leap forward in new directions.

50 Wild Ideas Activity

Let's put this into action – it's time for you to try on the Ideas Mindset. *(It's better, not cheating, if you ask a friend or two to join you!)* You have 10 minutes.

1. Grab a piece of paper, a whiteboard, or a stack of sticky notes.
2. Pick a problem you care about.
3. Now generate 50 ideas. Yes, 50!

Don't stop until you do. Because that's where the real ideas begin.

Applying Brainstorming Levers

You hit a wall. Your brainstorming session started strong, but then the ideas dried up. This is where simple shifts in perspective jolt your thinking into new territory. For example, what happens if you reframe the problem? What if you push yourself to solve it in 24 hours? What if you imagine the solutions you get by adding a five-year-old to your team? Great brainstormers know that when creativity stalls, it's not because they've run out of ideas, it's because they haven't shaken up their perspective.

In physics, a lever amplifies the force you can exert, giving you a *mechanical advantage* in pushing, lifting, or moving something beyond your usual capability. In the same way, *brainstorming levers* are conceptual levers you can use to shift your problem frame and boost the number of ideas you generate. As discussed in Chapter 6, the framing effect and semantic priming shape the type of solutions we generate.

Each brainstorming lever shifts the problem frame in subtle ways, prompting new associations between ideas. The words or prompts used in these levers activate different parts of your semantic network (the mental map of everything you know) helping you retrieve and connect concepts that might not otherwise come to mind. Neuroscience research shows that the greater the "semantic distance" between two combined concepts, the more likely the outcome is creative. This highlights how brainstorming levers help access remote or uncommon knowledge, expanding idea generation.

By altering your brainstorming questions you cue a broader range of unique and distant associations, leading to more creative ideas.

Let's explore how you can use brainstorming levers to generate a higher volume and more diverse range of ideas. As we introduce a few of our favorite levers, we encourage you to experiment and build your own library of levers. To illustrate the levers, consider the example of bicyclists crisscrossing the Stanford University campus. Two-wheeled traffic can become heavy, and certain intersections pose dangers for cyclists and pedestrians. Both groups recognize it as an issue without casting blame on either side.

We can reframe the problem as a question seeking solutions:

How might we reduce pedestrian–bicycle accidents on campus?

You might begin by brainstorming as many ideas as you can, quickly generating 10 or 20 options: separate bike lanes with barriers, speed bumps, removing trees that block visibility, narrow gates that slow bike traffic, and more. Soon, you might run out of steam. To avoid The Creativity Gap creeping in, you should give yourself new sparks of ideas by using something like The Twist Lever.

The Twist Lever

With The Twist Lever, you break down your original brainstorming question ("How might we reduce pedestrian–bicycle accidents on campus?") using these simple steps:

- Note all of the keywords – the most meaningful ones. In our example, it might be "reduce," "pedestrian–bicycle," "accidents," and "campus."
- Elaborate on each keyword with alternatives, similar words, opposites, combinations, and different scales.
- Create a new list of questions, variations of the original, by replacing the words with the alternatives.
- Start brainstorming on these new questions.

For instance, *reduce* could be replaced with *eliminate, slow down,* or *increase,* leading us to a question like – "How might we eliminate pedestrian–bicycle accidents on campus?" Similarly, *pedestrian–bicycles* could be replaced with *pedestrian, bicycle, automobile, bicycle–auto,* or *non-transportation,* perhaps giving us "How might we reduce bicycle–auto accidents on campus?" We can also get more prompts by changing "reduce" and "pedestrian–bicycle" simultaneously, such as "How might we *eliminate* bicycle accidents on campus?"

Original: How might we **reduce pedestrian–bicycle** accidents on **campus?**

- How might we reduce **bicycle** accidents on campus?
- How might we **eliminate bicycle** accidents on campus?
- How might we reduce **bicycle** accidents in **Palo Alto?**
- How might we **eliminate** pedestrian–bicycle accidents **globally?**
- How might we **lessen bicycle** accidents **statewide?**

Even if you only get ten new ideas from each of these questions, you'd be halfway done with the 100-idea homework we assign to our students.

If you keep going, you can substitute any combination of one, two, or all three keywords. Even only a few different adjustments can quickly give you many different prompts to work with. In practice, we often see that generating new prompts "on the fly" helps provide a new burst of creative spark to the team. Another way of finding creative sparks that seems counterintuitive is to limit yourself with constraints.

The Constraints Lever

Giving yourself complete creative freedom might sound like lowering the barriers to ideas, allowing you to generate with ease. We find that the opposite, constraints, are often more helpful to increase your generative ability by employing criteria such as money, timing/timeline, context, geography, or size (building vs. laptop; train track vs. ruler). For example:

- **Money:** How might we reduce pedestrian–bicycle accidents on campus for **$10 per student?**
- **Money:** How might we *reduce* bicycle accidents on campus **for free?**
- **Time:** How might we *eliminate* bicycle accidents on campus **today?**
- **Geography:** How might we reduce bicycle accidents in Palo Alto **near the library?**
- **Money and Time:** How might we *reduce* bicycle accidents on campus **for free today?**

The Persona Lever

Solutions are usually generated for a particular type of person or category, which we call a Persona. It's important to deeply understand the needs of the people involved, the stakeholders. However, when generating solutions, you can expand the number and variety of ideas by using a variety of Personas.

Typically, we find it helpful to consider the Age, Interest, and Experiences of the person you are developing to spark a generative brainstorm.

Here are some examples of mixing up Age, Interest, or Experiences to our campus safety example:

- How might we reduce pedestrian–bicycle accidents on campus **for undergraduate students?**
- How might we reduce pedestrian–bicycle accidents on campus **for grad students?**
- How might we reduce pedestrian–bicycle accidents on campus **for parents visiting campus?**
- How might we reduce pedestrian–bicycle accidents on campus for **new students in the first month of each year?**

The Designer Lever

In the same way that the Persona Lever lets you use your knowledge and associations with the potential user group for your solutions, you can use the same technique to imagine that you, as the designer, might be different – to design "as if" you were someone else. Consider the brands you commonly see day to day.

- How might **Coca-Cola** reduce pedestrian–bicycle accidents?
- How might **Disney** reduce pedestrian–bicycle accidents?
- How might **Apple reduce** pedestrian–bicycle accidents?

Each lever serves the same goal: sparking more ideas, encouraging unconventional thinking, and providing fresh starting points. They work through a process called "conceptual expansion," which pushes the brain to form new associations by activating the Semantic Network and engaging the Default Mode Network, which supports divergent thinking and the retrieval of unexpected ideas as we discussed at the beginning of the chapter.

Look at the impact of using each of these levers twice in our example with three keywords. Two alternatives for each keyword, two constraints, two personas, and two designers give 96 different variations. And three each for the same levers gives 432 possibilities! We are not suggesting even coming close to trying all the possibilities. The point is that you can quickly and easily generate variations in the flow of brainstorming.

As you try these, you will see they become easier to use with practice. You may find some levers are more productive or your personal preference. You may even discover new levers of your own.

Creating Levers

We were running a workshop with a group of C-Suite executives from several luxury and premium personal care brands on the Iterations Mindset. As often happens, while we were in the workshop it became clear that what they were working on required us to shift mindsets to the Ideas Mindset. We considered how we might come up with more wild ideas that related to their offerings and emerging technologies.

Putting that up as a problem statement and asking people to come up with solutions that include emerging technologies can be quite unproductive. Typically one or two ideas emerge. Asking people to brainstorm with a specific technology in mind, such as Artificial Intelligence or Virtual Reality, still leads to few results. In this room of executives, they came up with about one per named technology. At the end of the day most people don't deeply understand the technologies, and so it is hard to brainstorm with them.

We decided that we needed to create a new brainstorming lever. We focused on creating a list of emerging technologies on the whiteboard in the room, including a definition of the technology, and characteristics and affordances of that technology.

For example, for Mixed Reality, the definition was: Mixed Reality combines our physical environment with virtual objects by making them behave like real objects in the real world. The characteristics and affordances were: connects sound and lighting between two worlds, virtual objects reflect changes in the environment just like real-world objects would, virtual objects are responsive to real-world objects.

Turns out it is much easier for people who are not deep emerging technology experts to brainstorm off the characteristics and affordances of a technology. Within moments the executives were coming up with lots of wild ideas that combined the emerging technology on the whiteboard with their luxury skincare and personal care offerings. For instance:

- Interactive Virtual Mirror: Let customers test digital versions of real-world makeup in real time.

- Adaptive Tutorials: Use hand-tracking and object recognition so virtual assistants can demonstrate techniques in sync with real-world gestures, offering guided skincare routines in real time.

- Live Ingredient Overlays: When users hold or scan a product, virtual ingredient details appear as if they are physically attached to the packaging.

Since this workshop we have formalized this lever into a set of cards (now known as the Our Lady of Technology card deck), and we use them frequently with students and clients who have a need or constraint to focus on emerging technology ideation.

We created this lever in the moment when a brainstorm wasn't producing the kinds of ideas we needed. You can do this too. You have the freedom to make up a new brainstorming lever at any time, to fit the needs of the moment and support the generation of wild ideas.

Innovation-ish

Key Takeaways

More Ideas = Better Ideas

The best solutions don't come from finding one perfect idea but from generating many ideas. A high volume of ideas, especially wild ones, leads to unexpected breakthroughs.

Guidelines for Generating Wild Ideas

Suspend Judgment – Don't filter or dismiss ideas too soon.
Build on Other's Ideas – Say "Yes, And" instead of shutting them down.
Embrace Diverse Perspectives – Different viewpoints spark unexpected connections.
Focus on Generation, Not Decisions – Explore widely before narrowing down.

Use Levers to Unlock New Thinking

When stuck, shift your perspective with levers. Flip the problem, add constraints, or imagine how someone else (a five-year-old, Apple, or Disney) would solve it. Remember, constraints spark creativity!

Chapter 8

The Iterations Mindset

The Design for Extreme Affordability course at Stanford University's d.school challenges students to solve real-world problems on minimal budgets. A diverse teaching team, along with intentionally multidisciplinary students, ensures that projects are approached from a variety of perspectives.

In the mid-2000s, one team was tasked with designing a baby incubator for the developing world, using no more than $20 in materials. Many might have expected the team to jump into engineering solutions, purchasing materials and finding ways to generate heat for an affordable incubator.

This group took a different approach. They raised money to travel to Nepal to study the problem firsthand, speaking directly with the people who would use the incubator.

When they arrived, they expected to solve a technology problem. They assumed that hospitals lacked affordable incubators. However, when they visited the hospitals, they found something surprising: empty incubators. The real issue wasn't a shortage of medical devices, it was that premature babies weren't making it to hospitals at all.

Through conversations with hospital staff, they learned that many at-risk newborns were born in remote villages, too far away to survive the journey to the city. Traveling further into these villages, they discovered additional challenges: limited electricity and transportation routes consisting of rough footpaths rather than paved roads.

The team generated a wide range of ideas and iterated on them until they arrived at a simple yet effective solution: a small, insulated pouch (essentially a tiny sleeping bag) with a thermal "battery" made of wax. The wax, sealed in a plastic pouch, could be heated in boiling water and would retain warmth for about two hours, or the time it typically took to walk from the village to the hospital. If more time was needed, families could stop along the way, find or build a fire, and reheat the wax.

The project was a success, evolving into a company that has since saved thousands of babies worldwide. But the story didn't end there.

Iterating to Learn

Innovation doesn't happen in a straight line. It loops, spirals, and moves forward, backward, and sideways. The best innovators don't just test ideas once; they test, tweak, and test again. It's not "launch and learn." It's "learn, launch, learn again."

For the Embrace team, the journey involved many iterations. They tested different materials, refined the amount and shape of the wax, and adjusted the size of the pouch. Even after launching the product, they discovered a new challenge: mothers frequently opened the pouch to check on their babies. Each time they did, heat escaped, reducing its effectiveness.

It was understandable; new mothers needed reassurance that their babies were safe. Instead of ignoring this behavior or expecting mothers to change, the team adapted their design. They added a small plastic window to the front of the sleeping bag, allowing mothers to see their babies without compromising the warmth. This seemingly small change made a significant impact on adoption and usability.

This iterative cycle of learning and adapting is demonstrated by many innovative teams. Consider Nordstrom, the well-known department store chain. At one point, they explored a potential iPad app designed to sell sunglasses.

Nordstrom brought together designers, programmers, salespeople, and product marketers for a week-long rapid design session inside a store. Their concept was simple: an app that allowed customers to take photos of themselves wearing sunglasses, make notes, and compare options before making a purchase.

Innovation-ish

Much like the incubator team, Nordstrom's group started small. Instead of spending weeks coding an app, they began with paper sketches. They drew buttons, sliders, and features, then had customers interact with them as if they were using a real app. When someone requested a feature, the team quickly replaced the paper sketches to simulate its functionality. By the second day, programmers had turned the sketches into a working iPad application – with dozens of daily updates as feedback turned into features.

They quickly learned that customers didn't like the idea. More importantly, they didn't buy more sunglasses. Rather than wasting months on an expensive full production app and deploying it to hundreds of stores, Nordstrom saved time and money with a week-long sprint that showed them that they didn't have the right solution. Sometimes, the best outcome of engaging in the Iterations Mindset is realizing what not to build.

Engaging with the Iterations Mindset means seeing the world as a continuous process of learning, adapting, and improving. Every experience, action, and piece of feedback is an opportunity to refine an idea, or decide to retire it and move on.

It is also about taking opportunities to embody your cognition – that is leveraging the intelligence of our hands, eyes, and environment to enhance creative thinking. When people build a quick prototype, they are externalizing their thought processes into a physical form, and extending what their mind is capable of. Prototypes extend our memory and computation capacity. A simple diagram can hold multiple variables in view simultaneously, something very hard to do in bare imagination given working memory limits.

To engage it properly, you have to hold ideas loosely and be prepared to change everything frequently. In fact, you should embrace change and revision, viewing feedback as a valuable gift that facilitates improvement. Iteration should be part of your plan.

Consider an internal IT team at a large company tasked with modernizing an outdated intranet. Instead of launching a fully polished system on day one, they started with a basic prototype that was a physical representation of the idea and included lots of the little details such as buttons, search type, etc., They rolled out to a small group of employees. They actively collect feedback, learning that while the design is clean, navigation is unintuitive and some key features are missing.

Rather than feeling discouraged or defensive, the team embraces this insight. They make adjustments, refine the design, and introduce improvements over several weeks. Each update is informed by real-world feedback, making the final system far more user-friendly and effective. This approach not only improves the product, it also fosters a culture of continuous learning and innovation.

The Iterations Mindset is about seeking the opportunity to improve and change. Often by engaging with real people to test which ideas will work and which should be discarded. It's about seeing value in data-driven decision-making rather than relying solely on gut feelings.

Think of it like the IT team that launched a basic prototype, gathered feedback, and gradually refined the system or Nordstrom's team iterated rapidly inside a store for five days and determined the idea wasn't viable. By making that decision early, they saved time, effort, and resources.

Iteration is about testing ideas in the real-world as quickly as possible, filtering out what isn't working, and homing in on what truly resonates. In creative problem solving, we often hear phrases like "fail fast to learn quickly" or "fail faster, succeed sooner." This mindset means intentionally building things that will change, expecting setbacks, and using them as real-world tests. It's about actively seeking out failures to refine better solutions.

Ironically, one of the best ways to succeed is to quickly identify ideas that don't work and discard them. People often become stuck on an initial idea or an example solution and struggle to think beyond it – a bias known as Design Fixation. To combat this bias, we encourage our students and clients to explicitly seek disconfirming evidence during user research or prototype testing, thereby forcing them to take a look at what's not working, rather than focusing only on validating assumptions and what is working.

Intrinsic to the Iterations Mindset, are three core elements.

Innovation-ish

> **Expect failure:** Ideas are plentiful, good ideas are rare.
>
> **Seek the truth:** Honest feedback fuels better iterations.
>
> **Trust in evidence:** Make decisions with data, not opinions.

Expect Failure

As discussed in Chapter 7, adopting an Ideas Mindset allows you to generate hundreds, even thousands, of ideas once you frame the problem. The next challenge is filtering this large volume of ideas quickly to identify the best ones and persistently refining them to meet the real needs of people and businesses.

No matter how smart you are, most of the ideas you generate will fail. Even highly skilled teams at large, well-resourced companies regularly launch ideas that don't succeed. The website "Killed by Google," is a digital graveyard of discontinued products and services. The list includes Chromecast Audio (2013–2024), Google Domains (2014–2023), and the infamous Google Glass (2013–2015). Similarly, "Killed by Microsoft" features products like Windows Phone (2010–2019), Skype for Business (retired in 2025), and hundreds more.

These were fully launched products. Behind each of these product failures, dozens or even hundreds of ideas were abandoned internally before they ever reached the public. So, when we say most of your ideas won't succeed, you're in good company.

Unless you have a crystal ball, predicting which ideas will thrive is nearly impossible. Instead, embrace the Iterations Mindset and that to find a prince, expect to kiss a few frogs.

Seek Truth

Getting high-quality feedback to decide whether to refine or retire an idea requires finding the right people and sharing your ideas in the right way.

It's also important to build multiple versions of your idea. Consider my (Rich) daughter, who is seven and a budding artist. Every day, she brings home pages of drawings, cards, and pictures she has created at school, either for friends or for herself. She presents them to us with pride, eager for our reaction. We can always tell which drawings she has poured the most effort into. Without her even asking, we know we're expected to evaluate and respond to her artwork.

What she wants to hear is clear:

> "It's beautiful. I love it, my wonderful daughter. I wish we had more wall space to display all your amazing work. Thank you for sharing this gift with us. We cherish it as much as you do. And yes, we agree, it is special."

This is not a draft; it's a finished piece of art. So, we try to respond with an appropriate amount of praise, usually commenting on the process, such as the effort she put in, her use of color, her choice of technique. And, of course, how much we like it.

The lesson here is that if you only build one version of your idea, you risk receiving biased feedback. People generally want to be polite, especially when they don't know you well. If you present a single version of your idea (like its completed artwork) and ask for feedback, you'll likely receive vague encouragement about the effort you put in rather than genuine insights that help you improve.

Colleagues you work closely with are often better at providing frank, insightful feedback because you've built trust with them. However, it's crucial to test with the actual people you're designing for, not just your colleagues.

A better approach is to build several versions of your idea and test them all. A good rule of thumb is to create three or more.

- With one version, you ask:

  "Do you like this picture I drew?" → The answer is often just yes or no, which isn't very helpful.

- With two versions, you ask:

  "Which of these pictures do you like better?" → This gives a choice between A or B, but still lacks depth.

Innovation-ish

- With three or more versions, you ask:

  "What aspects of these pictures do you like before I make another?" → This invites detailed feedback and reveals valuable insights.

The third approach elicits responses like:

- *"I love the sun in this one and the tree in that one. I wonder what it would look like if you combined them."*
- *"The landscape with the mountain behind the meadow is nice."* (While ignoring the horse in the scene, which tells you the horse might not be important.)

These insights provide actionable direction for your next iteration. Instead of simply getting a yes/no response, you now understand what works and what doesn't, allowing you to iterate more effectively.

By putting the Iterations Mindset on, you are expecting to iterate. Seeking out honest feedback and expecting ideas to fail. It is about knowing that you will break it and build it again.

Trust Evidence

A Real Test of Value

During the pandemic a friend of ours, David, was missing the social connection of the wine and cheese cocktail parties he liked to throw. These parties had a familiar set of guests who loved getting together and learning about wine. This social outlet was interrupted by the medical lockdowns.

Dave is a serial entrepreneur with experience in super computing for National Labs, sports equipment, and consumer electronics. He saw an opportunity to unite sommeliers impacted by restaurant closures and his friends who also missed being more connected.

The service was called Connecting Flights and offered a group of six friends or couples, three bottles of wine and a zoom call with a sommelier to have a virtual wine tasting flight. The idea got great reactions from sharing it with friends, but David knew better than to invest in starting a business before proving the idea.

Hypothesis 1: The sommelier-led wine tasting over video conference provides learning and social connection during lockdown.

To test this idea, David found a sommelier who was willing to try it and shipped wine to several sets of friends and the sommelier. After each virtual tasting, he surveyed people and collected feedback. The results were mixed. He learned that while the sommelier was educational and personable enough that people enjoyed the experience, it did not hold up to a live tasting. Most guests reported that the wine and connection was the most valuable part of the experience.

There was enough positive feedback for David to move on to his second hypothesis.

Hypothesis 2: People want coordinated online social events like wine tasting with friends.

He created a website with wine packages and order forms. The service also provided coordination with guests. In reality it sent an email, and he would manually do the coordination himself by email. Then he ran a series of google ads to direct traffic to the website. The traffic from ads was very low and after a week, there were no signups – despite trying a variety of ads, search terms, and demographics.

Connecting Flights was a fun idea, yet there was no evidence that a coordinated online small gathering wine tasting was a viable idea in 2020. It might sound like a sad story of a small business that didn't make it. However David saw this as a big success. We agree. He saved himself a great deal of time and money by not pursuing an idea that didn't work.

The whole experience took just over three weeks from having the idea to having evidence that the service didn't have a market need. He invested a small amount of evening and weekend time to test the idea. He might have loved the idea and spent months lining up distributors, shipping contracts, building a list of sommeliers and writing a complex scheduling and e-commerce website.

Now, post-pandemic wineries host virtual tastings for people in their wine clubs. Websites ship tasting flights of wine, beer, and spirits based on your online profile and tasting notes. These are great ideas that do work in a different time and a different set of constraints. If David's passion was winetasting, he might have gone on to iterate and find an idea that worked. Trusting the data means collecting reliable data and letting it help you to make the revise or retire decision on your idea.

Dropbox, the now ubiquitous file storage service, originally launched as a simple prototype website. The website featured a video demonstration explaining how the service worked, along with a registration form to join the service. It was many months before the first invitations to this service started being sent by email. It turned out that the site initially visited was just a prototype. It was a test to see if users were actually interested in the service before Dropbox built the infrastructure.

Since you already know that most of your ideas won't work, by putting the Iterations Mindset on, you are seeking out collecting real data, not just opinions. Because, as our colleague Alberto Savoia says in his book, *The Right It*, data beats opinion.

Testing Your Ideas Early

Often, we fall in love with our ideas too easily. Afterall, they come from our own beautiful brains! Of course, they seem wonderful, but as we pointed out earlier, most ideas are not right, at least not at first.

Remember, no matter how much you love your idea, the ultimate goal is to design something effective that works well for users and meets a real human need and solves a real problem in the real world. Ideas need to be tested in the real world.

A very important reason for this is that ideas are inherently abstract. They exist only in our minds. Communicating them clearly can be tricky, so making them concrete is essential. An idea also has to stand on its own in the real-world, which means you need to present it in the most realistic way possible.

Imagine a shape with four sides, sharp corners, and parallel opposite sides. When you hear this description, you might picture a square. Without a visual representation, you could just as easily think of a rhombus or a parallelogram. Now, suppose we all decide to build this shape. We work on the frame while you cut the fabric. We all might be surprised when we bring our pieces together, because we weren't picturing the same thing. Without a concrete representation, our project is bound to fail.

A prototype clarifies an abstract idea by making it concrete.

Nordstrom's design team understood this principle well. They began with paper sketches, simple drawings that simulated an iPad app. By showing customers a tangible representation, they ensured everyone started on the same page. Using paper the size of an iPad, they drew buttons and sliders, allowing customers to "interact" with the app in a realistic way. Pressing a drawn button with a finger and swapping in a new sheet of paper to simulate the next screen was slow but mimicked the experience of using a real tablet application.

It would have been easy for the Nordstrom team to bring people into an office or an innovation center to test the app. However, testing live in the sunglasses department of one of their stores puts them directly in touch with their actual customers, who could immediately decide whether to buy sunglasses, making the test highly effective.

Whether it's a drawing of a square, a full-size prototype, or a paper model of an app, presenting an idea in context allows for meaningful feedback. The closer your test is to the real-world conditions, the more valuable your insights will be.

Testing involves collecting data from real users in the real-world by presenting them with a prototype. This makes the idea concrete, allowing users to explore and interact with it. When working with our clients, we emphasize that good tests have five key elements:

- **Generate a hypothesis** about the idea, how it functions, what it looks like, its price, and how users will interact with it.
- **Present the prototype** to users and observe their interactions.
- **Follow up observations** by asking users about their experience with the prototype.
- **Collect data,** not opinions or "likes."
- **Tally the data and evaluate** whether your hypothesis was validated or disproven.

The goal isn't just to validate your idea and move forward. You're aiming to identify what doesn't work so you can eliminate bad ideas quickly.

The Iterations Mindset means you are constantly testing, iterating, and refining multiple ideas at once. The longer you invest in an idea people don't actually want, the more resources you waste on a bad idea. Testing helps you identify the users who benefit most from your idea, understand their needs, quickly gather meaningful data, and refine or discard ideas that don't work.

When designing a test, we often recommend considering these aspects in the design of the test. These are all the different aspects of the test that could be variable to help you craft the most meaningful test:

- **Purpose:** what you are testing?
- **People:** who you are testing on?
- **Place:** where and how are you testing?

For example, you might vary the features you are testing, include people from multiple generations or background, or test both physical locations and online.

117

Managing Fidelity and Scale

When you listen to music or view digital images, you experience fidelity: a measure of how closely a reproduced sound or image matches the original. The first telephonic conversations by Alexander Graham Bell were a fantastic innovation, yet their sound quality was poor compared to hearing someone in the same room. Over time, telephone calls and recordings improved, and today, our technologies reproduce sounds almost indistinguishable from the originals.

Similarly, the prototypes you create to test your ideas exist on a continuum from low to high fidelity. At first, you begin with simple, low-cost models to determine whether there is a real problem. For instance, you might develop an Idea User Story that describes the problem, required data, settings where the idea would be used, and people who would interact with it.

Sharing this story with potential users provides essential feedback to validate your idea.

As you move up in fidelity, you start to focus on how users interact with your idea. You might create a storyboard that lays out the sequence of steps a user takes, ensuring the process is intuitive. Once the steps are set, you can build a paper prototype, presenting the idea in simple, tangible terms.

Through revisions and feedback, you may progress to a science fair project prototype or a mock up with more robust components that tests how users engage with the solution. Nordstrom's use of a pad of paper, chosen to mimic an iPad, is a great example of a low-fidelity prototype that provided immediate, actionable feedback.

The next step is to test the critical assumption of your idea, or the one element that must be correct for the entire concept to work. If this key assumption is invalid, further development is not worthwhile. Once that hurdle is overcome, you refine your concept with an in situ prototype that operates under real-world conditions, ensuring it integrates effectively into its environment.

Finally, you test the core function of your idea with a Minimum Viable Product (MVP) prototype. This stage confirms that the primary function is effective in the real world. Although the MVP may lack some features, it proves the idea works. After launching the product, testing continues at scale, gathering customer feedback to drive further iteration and refinement.

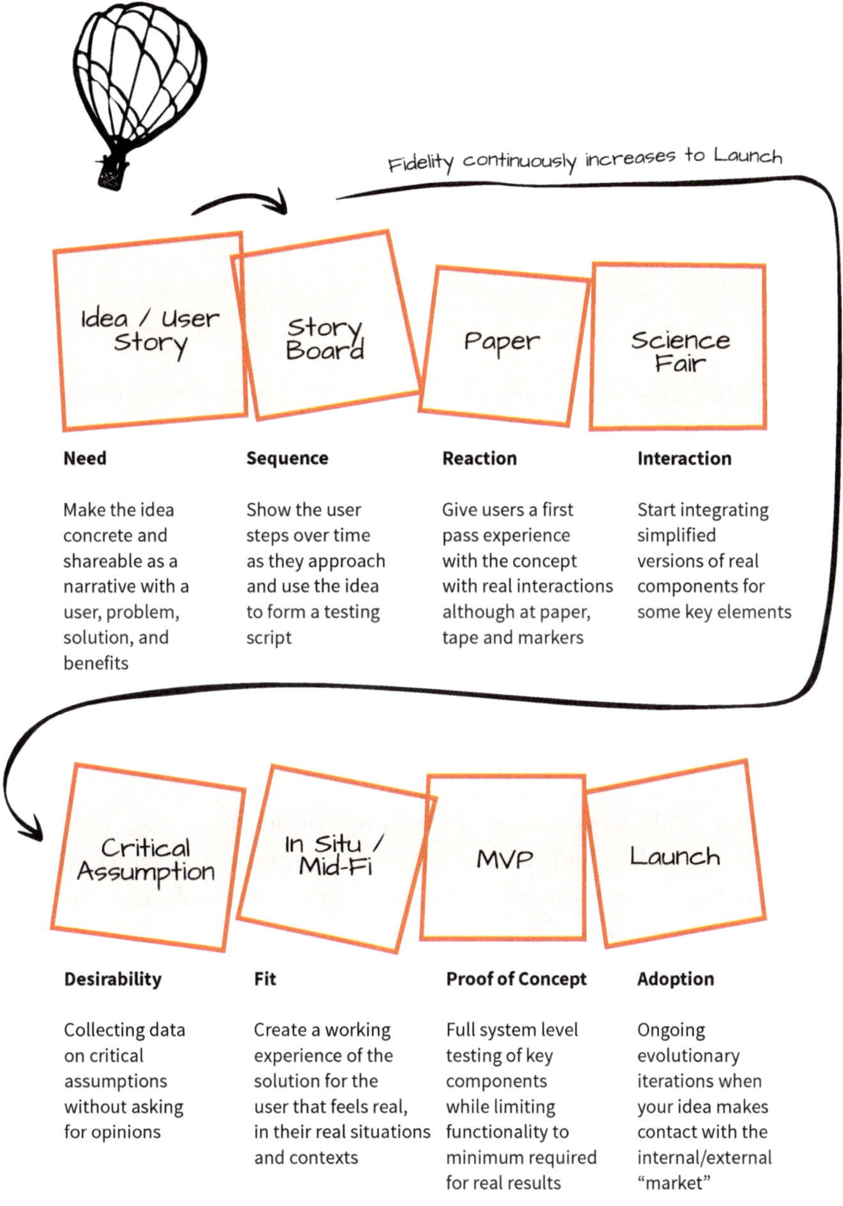

As ideas iterate from concept to launch the fidelity and scale of testing increases.

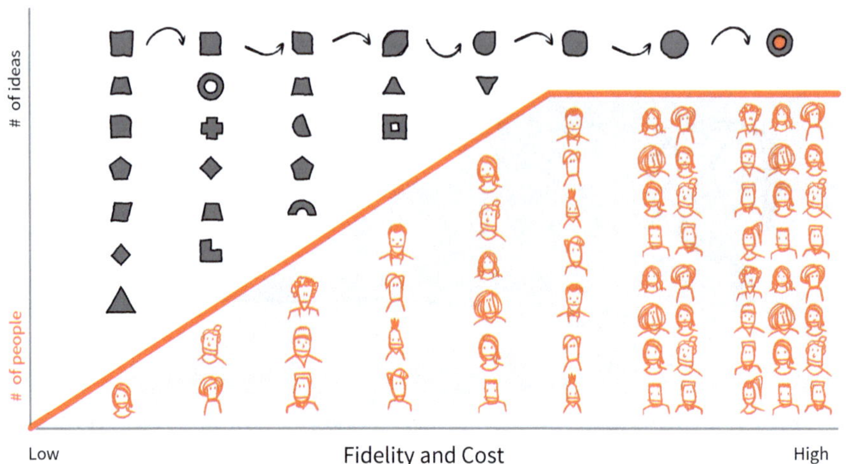

Over time, test fewer ideas with more people as the cost and fidelity increase.

This progression to higher fidelity in your prototypes has four primary components:

- The number of ideas you are testing.
- The number of people in your testing sample.
- The fidelity of the prototype you are testing.
- The cost in time and resources to create the prototype.

Starting with story-based and paper prototypes, you can test many ideas quickly with a few users. The opportunity is to gather quick feedback and then learn from a broader range of users by giving them something concrete to react to.

With each test, you stretch your understanding of the problem and uncover what aspects of the idea delight users. This delight comes from meeting their needs in a helpful and creative way.

Innovation-ish

Each round of testing allows you to:

- Reduce the number of ideas: Eliminate those that don't resonate with users.
- Iterate on the idea: Learn from users, making changes, and improving.
- Choose the level of fidelity: Increasing fidelity also increases the prototype and testing costs.
- Expand the number of users: A more broad group increases the robustness of the tests.

These principles help scale ideas while limiting risk and cost. This approach ensures that the ideas you invest in are the right ones, shaped by data from real-world testing.

Sometimes, none of your ideas are worth pursuing. That's a successful outcome, signaling that you need to reframe the problem or collect more insights. Regardless of the outcome, scaling an idea must be intentional and rigorous. This approach ensures you can back your decisions with hard data and report confidently to leadership or sponsors. Nordstrom's experience highlights the value of having concrete data. Since their prototype testing showed the idea didn't work, they could make trusted, informed recommendations for their next steps.

Thomas Edison's team of "Muckers" at Menlo Park used this exact process to develop the light bulb. They tested, gathered data, learned, iterated, and tested again. Edison famously said:

> "Genius is one percent inspiration and ninety-nine percent perspiration."

He also noted:

> "I will not say I failed; I will say I found 1,000 ways not to make a light bulb."

Key Takeaways

Test Many Ideas Early and Don't Fall in Love with Them

Most ideas are not right at the beginning. The best way to figure out which ones work is to test lots of them quickly. You are not trying to prove your idea is great; you are trying to learn which ideas actually solve a problem and discard the ones that don't.

Increase Fidelity as You Eliminate Ideas and Collect More Data

Start with simple, low-cost prototypes such as storyboards and sketches to test basic assumptions. As you eliminate weaker ideas and refine the promising ones, increase the fidelity of your tests. Move from low-cost experiments to more detailed prototypes only when the data justifies it.

Use Hypothesis Testing to Guide Your Iterations

Every test should answer a clear question: What do I need to be true for this idea to work? Define a hypothesis, put a prototype in front of real users, and observe what happens. Testing is not about getting approval; it's about gathering real data to make better decisions.

122

Innovation-ish

Chapter 9

The Inspirations Mindset

In 2009, Reshma Saujani became the first Indian American woman to run for Congress. Like most political campaigns, she visited many classrooms and noticed a disturbing reality. When she visited computer science and robotics classes, there were hardly any girls. She knew about the "boys club" of Silicon Valley but didn't realize that it started in high school.

This gap, preventing girls from going into this lucrative field, was why she started Girls Who Code. She didn't want an organization; she wanted a movement to try to solve that problem. What she didn't know was that teaching them to code would give them something beyond a path to a career.

Her degree was in political science and communications, not computer science. She later realized, and still believes, that this was an advantage. She started out with a fresh perspective instead of the typical biases that existed. It also meant that she spent two years meeting with someone at breakfast, lunch, and dinner to learn. She met with educators, PhDs in computer science, and business founders who hired programmers.

She learned that women had a strong role in programming from the beginning. The first programmer was a woman, and in the 1980s, 50 percent of programmers were women. Then, there was a 20-year dip in the pipeline of programmers, which she saw in her classroom visits. The problem she saw was a gender gap in the pipeline of girls going into programming.

She learned about this gender gap: when it happened, why it happened, and what interventions might close the gap. Then she started a pilot program, paying girls $50 to attend the summer sessions and giving them pizza every day. The girls learned to program, and "they blossomed." They told their friends, and the idea spread into a movement.

Her mission was to create a movement to change the gender gap problem. So, instead of products or profits, she focused on the story of the girls. The story *was what would happen if girls learned to code* – they would be healers, teachers, and presidents. In fact they would be anything and everything.

She knew that stories are what inspire people. The stories of her girls caused people to respond immediately with responses such as: Where do I write the check? Where do I volunteer and mentor?

Finally, ten years later, Girls Who Code had raised $100 million and had 18 percent global name recognition. Today, they have taught 670,000 girls, women, and nonbinary individuals how to code. They have learned that teaching coding is also a way of teaching girls bravery, which helps bridge another gender gap. This helps them succeed in technical careers and encourages them to follow their dreams.

Along the way, Reshma learned that you don't need to be an expert; you just need a passion for the problem. And as a founder, your story of how the world will be different inspires others and drives movements.

Reshma shares that by teaching girls bravery, they can pursue their dreams and change the world.

She demonstrates all the Innovation-ish mindsets, in particular the Inspiration Mindset.

Inspiring Others

You may not be starting a movement like Reshma. You might have a jump-shot or roof-shot problem that you are passionate about. No matter what the problem is, you need to inspire others to join and help you.

Imagine you're tasked with improving your company's expense reporting process. Along the way, you may need to inspire or persuade many different people. For example:

- An executive, who doesn't even do their own expense reports, to fund the project.
- A few managers to test your solution with their teams.

- The HR policy team to adjust the handbook.
- The finance and tax team to ensure compliance.

To engage those people, you need to inspire them with a vision of the world as you see it. Show them your passion for the problem and how they will benefit from that world. And tell them how they can participate to make it come true.

Who you need depends on the problem you are solving. One thing remains clear: collaboration is the engine of innovation, and a diverse team is essential to turn ideas into reality.

The Inspirations Mindset is about seeing the world as a place where stories create meaning and influence comes from emotional connection. When we've seen teams and leaders like Reshma fully embrace this mindset, they embody the following factors:

- **Create a human connection:** Humans connect through emotion and empathy.
- **Envision the future:** The vision we imagine creates possibility.
- **Share your passion:** When you believe, others feel it.

Create a Human Connection

Since humans drew petroglyphs on cave walls, we have created community through stories. Shared experience and empathy create strong feelings of belonging and identity. These psychological bonds help protect us and our social group.

Empathy is the ability to understand how others feel and to feel them as if they are your own. Imagining and experiencing how others feel fosters compassion and changes behavior. We can inspire others through this emotional connection. While you cannot control their emotions, you can share yours to build trust. And once established, you can share your excitement, hope, and enthusiasm with them.

Envision the Future

From a jump-shot to a moon-shot, your innovation is about creating a new future. Reshma often makes this point, saying that a founder shares their vision of how the world can be. You can create the future vision of your own idea, exploring it in your imagination. This gives you an opportunity to clarify and refine the idea and to share it with others.

You can create a vision of the future for anyone you may need to inspire – perhaps collaborators, partners or investors. For each of them, you might share a different version of the story that best connects with them. The story engages their imagination and they experience emotions as if it was real. This lets them create their own emotional connections to the characters and situations. This very human quality allows you to create excitement, and anticipation for your future vision.

To reach your vision, you need to motivate those collaborators and investors to join you. Including them and their role in your story helps them see their own participation in your vision and explore how they feel about it. It's that personal connection to your vision that inspires people to take action.

Share Your Passion

As Reshma did, you will likely start your journey solving a problem from a feeling. Perhaps it's a feeling of frustration with the current situation, of compassion for others, or of desire for a better future. No matter how it starts, problem-solving takes passion, persistence and grit to stay motivated. As time goes on and you learn more, motivation leads to hope and, eventually, excitement. This can sustain you through setbacks, failures, and learning along the way.

Your passion, motivation, and excitement are infectious. People are drawn to it, and that is the basis of inspiring others. As American poet Maya Angelou said, "People will forget what you said, people will forget what you did, but people will never forget how you made them feel." Sharing your passion for that vision of the future through a story creates a human connection that inspires others to feel that same passion and become drawn into your idea.

Innovation-ish

With practice and by adopting the Inspiration Mindset, you too can create stories with meaning. Then you can influence others to join you. The influence of story on influencing behavior is backed up with research.

Stanford University Professor Jennifer Aaker highlights research showing that stories inspire others because they effectively persuade people to take desired actions. In a study on donation behavior for the advocacy not-for-profit Save The Children, researchers tested two conditions by showing subjects two different ads. One ad focused on the problems of children in Africa, sharing some compelling statistics. The other told the story of one seven-year-old girl and her experiences of the problem. The results were clear: the story advertisement collected twice as many donations as the statistical ad.

Chip Heath, professor at the Stanford Graduate School of Business, and his brother Dan Heath, Sr. Fellow at Duke University's CASE center, explore this idea further in their book *Switch: How to Change Things When Change Is Hard*. They use the story about an elephant and its rider to illustrate the balance between our emotional and rational sides. The elephant represents our emotions, while the rider stands for our reasoning. When they conflict, the elephant often wins, showing how emotions can override logic. However, when both work together, they form a powerful team. This analogy, coined by psychologist Jonathan Haidt, highlights that to effectively influence people, you must appeal to both their emotional and rational sides.

Yes, you can directly appeal to the rational side of people with data, facts, and figures. However, it may not be persuasive if you ignore the elephant. Stories take people on a journey and engage their imagination. That is a way of eliciting emotional reactions to influence the actions they take.

This power of storytelling dates back to oral traditions in early civilization. Since then, authors have understood that people not only love to hear and read stories, plays, operas, and movies but they respond to them emotionally. These experiences make us feel our shared humanity validated and even more connected.

Stories are not only told with words, written or spoken. There are other sources of inspiration such as user reviews, images, and demos.

These can capture your attention and create lasting memories. Many times a single image, a set of art pieces, or a storyboard with no words at all can be more compelling than an inspiring speech. However the mechanism underneath them is rooted in the story.

Inspiration comes from giving someone a vision of the world as it can be. Inspiring others to join or take action means showing them their role in creating that world.

The remainder of this chapter deconstructs the principles for creating and using memorable stories to influence behavior.

Making Stories Sticky

Girls Who Code is a success story in creating impact, inspiring others, and creating a movement. It's problem-solving at scale. The movement provides a self-sustaining source of inspiration from the girls who graduate from the program. Reshma's story, indeed her movement, is due to the fact that these stories are memorable and sticky. This happens through four core elements:

Meaning: the story's meaning, which inspires the desired action.

Details: engaging the imagination that share the sensory and emotional experience.

Drama: dramatic tension that evokes emotions in the viewer or listener.

Narrative: balancing the structure with the emotion, which shapes the imagined experience.

Meaning

What was Reshma's story about, with a lower case 'a'? At its core, it's simply the plot:

Reshma saw that girls were not in programming classes, so she created programming classes just for girls.

It's accurate, sure, if not all that inspiring. Now, if we consider what that story is about, with a capital letter A, each listener may hear

Innovation-ish

several different meanings and implications. Some of the lessons we can learn from her story:

- Passion for the problem is required, not expertise in the area.
- As a founder you have a vision of how the world can be different.
- Story inspires others to join your cause creating a movement.

Recalling the story leads you back to the meaning at the end paired with the call to action – teach girls bravery. In that way, the story asks the audience to take action.

This concept is illustrated well in television commercial advertising. You may have an ad from your own history that was effective in persuading you. What was it that made it impactful? Can you identify where and when the call to action was placed?

Advertisers have a limited time to inspire viewers to take a desired action; usually to purchase a product or service. Influencing an audience with hundreds of alternative choices and distractions in under a minute is a challenge. Advertisers have honed their storytelling skills beyond entertainment to persuasion.

The public service announcement "Embrace Life – always wear your seatbelt," by Sussex Safer Roads Partnership: is a good example of a call to action.

> The video shows a father pretending to drive a car while sitting in a small chair in what appears to be the daughter's room. He is smiling at his wife and daughter sitting at the side of the room. His expression changes from joy to panic, and he kicks the table in front of him, sending glitter into the air, indicating shattered glass. The family surrounds him, clasping him in their arms shaped like a seatbelt holding him in the chair. The call to action, Embrace Life, is to always wear your seatbelt. It appears for the last ten seconds, and the seatbelt has now turned into a family embrace.

This simple story uses no dialogue yet elicits an emotional reaction from most people before delivering a concise call to action at the end.

As we mentioned above, inspiring people comes from storytelling. Not every story uses words.

Details

What elements do you recall from Reshma's story? The items that stand out in your memory are the ones that are sticky.

- She was shocked that she didn't see girls in the computer science classrooms.
- She was political science, not computer science.
- She raised $100M in 10 years.
- She bought pizza for the girls and they blossomed.
- The story of the girls makes people donate and volunteer.

They are details that bring the story to life and activate the imagination of the audience. It allows them to experience the events as if those events happened to themselves and create a personal connection. That connection comes from empathy. Cognitive empathy is the ability to understand another person's perspective and emotions intellectually. Affective empathy is the ability to feel another person's emotions as if they were your own. When you consume media – books, plays, movies – those kinds of emotional reactions are common. Joy, sorrow, fear, and anxiety are not special "story emotions"; they are real emotions that you are experiencing.

When you intentionally craft your story with details that can shape someone's emotional experience, you can directly address the listener's elephant. Now, you can't force or control their emotions, but you can set the conditions where you are likely to get a certain set of responses.

These categories of details commonly enhance a story's emotional content:

- **Numbers** – one or two important or surprising numbers.
- **Emotions** – evoked in the audience or described about the characters.
- **The senses** – what you see, smell, taste, touch and hear.

By integrating the right amount of detail into a story, you increase the emotional experience of the audience and make it more memorable. You might remember an ad from childhood that stuck with you for years. What made it so memorable? Chances are you can remember enough details from the ad to share with someone today.

To illustrate, let's compare two ads of similar products from 2010. (Of course, neither represents all of the advertising by either company.) One of these products was wildly successful and still available today, the other stopped production a year later.

The first ad is for the music, video, and gaming device the Microsoft Zune HD, titled Portable Perfection.

It opens on the Zune HD logo before the product fades in. The device is shown from several angles with a variety of visuals and media, with a voice-over listing each of the features.

> Zune HD is a next-generation entertainment experience with HD radio, HD-compatible video, and an elegant multi-touch OLED screen. Enjoy new levels of clarity with HD radio and a wider array of formats from your favorite stations at no extra charge. Experience the ease of quickplay, which puts your favorite media at your fingertips. Dig into history, photos, and related bands from an art artist's point of view. Play games, browse the internet, download your favorite music, and sync with your PC wirelessly. Zoom HD, it's a premium portable entertainment experience.

The second ad is for a contemporary music, video and gaming device combined with a phone, the iPhone 4, Apple ran an ad titled Meet Her.

> The ad opens with an older man video-calling what looks like his son. The son asks if he's ready and then shows his new daughter in his arms. The grandfather choked up and said, "She's beautiful, she's perfect," and then, "How's it feel being a father?" The son asks how it feels to be a grandfather, and he replies, "It's incredible; how's it feel being a father?" The son replies, "Pretty good."

The Inspirations Mindset

The contrast between these two ads is stark.

The first ad has few if any, story details as described above – no numbers, emotions, or senses. In contrast, the second ad directly appeals to cognitive and affective empathy. It vividly shows feelings and engages both your visual senses and those of the characters in the story.

This illustrates the point Aaker's research described above, which is that the appeal to emotions was more effective in persuasion. She shares a second research study that examines the impact of emotion on memory. In that study, participants were asked to create a 1-minute pitch. On average, the participants included 2.5 statistics in their pitch. Only 1 in 10 included a story.

Ten minutes after the pitches were presented, the researchers asked participants to write down everything they could remember about the pitches. Only 5 percent of the participants had written a statistic, and 63 percent of them had written a story. In fact, she reported that stories are up to 22 times more likely to be remembered.

You can try it yourself right now reading this book. Without turning back a few pages, what do you remember about the Zune HD ad? And what do you remember about the iPhone 4 ad? Which one uses the same ideas as the childhood as you recalled earlier?

The details in stories evoke emotions in the audience, making them easier to remember. Recalling the story engages their imagination, reinforcing its meaning and call to action. However, details are not the only way you can inspire emotions in a story.

Drama

You can also make a story more memorable and persuasive by increasing the emotional intensity through drama. Drama is created in the structure of your story and the particular order of events. There are three main ways you can add drama to your story:

- Surprise.

- Suspense.

- The third way is the one we will reveal below...

Surprise comes in when you let the audience in on specific information that was previously concealed. For example, imagine you are watching a crime drama. The gangsters are sitting in a secret meeting place, playing poker around a table. They banter as gangsters do – and all of a sudden, there's an explosion! We eventually learn that it was retaliation for some actions that they took earlier in the movie, but there was nothing to indicate that this was the time and place that the retribution was going to take place. This big narrative event is a surprise to both the audience and the characters.

In Reshma's story, she was surprised by the lack of girls in the classroom she was visiting, yet it's unlikely that it was surprising to you as the reader.

Surprise leaves the audience thinking: "I didn't see that coming!"

Suspense usually suggests the audience knows something that the characters do not, and they get anxious waiting for it to happen. If the crime drama scene was written with suspense rather than surprise, it might go something like this: the camera focuses on the bomb strapped to the underside of the table, then pulls back slowly to the cards on the table. The gangsters play poker and exchange banter, but the bomb does not go off. The camera might cut away to other scenes and then return to the poker. The time that passes with the bomb not going off keeps us in suspense.

Suspense leaves the audience thinking, "Is it going to happen?" Or, "When is this going to happen?"

We said there were three types of drama, yet we have covered only two. This might leave you thinking, "What is the other type of drama?" And the answer is. . . Mystery.

Mystery is when the author indicates to the audience that there is something missing but doesn't reveal what it is until later in the story. In retelling Reshma's story, we used mystery. We told you at the beginning that teaching them to code gave them something beyond a career. What we didn't tell you initially was what it was.

The Inspirations Mindset

Mystery compels the audience to keep asking, "Is that the
missing piece to the story?" Over and over until it's finally
revealed.

At the end of the story, we revealed that teaching them to
code taught them to be brave. That bravery helped them beyond
their career; it also helped them to pursue their dreams and
change the world

Suspense, Surprise, and Mystery are interactions with the audience. The structure you use in the story can produce emotional
reactions in the audience. Adding drama evokes an emotional connection between your audience and the story. By increasing the
emotions, it makes the story more memorable. The point of storytelling is to communicate persuasive ideas in a way that people can
relate to and remember.

If you want to inspire others to join your project, cause, or mission, you need to help them see their role in the story and engage
them emotionally. You need to align the rider and the elephant.

Narrative

Details and drama, or the *color* of the story, play an important role in
making a story memorable and persuasive. To be effective, you also
need a good narrative structure. The structure helps the story move
along and makes it interesting. What you need is a good balance
between narrative and color.

Many different frameworks and methods exist for creating a narrative structure. While we are going to introduce one simple-to-
use one, we encourage you to explore others. In his book *How
to Improvise a Full-Length Play: The Art of Spontaneous Theater* by
Kenn Adams, he introduces the story spine. This same structure
became so useful and popular at Pixar that now many people call
it the Pixar Pitch.

The story spine gives structure to a story and can help you find
the balance between narrative and color. The spine itself guides the
narrative and ensures that the story moves ahead in a connected way.

The structure works as a series of sentence starts for you to complete as follows:

1. **Once upon a time...**
2. **Every day...**
3. **But, one day...**
4. **Because of that...**
5. **Because of that...**
6. **Because of that...**
7. **Until finally...**
8. **Ever since that day...**

Completing each sentence of the Story Spine guides the narrative of a story.

You can see the spine in the story above. If reset in this form, it would be written:

- *Once upon a time* Reshma ran for Congress.
- *Every day* she would campaign, often visiting classrooms.
- *But, one day* she noticed that the "boys club" of Silicon Valley actually started in high school.
- *Because of that* she decided to start a movement to teach girls to code.
- *Because of that* she spent two years learning about the problem.
- *Because of that* she saw girls blossom and shared their stories.
- *Until finally* after 10 years, she had taught over half a million girls to code.
- *And ever since that day* she taught girls code and to be brave to improve their lives.

The Inspirations Mindset

As you can see, the longer story above follows the structure of how it was told. The story spine is just the outline of a story. Each line intentionally connects to the previous line. This propels the story forward without wandering off track. You can see in the table below that there are essentially three main sections.

The Three Sections of the Story

Section	Narrative	Description
1 – The platform	Once upon a time. . . Every day. . .	The setting and the main characters of the story. It establishes the normal routine every day for those characters.
2 – The tilt	But, one day. . . Because of that. . . Because of that. . . Because of that. . .	Something out of the ordinary happens – this is why the story is about this particular day. The shift sets off a chain reaction that sends the story, the characters, and the reader on a journey until the narrative reaches the peak or the climax of the story.
3 – The resolution	Until finally. . . And ever since that day. . .	A new normal is established. We learn that the characters have changed from their experience and how they will be different, and the meaning of the story becomes clear. In a series of stories, this new normal also becomes the platform of the next story.

Innovation-ish

These three main sections – the platform, the tilt, and the resolution – work together to create the narrative journey. If you take the Story Spine literally, it might feel too much like a fairy tale for your needs. In a workplace presentation, for example, a different tone or wording may be more appropriate. What matters most is the power structures in crafting a compelling and impactful story, not the specific language used.

For example, here are some "Once upon a time" alternatives: "As you all know…," "For the past year…," "When we started the project…," "Ten years ago…"

All of these situate the reader or listener in a context so they have a sense of the background. That is expanded upon by the "Every day…," which can also be varied; for example:

> "As you all know (Once upon a time), we have been working toward the goal of improving patient satisfaction. At the beginning of the year (Every day), we focused on treating as many patients as possible to reduce waiting times."

This is how and why the story spine can be an effective tool for creating a narrative for almost any situation. It's the intention and the structure, not the specific language, that is important. This is good because if you began every story with "Once upon a time…" it would get old pretty quickly.

The problem with the story spine described above is that it's a bit dry. There are no details, no drama. Nothing to hang on to and make it sticky. Those qualities have been lost from the original version; we need some color. As we saw earlier, research shows that adding color brings a story to life and makes it memorable. Without it, Shakespeare's *Romeo and Juliet* boils down to two teenagers falling in love, disapproving families, depression, and an untimely end. True, but not much of a story.

A simple way to extend the original story spine is to simply add a second sentence after each start in the spine. This makes

The Inspirations Mindset

the total number of sentences 16 instead of eight and looks like this:

1. **Once upon a time...**   Color sentence.
2. **Every day...**   Color sentence.
3. **But, one day...**   Color sentence.
4. **Because of that...**   Color sentence.
5. **Because of that...**   Color sentence.
6. **Because of that...**   Color sentence.
7. **Until finally...**   Color sentence.
8. **Ever since that day...**   Color sentence.

Balance narrative with color to create memorable stories.

Expanding our example looks like this:

- *Once upon a time*, Reshma ran for Congress. She was the first Indian American woman to run for Congress.
- *Every day* she would campaign, often visiting classrooms. In the computer science and robotic classes, she did not see any girls.
- *But, one day* she noticed that the "boys club" of Silicon Valley actually started in high school. She was passionate about changing the gender gap that kept girls from technical careers.
- *Because of that*, she decided to start a movement to teach girls to code. Having a political science degree instead of a degree in computer science she found to be an advantage.
- *Because of that*, she spent two years learning about the problem. She discovered that in the 1980s women held 50 percent of programming roles and that rate then dropped over the next 20 years.
- *Because of that*, she saw girls blossom and shared their stories. Their stories inspired people to donate and volunteer, wanting to support the movement.
- *Until finally*, after 10 years, she had taught over half a million girls to code. She had created 18 percent global brand recognition and raised $100 million in funding.

138

Innovation-ish

- *And ever since that day*, she taught girls code and to be brave to improve their lives. Her movement helps change culture by teaching girls lessons often still taught only to boys.

Telling this story in 16 lines is more memorable and more interesting, but it's still not as compelling as the first version. That's for two primary reasons. First, the structure of the story, which has one narrative line and one color line, sounds too rigid in form. It follows the narrative formula too closely instead of using it as a guideline. Second, the balance of narrative and color is off. Making it 50 percent color is still not enough to bring the story to life. This balance, the percentage of narrative, is a key to getting a story right.

There is no strict formula for the right amount of color. And it is subjective, a matter of personal preference, so it's the balance that you need to experiment with. In writing, we call this editing. Writing a draft, reviewing, and making changes are all common in any kind of writing.

Even my (Rich) daughter in second grade starts with a "first draft" and then finally has a "final draft" for her assignments. This process of refinement is at the heart of the discipline. You can use a similar process when telling stories and asking for feedback.

Creating a story that is memorable and meaningful is a powerful way to persuade others to join you in your efforts or invest in your project. Pairing your meaning with a clear call to action at the end of your story can have a significant impact on decision-making. Adding color, detail, and drama to your story activates empathy through emotional connection. Crafting stories that combine these ideas takes time and a few iterations to ensure they are effective. To give yourself the best opportunity to persuade your audience, you need to tune your story to connect with the specifics.

Understanding Your Audience

We tell stories to connect with others – the audience for our stories. In this case, we are using the word audience to mean anyone who receives the story – the listener, the reader, the consumer, the partner, the board member. Depending on the person you are trying to reach, that is your audience.

The Inspirations Mindset

When presenting to the board of a not-for-profit organization, your narrative might focus on the mission and the organization's connection with the people it serves. Later, when speaking to a leader at a foundation considering a grant, your story might emphasize a specific social program, its effectiveness, and ways of tracking beneficiaries. Though both audiences cared about the mission and the proposed new program, each needed different details to make the story sticky. By tailoring your story to a particular audience, you have the best chance of connecting with them.

This is where it's helpful to use a tool like the story spine, so you can quickly sketch out the main idea of each story. You can also add a bit of color to emphasize the most important parts. By comparing the different versions for different audiences, you can have a meaningful discussion with others about the shape of the stories and their effectiveness – before spending a lot of time expanding on details, making slides, or writing long drafts.

By understanding who you are trying to communicate with, you can craft stories that connect and drive action.

Key Takeaways

Passion and Emotion Are Contagious
When you believe in your idea, your energy and excitement inspire others to join your mission.

Stories Are More Memorable and Persuasive Than Facts
People are up to 22 times more likely to remember a story than a statistic. Facts appeal to logic, but stories engage emotions, making them more effective at persuading people to take action.

Crafting Impactful Stories: Structure and Emotion
A strong Story Spine keeps your narrative focused, while sticky details make it memorable and emotionally engaging. The structure provides clarity, while vivid details create connection, and together, they make stories persuasive and unforgettable.

Chapter 10

The Implications Mindset

In the 1930s, wolves were eliminated from Yellowstone National Park, triggering a chain of unexpected ecological consequences. Over the following 65 years, elk populations surged, leading to overgrazing that destroyed willow groves. In 1995, the wolves were reintroduced. A horse trailer carrying 12 wolves from nearby Canada was released into Yellowstone, setting off a cascade of significant and unforeseen impacts on the ecosystem.

The elk population, now under predatory pressure, moved to higher-altitude grazing grounds and foraged less aggressively. As a result, willow groves began to recover in the lower valleys. These healthier willow groves created a boon for beavers, whose population soon began to grow. With more beavers, there were more beaver dams, altering the park's water system. Water levels in ponds rose, creating better habitats for fish and songbirds. Meanwhile, reduced riverbank erosion led to deeper, more stable streams, reshaping the park's geography.

Furthermore, the wolves' presence kept coyote populations in check, which in turn allowed rabbit and mouse populations to flourish. This increase in small mammals provided a richer food source, attracting hawks, weasels, foxes, and badgers back into the ecosystem.

This cascade of effects demonstrates how a single event can ripple across an entire ecosystem, just as innovations do. When you adopt an Implications Mindset, you become more aware of the interconnectedness of systems, carefully evaluating how your decisions might affect people, environments, industries, and institutions.

Engaging in this mindset requires stepping back from the excitement of a new solution, setting aside assumptions, and scrutinizing how an idea will interact with the broader context.

In many ways, an Implications Mindset is a form of Systems Thinking, where you recognize that every innovation exists within a broader network of influences. When you identify negative implications (which you inevitably will), this isn't a sign to abandon the idea. Instead, it's an opportunity to adjust your strategy, mitigate risks, explore alternatives, and weigh different options.

In our experience, stepping into an Implications Mindset can be difficult. Dual-process theory suggests that the mind operates using two distinct systems for thinking: a fast, automatic mode that favors simple, straightforward stories, and a slower, more thoughtful mode that digs into details. Fully considering all the ripple effects of a new idea is difficult because it forces you into that slower, more effortful thinking process.

The core of the Implications Mindset is opting into this deeper level of analysis, even though it requires more effort. The good news is that the more you engage in this type of thinking, the better you become at it. Once you start practicing systems-level analysis, you naturally begin asking critical questions, such as "Should we do this?" and "Can we do this?"

Asking "Should We?" First

When we take on a challenge and create new solutions, those solutions enter a conceptual ecosystem. The impact of innovation can be wide-ranging. It is not enough to ask ourselves, "*Can* we solve this problem?" We must also ask, "*Should* we solve this problem in this way?" With advancements in technology, science, and access to capital, the answer to "Can we?" is often yes. However, the answer to "Should we?" is rarely that simple. An Implications Mindset ensures that feasibility and viability are assessed only after the ethical and practical responsibilities of an innovation have been considered.

In the Yellowstone wolf reintroduction example, many of the effects were considered positive. However, not all impacts benefited

Innovation-ish

every stakeholder. While beavers thrived with the return of willow groves, elk and deer faced increased predation threats. Similarly, innovations often benefit some while are disadvantageous to others. The "should we" question is important when initiating a top-down intervention like this on a system.

Keurig, the German manufacturer of instant coffee machines that holds about 5 percent of the global coffee market, provides an example of cascading impacts in the marketplace. Single-serve coffee seemed like an obvious solution to a common problem. Previously, French presses, drip coffee machines, and stovetop pots could brew up to ten cups at a time, which was inefficient for those wanting just a single cup. As a result, coffee drinkers were routinely over-brewing coffee for their needs, leading to excess wastage in energy and water. Keurig revolutionized coffee with its single-serve K-Cups, providing precise portions and flavor variety. However, Keurig's success created a massive plastic waste problem since the system relies on single-use plastic pods.

This example highlights how innovation exists within a system. Changing one element can unintentionally disrupt another. If innovators do not step back at some point in the process to examine the whole system, they may impact it in ways they had not foreseen. Those impacts might be beneficial or detrimental and may affect people in unanticipated ways.

Consider another example in the process of hiring personnel. A company implementing an applicant tracking system may decide to integrate LinkedIn's Easy Apply feature, allowing candidates to apply with one click. At first glance, this simplifies the hiring process for candidates and expands the recruiter's talent pool. However, the downstream impacts were unexpected. More applicants flooded job postings, including those who were not truly interested or qualified, because the barrier was much lower. As a result, recruiters received far more applications than they could process. Many applicant tracking systems began filtering out Easy Apply applications altogether. Consequently, some highly qualified candidates who applied through Easy Apply were never even considered, limiting both their job prospects and the recruiter's ability to find top talent.

This does not mean that the Easy Apply button has not worked. For some people and organizations, it has been a beneficial and valuable feature. However, it illustrates that every innovation can have unintended consequences.

And, what if those cascading impacts produce an outcome that was not intended?

When we ask this question to students, many initially respond, "Well, it won't; we have considered everything." This reaction is an example of cognitive biases, firstly overconfidence bias, or the tendency to overestimate our understanding of complex systems, and secondly simplification bias, the tendency to reduce incredibly complex dynamics into small chunks. The human brain loves to simplify problems to make them more manageable.

Cognitive load, or the amount of information we can process at a given time, is finite, leading us to unconsciously compress complexity into digestible pieces. This tendency can create the illusion of a full understanding when, in reality, important factors may have been overlooked.

That is why students and even experienced innovators struggle with "Should we?" thinking. Because they both simplify complex systems into digestible chunks, and overestimate their understanding of it.

Fortunately there are several strategies that we find helpful to overcoming these biases and honestly ask ourselves the question "Should we" and they are to engage **diverse perspectives,** consider **real-world** contexts, and to do it **responsibly**.

Diverse Perspectives

Once you are mindful of these biases and anticipate that they might happen, you can actively counteract it by incorporating diverse perspectives.

For example, while working with New Profit, a US-based venture philanthropy firm, to develop a tool that used IRS nonprofit tax data to build a pool of potential grantees, we needed to consider all potential downstream impacts. To evaluate this, we held a workshop focused entirely on identifying unintended consequences.

During our workshop together, the conversation focused on responsible use of the tool. It was important to the stakeholders involved that the tool not be thought of as simply the output of a "technology project" but as an addition to the organization's overall portfolio efforts.

We invited outside experts beyond the core project team to challenge assumptions and considered both positive and negative ripple effects of the tool's implementation. The team had such significant diversity of thought – from a systems engineering PhD, a former strategy consulting partner, an expert in grantmaking, a leader in the subject matter, a finance representative, and more. Different members of the team asked different questions, and revealed different insights informed by their preexisting mental models and backgrounds. This approach led to a more honest and well-rounded understanding of potential impacts, influencing guidelines for ethical use.

Research supports this practice. Teams with diverse perspectives are better at uncovering hidden risks, engaging in productive debate, and are less likely to succumb to group think. Actively seeking different viewpoints helps counteract simplification bias and overconfidence.

In New York, the High Line is a widely popular 1.45-mile elevated park and greenway built on a former New York Central Railroad spur on Manhattan's West Side. Its success story began when two neighborhood residents formed Friends of the High Line in 1999, initially just to prevent the abandoned railway's demolition. What happened next demonstrates how diverse perspectives can systematically uncover hidden risks and counteract simplification.

Through their organization, Friends of the High Line, they created a structured community input process that brought together residents, design professionals, and community advocates. Each group, viewing the same abandoned railway through their unique lens, spotted potential problems that others had missed.

For example, community activists raised early concerns about gentrification that the design team, focused primarily on the physical space, hadn't fully considered. Meanwhile, environmentalists highlighted the importance of preserving the wild, unplanned nature of the space that had emerged over time – a perspective that significantly influenced the final landscape design.

However, perhaps the best part of this story is that several years after the project was completed the founding team said that they now wish they had included even more diverse voices across the whole community since they have since recognized unintended impacts they had not considered, specifically that the High Line serves tourists and office workers more than the communities that bookend it.

Breakthrough ideas do not exist in isolation. They interact with complex systems, affecting people in ways that are often difficult to predict. Before bringing an idea into the world, it is important to ask what unintended consequences may arise, who benefits, who might be harmed, and whether we are overestimating our understanding of the system. By engaging in deeper, more critical thinking with a diverse group of people, innovators can design solutions that work well for everyone and everything they impact.

Consider the Real World

In Saint-Nazaire, France, is the Chantiers de l'Atlantique shipyard, where the world's largest cruise ships take shape. Massive steel hulls rise from docks, engineered to carry thousands of passengers across the open ocean. These floating cities are designed for luxury and efficiency, with each new generation pushing the limits of what is possible. The oceans they navigate impose real-world constraints on how innovations come to life.

Newer ships are taller than ever, featuring multi-story glass atriums, water parks, and open-air skywalks. This extra height shifts their center of gravity, making them more susceptible to rolling in rough seas. Older ships relied on sheer mass for stability; however, modern designs require new engineering solutions to stay steady. To counteract these forces, engineers refined stabilizer fins that are like giant wings that adjust in real-time to keep the ship level. The unpredictability of the ocean doesn't stop innovation, but successful innovations must account for these realities.

Real-world considerations can be obvious, like the ocean is for the ships of the Chantiers de l'Atlantique shipyard. But, they can also be nuanced and very specific to a particular setting.

Remember Tom from Chapters 5 and 6, and the project that shifted from saving labor in the back room of a restaurant, to finding productivity and efficiency across the supply chain? Well as part of the next phase of that project, we were helping Tom prototype tracking inventory through their supply chain using RFID. RFID identifies objects from a distance, making it a great candidate for tracking inventory. It worked great through several prototypes. That is, until it met chicken.

Chicken processing plants operate under heavily sanitized conditions. The production lines, made primarily of metal, are constantly cleaned with chemicals and water. While essential for public health, these sanitation requirements created a unique challenge. The equipment designed to place RFID tags on each case of the product had to be moved away from its intended location to accommodate stricter cleaning procedures. Additionally, the tagging equipment itself needed to be cleaned regularly due to its proximity to raw chicken.

After repeated cleaning and slight shifts in positioning, the tags began falling onto the floor instead of adhering to the boxes. The tracking system then registered that a box of chicken had been sitting on the floor for three days when, in reality, the tag had detached while the box moved untagged through the line.

Even when an elegant solution works well in many contexts, it may not be ideal for every scenario. The RFID system provided tremendous value in other environments. However, when it came to chicken processing, there were additional considerations. Unique and nuanced constraints help determine when and where an idea fits.

All of these stories reinforce the same truth: real-world considerations are not *barriers*. They are *critical inputs* that shape whether and how a project should move forward. By recognizing and adapting to these conditions, you can determine whether your idea truly belongs and, if so, how to bring it to life.

Do It Responsibly

That's why, with any innovation, we prompt our clients and students to do "responsibility checks" as a way of intentionally putting on

The Implications Mindset

the Implications Mindset, building these moments of reflection into the process to ensure that key impacts are not overlooked, biases do not creep in, and real-world considerations are factored into decision-making.

Far too often, an innovation is designed to improve efficiency, accuracy, or operational costs, only to later reveal cascading unintended consequences, just like the Yellowstone wolves, K-Cups, and the Easy Apply button. Similarly, a solution may fail because it does not account for critical real-world elements, such as the ships in the Chantiers de l'Atlantique shipyard or the durability of computer hardware in a harsh chemical environment.

Responsibility checks are a fundamental part of responsible innovation. They improve the quality, rigor, and integrity of the work while helping to prevent unintended consequences that may require additional fixes later. They also surface real-world considerations early, preserving trust, momentum, and effort.

Responsibility checks help answer the crucial question: "Should we?"

Then Asking "Can We?"

"I'm an ideas person!" is a phrase we commonly hear, often playing right into innovation mythology. And you can see why it's so appealing. Who wouldn't want to be the brilliant thinker who comes up with winning ideas?

However, as we have discussed in Chapter 7, generating ideas works best as a collaborative process. It typically takes many ideas, built upon and refined through iteration, to find and develop the right solution for a problem. Besides, what good is being an "ideas person" if you can't turn a concept or prototype into an implemented solution?

Geoffry Moore, in his book *Crossing the Chasm*, introduces the concept of the device versus the whole product. The device is simply the technology or app. The whole product encompasses everything that shapes the customer experience: packaging, user manuals, support information, customer service, customization, consulting, and more.

The right idea is like the device. You might have tested and validated your idea, but it still needs to go through multiple steps with various stakeholders before it's ready to be introduced to the world. For a consumer product, this might involve manufacturing partners, distribution networks, sales and marketing teams, investors, customer service infrastructure, and an e-commerce platform. For an internal process improvement, you might need executive support, a business case, change management strategies, and coordinated adjustments across multiple departments. In that case, you would also need project or program management, budgets, forecasts, and effective communication plans.

This mindset is about considering the full implications of an innovation, including how it affects all stakeholders and how the whole product comes to life. It involves more than just generating ideas; it requires substantial business and financial planning. We often encourage our students to break the question of "Can we do it?" into three key parts: **Financial Viability, Team Capability,** and **Technological Feasibility**.

Financial Viability

Do you have the financial resources, a realistic business model, or a path to sustain the idea?

Patagonia had a pretty cool idea; to create a worn clothes repair offering. In order to launch their Worn Wear repair program, they faced a fundamental business challenge. They needed to determine whether they could make fixing clothes as financially viable as selling new ones.

Starting with one repair center in Reno, they had to create a completely new business model. They developed standardized repairs, trained specialized technicians, and offered trade-in credits for used items. Within only a few years, they were completing over 100,000 repairs annually, proving that this offering could be financially sustainable.

This goal of sustainability – through funding, a business model, or other pathway – prompts you to assess whether you have the funding necessary to bring your idea to life and sustain it over time.

Many people assume this refers solely to venture capital investment; in reality, it often means departmental budgets, philanthropic grants, or revenue from sales. Even low-tech innovations, such as a novel staff rostering method at a childcare center, require financial sustainment, including labor costs to implement and maintain the system.

Consider a novel staffing roster at a childcare center. While the new approach won't require venture capital, it still has financial considerations. They will have to craft a budget proposal for approval, outline the return on investment, and demonstrate what the organization would gain from allocating resources in this way. They may also have to make trade-offs, determining which initiatives could be funded in the current budget cycle and which needed to be deferred to the next financial year.

One tool we often find especially helpful is the *Business Model Canvas* from Alexander Osterwalder and Yves Pigneur's *Business Model Generation*. This framework helps analyze customer segments, value propositions, distribution channels, revenue streams, key partnerships, cost structures, and other essential factors. While originally designed for ambitious, high-growth ideas, it also works well for smaller-scale projects.

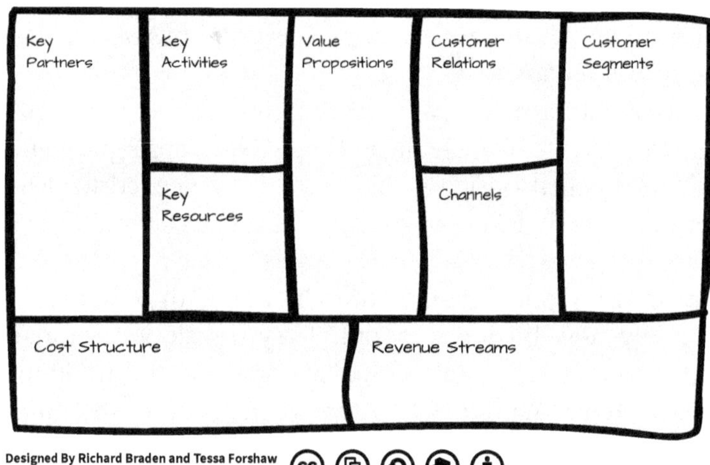

The Business Model Canvas

Any structured approach that encourages thinking through these elements is valuable for answering, "Can we do it?" Since bringing ideas to life and sustaining them always incurs costs, it's crucial to assess what that means for you and your idea.

Team Capability

Does your team have the right expertise, skills, and support to bring the idea to life?

This question addresses whether you have the necessary expertise and backing to execute your idea successfully. It's one thing to develop a great concept; it's another to implement it effectively.

One common challenge is founder syndrome – a phenomenon where the founder's skills don't align with the needs of scaling the organization. This phenomenon has been depicted extensively in shows like WeCrashed, which explores the rise and fall of WeWork.

Most of the time, expertise gaps aren't as dramatic as founder syndrome. The underlying issue is ensuring you have the right skills and support is critical to making your idea a reality. Bringing an idea to life often requires assembling a well-rounded team with a range of complementary skills, such as:

- Project and program management to coordinate timelines and budgets.

- Financial planning and business modeling to develop sustainable funding strategies.

- Marketing and communications to promote the solution and engage the audience.

- Regulatory and legal compliance to navigate laws, standards, and risk management.

- Change management to facilitate internal transitions and align stakeholders.

- Operations and supply chain management to ensure efficient production and distribution.

The Implications Mindset

This list is not exhaustive, and sometimes your needs will be more specialized. For example in the organizations we have worked with we have seen:

- A humanitarian nonprofit needing to train their existing coaches and mentors in the new leadership program they were rolling out to ensure continuity.
- A skincare brand considering blockchain integration in its supply chain needing to secure blockchain development expertise.
- A bakery launching a subscription-based pastry delivery service with an automated ordering system needing a system integrator.

In the case of LogicMonitor, a cloud-based IT monitoring firm, leadership recognized that sustaining growth required more than just great technology. In 2022, they added key leadership roles, including a Chief Performance Officer and a Chief Customer Officer, to enhance operations and deepen customer engagement. By 2024, LogicMonitor's annual recurring revenue had exceeded $150 million, reflecting a 300 percent increase over three years. Their success underscores the importance of continuously strengthening a team's expertise at every level.

Sometimes, you'll have the skills you need in-house. Other times, you'll need to hire, partner, or upskill to fill gaps. The key is to be honest about what's missing and proactive about finding the right expertise to move forward.

Technological Feasibility

Does the technology or core capability exist to support the solution in reality?

As we drove down University Avenue in Palo Alto toward the Stanford University campus, we often passed under a train bridge. For many years in the early 2010s, a banner advertising Theranos hung from that bridge. People were excited about the company, and landing a job there was a dream for many students. The company's premise was to develop technology capable of running over 200 blood tests from a single drop of blood, an undeniably bold vision that could have transformed healthcare. Except, it didn't work.

While she was a student at Stanford, founder Elizabeth Holmes met with Dr. Phyllis Gardner, a Stanford professor of medicine, who pointed out the lack of scientific support.

We know it isn't exciting or flashy to say, but sometimes an idea just isn't possible, or at least not yet. And when that is the case, it is important to factor that into how you answer "Can we?"

Like Theranos' blood test, millions of people might want it, it might have a sound business model and future profit potential, and it might even have many working components. Yet if some fundamental science, technology, or capabilities don't exist, that is a moment to pause. Ignoring this reality led Theranos to face some significant consequences. Had the company not been so focused on delivering 200 tests, it might have succeeded with a smaller set of tests that did have scientific backing, such as rapid HIV tests, cholesterol checks, diabetes screenings, and iron level assessments.

This challenge was something founders Reed Hastings and Marc Randolph considered in their launch of Netflix. When Netflix launched in 1998, they wanted to deliver movies online directly to customers' computers. However, internet infrastructure at the time was still developing, and most connections were too slow to handle streaming. So, they pivoted to mailing DVDs instead. This allowed them to build a customer base while waiting for broadband to become more common. Once broadband was widely available, they were ready to introduce the streaming model that revolutionized how we watch television and movies.

Before launching an idea, ask:

- Financial Viability: Can we fund and sustain it?
- Team Capability: Do we have the right expertise?
- Technological Feasibility: Does the core technology exist?

Ideas need the right timing, support, and conditions.

Key Takeaways

The Impacts of an Innovation Cascade

Every idea triggers ripple effects. Wolves in Yellowstone, Keurig pods, and Easy Apply all had unintended consequences that shaped their success or failure. It's essential to consider these before embarking on bringing your idea to life. Diverse voices and intentional spaces for thinking through helping you innovate responsibly.

Execution Needs Money, Skills, and Feasibility

To bring an idea to life, ask: Do we have the financial resources to sustain it? Do we have the right people and expertise? Does the necessary technology, science, or infrastructure exist?

Ask "Should We" Before "Can We," but Do Ask Both!

The Implications Mindset ensures ideas are both responsible and feasible. "Should we?" forces us to consider ethics, impact, and real-world constraints. "Can we?" pushes us to think about funding, skills, and execution. Strong innovation balances both so solutions aren't just possible but sustainable and effective.

Innovation-ish

Moves

Moves Are Actions

"Think about a problem you're facing today, a problem so big and complicated that you haven't even been able to get started. You've been putting it off, not intentionally. You're planning to do it later. But, somehow, you never seem to get started. It's a problem that's stuck. Now, we want you to start solving that problem right now."

We announce this at the beginning of our course for business professionals, graduate students, and other adult learners.

"Gah – what should we do?" They start shifting in their seats, glancing at each other. Some, after an initial scan of the room, look back at us. We can tell they're wondering: Do they really mean it? Do we really have to tackle that problem, the one that has felt overwhelming for so long?

If this feels familiar, it's because we all have problems like that. Problems we put off because they're unfamiliar, too complex, or have never been solved before. Or perhaps we lack the budget or don't feel we have "permission" to take action.

Remember that it doesn't need to be a moon-shot problem; it might be streamlining your ordering process, launching a new business, organizing your attic, or perhaps changing careers.

No matter what problem you choose, you may be wondering: How am I going to solve this one?

The answer: By starting somewhere.

Remember Start Somewhere

Remember the "Start Somewhere" questions from Chapter 3? These questions help you push past analysis paralysis and overthinking, guiding you into organizing your thoughts so it's easier to take action.

Revisit Start Somewhere Activity

Either revisit your notes from this activity or spend one to two minutes brainstorming answers to each question. Write down your ideas before moving on to the next question.

- How can I better understand the problem?
- How can I activate other people to help me solve the problem?
- How can I generate lots of potential solutions to the problem?
- How can I learn how other people experience the problem?
- How can I experiment with my ideas to see how they address the problem?
- If I could eliminate my problem today, how would I know it was solved?

You can use these six questions for any problem, at any time. You don't need special materials or training, just a willingness to think and take action. This is a simple way to start being Innovation-ish right now. Let's explore how these questions help get you moving in the Innovation-ish approach.

It's Called a Move

Every idea you generate in response to these questions is what we call a move. A move is a small, concrete action you take toward solving a problem, whether it's a minor obstacle you've been tripping over or a major challenge that's been holding you back.

We'll show examples of moves and why they matter; for now, let's examine your responses to the Start Somewhere questions.

After brainstorming potential moves, pause for a moment and reflect on the problem. What do you notice? Does the problem seem different now?

We often hear:

- "The problem looks smaller now."
- "It's not as big as I thought."

158

Innovation-ish

- "I have a plan for getting started."
- "It doesn't feel as scary."
- "I know who can help me."

Some of the overwhelming feelings of uncertainty and fear – the cognitive caution – are replaced with confidence and motivation, even though you haven't actually solved the problem yet. What you have done is take a small and significant step forward.

Looking at your answers. Are you surprised by how many ideas you generated? The goal of these six questions is to show that you already possess a vast set of problem-solving tools. You have a lot more than you realize.

Notice that your list likely includes actions you already know how to do. For instance, your response to How can I better understand the problem? might include:

- Writing about it.
- Organizing your thoughts on sticky notes.
- Creating an outline of key points .
- Making a spreadsheet.
- Reading about it.

These are all familiar skills.

Similarly, your answers to How can I activate other people to help me solve the problem? might include:

- Talking it over with a family member.
- Convening a group of friends.
- Posting about it online.
- Finding people with expertise on the issue.

Again, these are actions you already know how to take.

When you step back and review your brainstormed list, you'll see that you possess a wealth of useful skills (moves), perhaps

Moves are Actions

even recalling some you'd forgotten. People often underestimate themselves, failing to tap into their own storehouse of knowledge and experience.

We can't begin to guess the specific problem you're grappling with. The range of challenges our course participants have faced is vast. Let's say one of your answers to "How can I activate other people to help me solve the problem?" involves gathering input from people you don't know.

For example, perhaps you're trying to get your city to redesign a dangerous intersection. You realize you need input from others in the neighborhood, so you consider gathering their thoughts. At first, this might seem anywhere from daunting to impossible.

This exact issue, and the feelings of nervousness and cognitive caution that come with it, often arises in our courses because we frequently ask students to go out and interview strangers.

You can probably imagine what that feels like. Picture yourself in our sunny second-floor classroom, looking out the window at the people hurrying by on the sidewalk. You wonder, "How on earth am I supposed to stop them and get them to answer my questions?"

In one class, the assignment was to redesign campus tourism. We asked students to interview local residents, shop owners, and students to understand their perspectives on visitors and their own interests and concerns. As we've emphasized, gathering input from potential users before developing solutions is crucial. In this case, we had an additional goal: we knew that talking to strangers is difficult. That's precisely why we wanted our students to confront that fear, figure out how to engage people quickly, and then reflect on how they overcame the challenge, facing cognitive caution head on.

This experience highlights the importance of breaking down daunting tasks into moves.

Moves are intentionally small steps. It is through small steps that you build an Innovation-ish habit. Neuroscientifically, each small accomplishment of a move triggers a reward response: even tiny "wins" can elicit dopamine release, the brain's reward neurotransmitter, leading to a "feel-good" boost that reinforces further effort.

Innovation-ish

With regards to creativity specifically, this phenomenon was termed the Progress Principle by organizational psychologist Teresa Amabil, who showed that recognizing small daily progress increases engagement and creativity.

The feel-good boost and quick win help overcome the paralysis from Innovation Hesitation that often accompanies starting an Innovation-ish practice. Since moves are small and about a single small step, they lower the stakes because there isn't such a thing as failure with a move, except by not doing it.

Apart from being small, how else do we define a move? Let's find out.

Understanding Move Characteristics

Imagine a massive, government-run repository of personal protective equipment, maintained in case of future pandemics. Stanley, a manager, oversees general operations, supervising a team of submanagers, each responsible for a group of workers on the floor.

When we first meet Stanley in one of our Innovation-ish courses, he is full of enthusiasm. He tells his classmates that he is already ahead of them; he is just refining his established innovation skills because he has already innovated. During a solo "retreat," he identified a challenge with his submanagers: the accuracy and analysis of performance data they collected and reported weekly. As a self-proclaimed "spreadsheet expert," Stanley spent weeks creating complex spreadsheets to optimize the process. Passionate about his solution, he excitedly explained how his process was faster, more accurate, and would save the company significant costs.

At first glance, you might assume Stanley's actions exemplify Innovation-ish. But were they moves?

We asked him if he had already invented such a great tool, why had he enrolled in our Innovation-ish course? What more did he hope to accomplish?

He admitted he had an implementation problem: his submanagers and floor workers were resisting his spreadsheet, despite his insistence that they use it. He wanted ideas on how to get them to

Moves are Actions

adopt his invention, yet no matter how many times he explained or demonstrated it, they continued to resist.

Stanley's struggle presented a fascinating problem for the class, and a perfect opportunity to refine our definition of a move. While Stanley's spreadsheet was a classic example of a traditional problem-solving approach, his actions weren't moves.

Remember our preliminary definition of a move? An incremental step, often a small one. Big problems rarely disappear overnight; they unravel through small, often nonlinear steps. Moves guide us from step to step along this often unpredictable path.

You might wonder: Didn't Stanley take some steps toward solving his problem? Weren't his expertise and experience moves? Let's take a closer look.

Remember, Innovation Mythology tells us that breakthroughs happen in the minds of lone inventors, despite historical narratives suggesting otherwise. But Innovation-ish, the kind of innovation you need in your work and life, requires collaboration.

That's why a move must be:

Definable: It has clearly defined boundaries and actions.

Actionable: It can be started immediately; the team can take action right away.

Shareable: It produces meaningful results that are useful to others.

Reusable: It can be reapplied by other teams or adapted to different problems.

Stanley's spreadsheet might have been an impressive technical solution; however, it failed the move test because it was not developed collaboratively with a series of moves. He didn't engage his sub-managers along the way. It was his own idea, that he identified, developed, finalized, and launched that solution one big step.

The best innovation doesn't happen in isolation. It happens through iterative, incremental moves that involve real people, real collaboration, and real-world testing.

The four characteristics of a move.

Definable

When you come up with a move, you need to be able to describe and explain it to your team members, whether your team is formal or informal. A move must have a clearly defined beginning and end, with specific steps, constraints, and logistics so the team can evaluate its usefulness. Everyone involved must be able to grasp the contours and dimensions of any move you propose.

The team also needs to determine the specifics of how the moves will be used – who will implement it, how often it will be used, and the time frame. A move does not involve unlimited practice; it's a bounded activity that starts, is utilized, and then stops.

For example, a gut feeling is not a move because it isn't definable. There's no evidence-based way for a team to evaluate a member's instinct. While gut feelings may sometimes be correct, they are ultimately just guesses. A statement like, "After talking with all of these people, I think they need. . ." is vague and untestable.

In contrast, a move could be having the whole team extract direct quotes from interview notes onto sticky notes and clustering similar ones to identify themes. This is a clearly defined process: who will do it, how much there is to do, and what the expected outcome will be.

Moves are Actions

Actionable

A move should be something a team member can act on immediately. If no one can implement it right away, it isn't a move. For instance, "Let's wait until our next meeting" or "We'll address this at next year's conference" are not moves. The team must be able to execute the move in real time. If they can't, it needs to be reconsidered.

A statement like, "I've been in situations like this before, and nothing we do will work," is also not a move because it lacks actionable steps. On the other hand, the sticky note clustering example allows team members to immediately begin sorting their notes and writing out quotes. They don't need to wait for additional interviews, they can prepare now and refine their work later as a group.

Shareable

The results or output of the move – whether data, insights, new ideas – must be shareable to other people.

Actions like spending time thinking about the problem or reading a report on production line performance may be valuable; however, they are not moves unless they produce tangible, shareable results.

For example, Stanley going on a solo retreat and thinking about the problem is not sharable, it cannot be examined, expanded, or shared in a meaningful way. However, if he mindmapped his assumptions, and then showed it to his team members as a conversation starter to capture their reactions, that would be a move. Team members, whether present from the beginning or newly onboarded, could explore his mindmap, and discuss, refine, and challenge the assumptions, adding more or reorganizing.

A move should allow others to engage with its results.

Reusable

For an action to be a move, it needs to be adaptable and applicable to multiple projects across different teams and contexts.

When a move is reusable, teams can get faster and more efficient at implementing it if they choose to reuse it. Instead of constantly inventing new processes, they refine and improve the ones they already use. Each time a move is applied, it may take on a slightly different meaning, adapting to the team, the problem, the impacted stakeholders, or even the business context.

However, it is important to consider here that just because you have used the move before and it worked for you, that doesn't mean it is the right thing to do at this moment. It's common for people to use a familiar solution even when a better approach exists, simply because their past experience "primes" them to stick with the known method. Knowing something isn't the right reason to reuse it.

If an action isn't definable, actionable, shareable, and reusable, it's not an Innovation-ish move. These four characteristics form the foundation.

In our class with Stanley, we decide to set his problem aside for a few days while the students go through the process of learning about the six questions and moves. We send them into the streets to interview strangers, help them think through the process, and discuss the moves they develop.

When we return to Stanley's problem, his classmates have gained new insights. They now recognize that many of his actions weren't actually moves. Taking a solo retreat, for instance, wasn't a move because it wasn't definable or shareable. Creating a spreadsheet wasn't a move either, because it wasn't actionable or shareable.

Stanley's classmates helped him develop questions he hadn't considered. His first step should have been gathering a team to brainstorm ways to understand the problem and determine whether a problem even existed. These ways of understanding the issue should have been his first moves.

Next, he should have asked:

- How can I activate other people to help me solve the problem?

- How can I generate multiple potential solutions?

- How can I learn how different people experience the problem?

165

Moves are Actions

- How can I experiment with my ideas to see how they address the problem?

- If I could eliminate my problem today, how would I know it was solved?

The answers to these questions would have formed his next set of moves.

Getting Your Hands Dirty

Walk into the kitchen of a fast-food restaurant, and you'll often see a bin in the back where employees discard food that, according to food safety rules, wasn't served quickly enough after preparation. If a hamburger is grilled and sits unsold past its allowed time, it becomes waste. It has to go into the bin. Restaurants must use this waste for accounting and environmental purposes. In many kitchens, you'll find a clipboard with lined paper and a pencil taped to a string near the waste bin, where employees record discarded items.

During busy times, employees don't always take the time to write down what they're throwing away, so managers must periodically check the clipboard against what's in the bin. Most days, this means someone gets the unenviable task of "gloving up," digging through the trash, and counting every discarded hamburger and chicken tender.

Fast-food restaurants are among the biggest first-job employers, so the "someone" is often a young employee in an entry-level role. Many restaurants struggle to retain these young workers. We were brought in to help address this challenge.

We gathered a diverse set of stakeholders to get as many perspectives as possible. Through brainstorming, they generated dozens of potential solutions.

One idea was to use a voice-recognition system. A similar system was already in use at the distributor, allowing employees wearing headsets to track orders loaded onto pallets. Having a voice system near the waste bin would let anyone walk up and say, "I'm wasting two burgers," to record it. No pencil required.

It was a brilliant idea – both low-tech and high-tech at the same time. It had a buzz. Of all the ideas put forward, it seemed like the clear winner.

The team excitedly began pricing the solution to determine how much it would cost to implement across all restaurants. We've seen this before; people get so energized about an idea that they want to roll it out immediately. It solves a big problem, and the potential savings seem too good to ignore!

And that is the trap many companies fall into. The idea is so compelling, with so much perceived upside, that they make a fateful decision: Let's do it! They implement the idea without further testing.

Here's where the team made a crucial decision.

One team member asked, "How could we experiment with our idea to try it first?" After discussing a few moves that could help answer that question, the team used an Innovation-ish move called a critical assumption prototype.

The critical assumption prototype move involves creating a prototype that is robust enough to test the most critical aspect of an idea, and can be built quickly and at a low cost. The hypothesis for this test was:

> "If we provide a hands-free tracking system, the crew's compliance and waste accuracy will improve."

It was a move because it was:

Definable: The team could define the requirements in terms of cost, effort, and functionality, ensuring the prototype was effective without being too time-consuming or expensive.

Actionable: The team could start working on it immediately, sometimes building it in just a few hours with readily available materials.

Shareable: The prototype could be tested by many different team members, and then get back together to share the results for feedback and discussion.

Moves are Actions

Reusable: Once familiar with this move, the team could use it repeatedly in later phases of the project, on other ideas, or in different projects if they choose.

The team visited a storefront maker space and recruited student programmers to build a simple version of the tool. In just one afternoon, they had it up and running. They used an off-the-shelf Amazon Echo, something familiar to many of them for ordering pantry items at home. While it wouldn't withstand the harsh environment of a commercial kitchen, it would work long enough to test the idea.

Two team members who owned franchises installed the prototype in their restaurants and observed employees to ensure proper use. To verify its accuracy, the owners themselves got their hands dirty. They "gloved up" and combed through the trash.

Expectations were high.

Yet, the team found that the prototype Alexa was no more accurate than the clipboard-and-pencil method. The prototype worked well in the quiet maker space environment, but commercial kitchens are noisy. People move and talk fast, and there are wide variations in language and accents.

This might sound like a story of an idea's failure. And, truth be told, it is. More importantly, however, it's a story of Innovation-ish success!

Why? Without the critical assumption prototype move, the team might have moved forward aggressively with what seemed like a brilliant solution. Realizing that Alexa wasn't suitable for the kitchen, they might have commissioned a more robust, professional-grade, grease- and drop-proof device. Imagine the cost of developing that technology; hardware, software, compliance, back-end integration, and installation across thousands of restaurants in multiple countries.

Many companies fall into this trap, spending millions to create and launch "bulletproof" ideas. If those ideas fail, they incur even more costs trying to fix or ultimately replace them.

The critical assumption prototype is a powerful move that reduces risk. It allows teams to quickly determine, with minimal investment, whether a big idea will actually work.

Key Takeaways

Start small with moves to get unstuck.
A move is a small, concrete action toward solving a problem. Instead of waiting for the perfect plan, taking small, definable steps builds momentum and reduces overwhelm.

Good moves are definable, actionable, shareable, and reusable.
Effective moves should be clearly structured, able to be implemented immediately, generate meaningful results, and be adaptable for future challenges.

Chapter 12

Using Moves

We define a move as an incremental action, based on your own knowledge, experience, and skills, that you take to drive toward a solution to a problem.

You should note an important phrase in that definition: "your own." When we refer to *"your own* knowledge, experience, and skills," that's because we know that you have what you need already to at least get started at solving the problem. Moves can come from any discipline, and as you find them and use them, you are building your repertoire of skills.

Erika, a marine biologist, National Geographic Explorer, and founder of The Hydrous, gained extensive knowledge about trophic cascades while completing her PhD, focusing on coral reefs at the Great Barrier Reef in Australia. So much so that it was a concept she often thought about in her work, even when it wasn't directly related to biology. In fact, Erika wanted to understand some of the unintended consequences of different designs on marine pollution; she used her deep understanding of trophic cascades to inform her approach. This knowledge became the tool she relied on to assess the impacts.

This is exactly what it means to use a "move" from the toolkit you already have and use often.

But, sometimes you're looking for a move, and nothing comes to mind right away.

It happens to all of us. So don't throw up your hands and give up. You can find moves all around you, and make them your own. Here are four places we ask our students and clients to look to find them:

Historical moves: Moves that come from your own history and experiences.

Customizing moves: Moves that come from other people or external sources, that you make your own.

Translatable moves: Moves that you often use with one mind-set and then decide to use in another.

Analogous moves: Doing moves in similar contexts when you can't answer your question on your own.

Continuously growing, learning, and evolving is why Innovation-ish is a practice, not a process. We believe each person will develop their own collection of moves and follow their own steps to creatively solve problems. That's what it means to be Innovation-ish.

Using Historical Moves

The first thing you do, whether you realize it or not, is reach deep into your past experiences to find tools or skills that might help you face the challenge. We don't only mean the tools that seem obvious to you, like Erika and the trophic cascades, we also mean the ones that are deep in the history of your knowledge and experiences. Maybe you learned them at work, perhaps by participating in a community organization, raising children, or while in a program, school, or university.

Examples of Moves from all parts of life

Aspect of Life	Move Example	How it is Innovation-ish
Community Organization	You volunteer at a cat adoption clinic, and that involves taking photos and writing captions that highlight each cat's unique story.	This same move can help "humanize" a product, idea, or service, by creating genuine empathy and buy-in by sharing personal narratives and real-life details.
Raising Children	When inventing new bedtime stories every night, you notice which parts excite your kids and build on that feedback.	This same move can help you nail your pitch. You can pitch ideas in small chunks again and again, while revising instantly based on feedback.
High School	In high school you were the yearbook editor. You gathered snapshots and information about each student, and then clustered them thematically into groups.	This same move can help you sort through the stakeholders or customers in your Innovation-ish system.
Summer Job	At your summer job in a local restaurant, you had to notice what was going on. You needed to make sure everyone had what they needed, that people would not leave without paying, and that you were generally aware of the room at all times.	This same move can help you continuously observe your problem's context and the people within it to spot hidden needs or emerging problems.

Using Moves

Moves are personal. They come from all sorts of places and experiences, and you already have more than you know in your toolkit.

For example, one of our students protested that she wasn't a trained interviewer and wouldn't know how to "get the right information" from people she approached. Until she remembered that she had once worked at a fast-food restaurant.

We asked, "Did customers always know exactly what they wanted when they got to the drive-up window?"

"No," she said. "Sometimes they'd be like, 'I'm not sure what I want.'"

We discussed how she had helped those customers by asking, "What are you in the mood for?" and letting the conversation unfold until they made a decision. In essence, she already had a move she could use – entering into soft discussions to gently prompt people to reflect on their preferences.

Aha! A light went on. She realized she didn't need specialized tools or training to start interviewing potential users; she just needed to dust off the move she'd already been practicing at the drive-through.

You may not have worked in fast food; your experience talking with strangers might have come from school fundraisers, a science fair, or working a booth at a conference.

Another example comes from one of our courses. Students were wrestling with how to make sense of or create order out of all the possible solutions they had brainstormed for a design problem when a student spoke up. She was new to innovation and design although wasn't new to creative thinking. She switched careers after years of practical work as a psychologist in challenging situations.

In class, she suddenly saw a connection between her past career and the design thinking process we were exploring. She told us how she had learned how useful it can be to make visual maps of sprawling blended families – aunts, cousins, adoptees, foster children – to understand relationships and find potential solutions to conflicts. "I used to do this all the time," she said. "In my world, it was called 'family structure analysis.'" She saw that the kinds of maps she once created for families could be used to evaluate the sprawling range of design solutions the class was considering. This was one of her moves – an action she already understood, and she could confidently apply it to a new innovation challenge.

"Family structure analysis" is not a design thinking tool. It was, however, a Move she already knew, and it worked perfectly with her project. That Move gave her team the understanding they needed to gain key insight and move the project forward. This Innovation-ish approach elevated her "design thinking" work by expanding the definition of what tools she could use to search for solutions.

Was it "design thinking?" – maybe not. Was it helpful? Easier? Beneficial? Innovation-ish? YES!

That's precisely the kind of small breakthrough we'll show you how to achieve: drawing on your own abilities and applying them to new situations.

Beyond first jobs, high school, raising kids, and everyday life, many people have specific capabilities honed through experience in particular vocational fields. These can also be extremely valuable to being Innovation-ish.

For example, we've seen students and clients apply:

- Machine Learning: Algorithmic Problem Analysis – Students used their ML knowledge to run complex algorithms to analyze problems.

- Marketing: Stakeholder and Interviewee Mapping – Marketing students mapped out who might be impacted by a problem and created lists of potential interviewees.

- Videography/Visual Arts: Narrative Visualization – Videographers and visual artists used storytelling techniques to explain both problems and solutions clearly.

- Biology: Ecological Modeling – Biologists applied ecological models to assess the potential unintended consequences of their ideas.

Their familiarity with these tools helped them confidently apply existing moves to new problems.

By recognizing the moves you already have and those you can learn from others, you can take control of the innovation process. Innovation doesn't require starting from scratch; it starts by leveraging what you already know and applying it in new ways.

Using Moves

Regardless of your background, you have familiar tools, frameworks, and methods that can serve as *Innovation-ish* moves.

This cognitive process of intentionally reaching into our existing skills and abilities and applying them to a new problem is called learning transfer. It's just like what the GM workers in Indiana did when they started building ventilators as we discussed in Chapter 6.

More often than not, we have knowledge, skills, or experience that can help us get started. We are never starting from zero. Let us say that another way: you already are Innovation-ish and have some of the skills you need to get going on your creative problem-solving journey right now.

If you feel stuck, intentionally ask yourself, "What do I already have that could apply here?" and if you need a little bit more of a push you can also ask your partner, friends, manager, peers, team mates, – anyone who knows you – what skills they think you have that could help you solve this problem. Turns out other people are a great resource at helping us transfer our learning into a novel context.

By tapping into your past experiences – with the help of others – you build a toolbox of reliable moves that forms the foundation for tackling any problem head-on.

Customizing Moves

In 2003, when I (Rich) finally committed to fulfilling my long-time dream of hiking the entire 2,653-mile Pacific Crest Trail (PCT), I didn't expect it to have anything to do with innovation or with moves, but it did.

Once I decided to go, I started preparing. One of my decisions was to make as much of my gear as possible. My grandmother had taught me basic sewing skills when I was growing up, so with a $50 second-hand sewing machine, I began the process. I tried, failed, and iterated my way through making my own backpack, sleeping bag, tarp-tent, and most of my clothing. I must have ripped out every seam at least once as I worked to create ultra-light backpacking gear.

However, it wasn't until I got on the trail that I realized the most valuable aspect of making my own gear: I could modify it at any point.

One day, while cutting a hole in a brand-new pair of running shoes, I had a realization. By necessity, I had purchased some of my gear rather than making it myself. Before this trip, if a buckle broke or I tore a hole in something I had bought, my instinct was to consider it broken. I would either send it back for repairs or dispose of it entirely.

Out on the trail, I had a different perspective. This gear was mine. I owned it, and I could use it however I wanted. I could change it, fix it, or modify it to suit my needs. I was no longer bound by the thinking of the designer, inventor, or manufacturer. I made it my own.

The same applies to innovation work. When you consider the skills, tools, and frameworks you have in your experience, you are free to adapt them to fit your project. They already belong to you, and you can modify them as needed.

This principle extends to any move. There are countless books, courses, podcasts, and online resources filled with innovation moves that others have used and described. You can make those your own, modifying and adapting them however necessary to solve your problem. Many resources outline specific sequences or frameworks for these moves. You are just as free to follow those patterns or create your own. Once you have made them your own, they become part of your personal toolkit.

Move inspiration comes from your teammates. Moves can be found, acquired, adapted, learned, and experimented with from others, because, as we often point out, innovation is a team sport just like soccer. It requires collaboration and multiple perspectives. A move you make may combine with a teammate's move to create something entirely new. Something neither of you would have developed alone, but which turns out to be the perfect solution for the problem at hand. That's why two of the six questions we asked in Chapter 11 are:

- *How can I activate other people to help me solve the problem?*

- *How can I learn how other people experience the problem?*

Or Move inspiration may come from anyone you interact with such as people you've had conversations with, authors of books you've read, instructors of courses you've taken, or anyone you have had a meaningful conversation with.

Using Moves

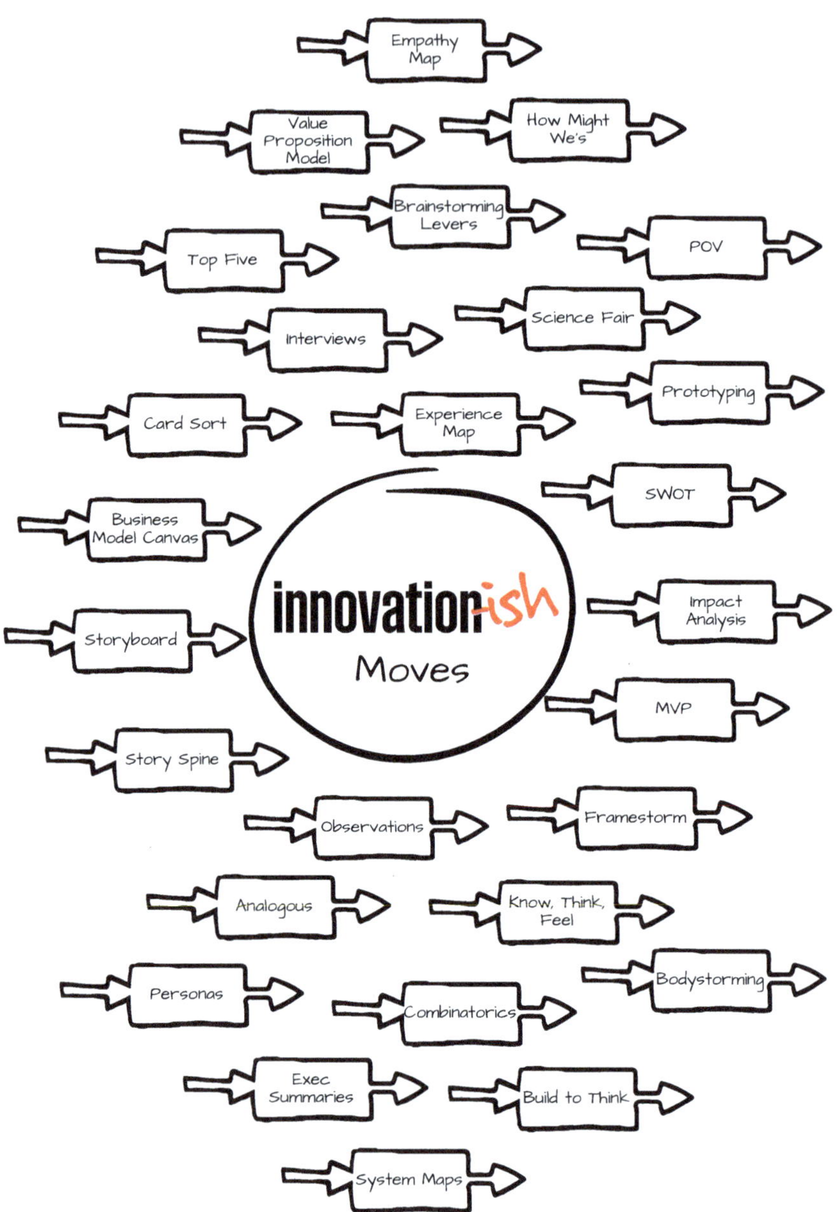

Adopt moves from any toolkit or method, and make them your own Innovation-ish moves.

This also means that moves from any innovation, design, creativity method can become your own. The *Innovation-ish* approach embraces any tool, skill, or move that helps you move forward. In reality, many established innovation processes include great tried and true techniques that can be adapted as moves. You can mix and blend moves from multiple methods, processes, and experiences to create your own *Innovation-ish* approach.

Like customizing gear on the PCT, you can customize your moves. Doing so requires you to embrace being adaptable and cognitive flexible. You need to adjust moves to fit your parameters and your context – not just adopt them as written or used by someone else.

Translating Moves

"Come on up and place a piece of tape connecting the move you just learned to the Mindset you can use it in," we told our class.

On the board, the Six Mindsets are arranged in a circle. In the center was the move we had just introduced; the user journey map.

A user journey map is a tool that helps us understand the user experience. As users share their stories, you document events and add visuals to explain or augment their experience, capturing the sequence of steps they took. It's the plot of their story. You might co-create this map on paper with the person you're interviewing or develop it yourself based on their responses. Explicit emotions, either those they mention or those you infer, should be incorporated. The goal is to uncover both pain points and moments of delight.

To bring this to life, imagine mapping an airplane travel experience. Where did the journey begin? What actions did the traveler take? Where did they go next? What happened along the way? Document every step and include the emotions they experienced at each point. Sometimes, the smallest details reveal the biggest insights.

Once we'd written the title of the move, User Journey Map, on the board, we stepped back and waited. Slowly, one student and then another approached the eight-foot-tall foam core board. The first student quickly grabbed a piece of colorful tape and stretched it from the User Journey Map to the Insights Mindset.

179

Using Moves

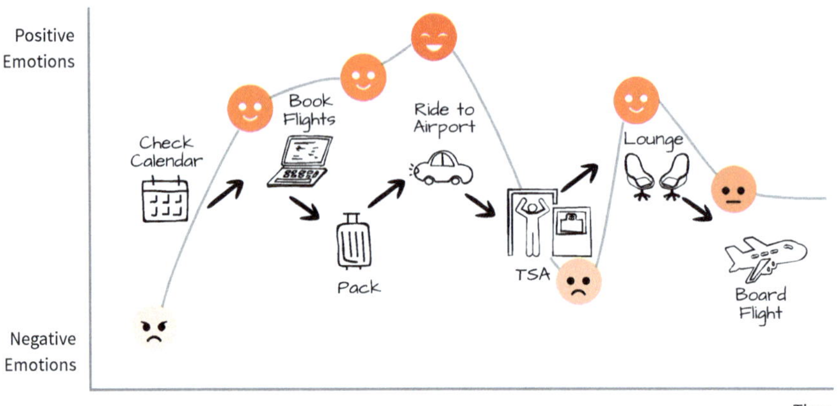

A User Journey Map explores the user's experience to discover insights.

The next student hesitated, glancing at us to see if the first student had mapped it correctly and, in turn, if they could safely return to their seat. We smiled and encouraged them, "Go ahead, put it up." This time, the student linked the move to Interactions, then suggested that allowing interviewees to co-create illustrations during the conversation, perhaps even handing them the pen, could make the discussion more engaging.

"Yes, that's a great way to use it!" we responded enthusiastically. Soon, more students stepped up, placing more moves and more tape on the board. They mapped moves to mindsets, each move connecting to at least three mindsets.

This was the moment we had been hoping for! This was ownership. These were their moves, and they realized they could use them however they saw fit. They learned that being taught a move in the context of "interviews" or "empathy" didn't mean they were limited to that application. That was just *one way* to use it.

With each explanation of how they would adapt, shift, or change a move, their understanding expanded. In a single session, the number of moves they had formulated multiplied. The move they initially associated with Interactions suddenly had three, four, or even five new applications. Their toolkits grew, along with their confidence.

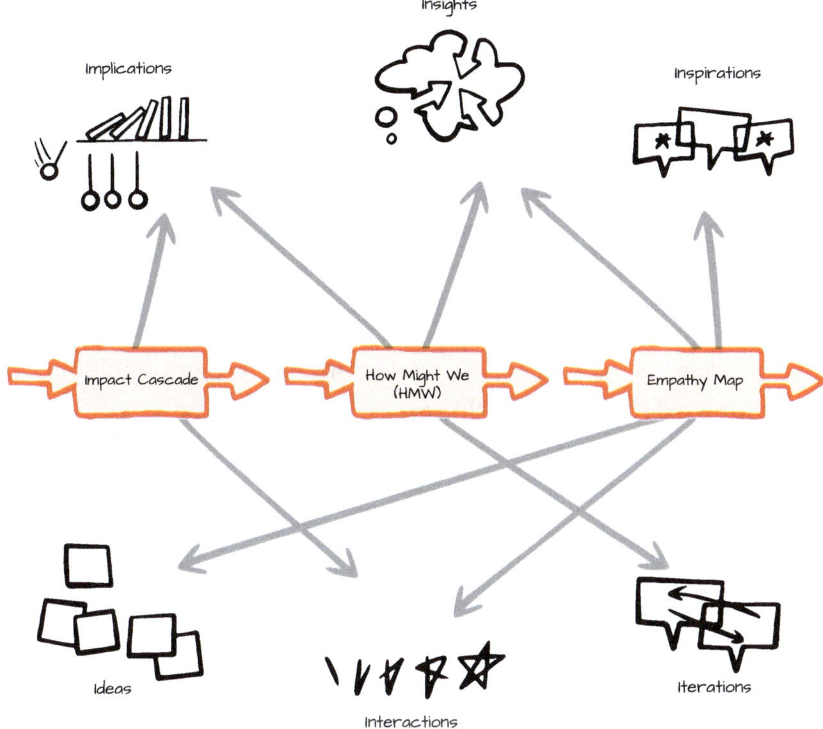

A move can be used in several or all mindsets.

This ability to translate moves across different contexts is an important skill for Innovation-ish thinking.

Try Translating Some Moves Activity

1. Write down five moves you've used in your life.

2. List two or three creative problems you need to solve.

3. Draw lines between the challenges and the moves to explore how you could repurpose them.

A single move can be used in many different mindsets.

Using Moves

Take storytelling as an example.

While storytelling is a common move used with the Inspiration Mindset, it can also serve other purposes:

- In Interactions, it can elicit reactions, generate ideas, or function as a collaborative tool where participants co-build the story with you.
- In Iterations, it allows for rapid adjustments, refining each idea through new versions of the narrative.
- In Ideas, it can act as a brainstorming prompt, helping to explore different possibilities.

Or consider the User Journey Map:

- As an Interactions move, it engages users in mapping their own experiences.
- As an Insights move, it helps synthesize participant data into a cohesive journey.
- As an Iteration move, it visualizes different versions of an idea, showing its evolution over time.

Moves are not confined to a single mindset. They are cognitive strategies that produce different results depending on the mindset, or cognitive framework, you apply them within.

Finding Analogous Moves

When you're stuck on a problem, analogies can be a powerful way to discover new moves. They work by drawing a comparison between two things that are seemingly different and that have particular similarities.

More than just useful communication tools, analogies help break through conceptual barriers and reveal problems from entirely fresh perspectives. They're especially valuable when you can't find a way

Innovation-ish

to answer your question in your real-world problem context. Or, at least, not yet.

Because of this broad applicability, when working with organizations that have been stuck on a problem for a long time, our first instinct is often to turn to analogies to help them move forward. Often doing a move in an analogous context can feel like less of a high bar than in your real-world one.

The key is to look beyond surface level similarities and focus on finding situations that share deep structural patterns with your challenge. For instance, when we worked with a Sharing-Economy Technology Company to improve team performance, we explored Navy SEAL teams and Formula One pit crews because they dealt with similar underlying dynamics of coordination, role clarity, and high-stakes performance. They didn't want to involve their stakeholders yet in what they were thinking so looking to an analogous context and seeing what move might work there was an easy way for them to keep moving forward.

This process involves identifying your core challenge and then exploring how others have solved similar problems or moved forward in their Innovation-ish journey in completely different contexts. By immersing yourself in these analogous situations, you can uncover moves and approaches you might never have considered.

To illustrate this concept let's look at an analogous move we used in our work.

In early 2020, as the COVID-19 pandemic emerged, we worked with the Australian Government on leadership challenges in this unprecedented situation. Because there was no direct historical precedent for managing a pandemic at this scale and we couldn't very well go and disrupt teams currently working on pandemic response, the team struggled to find how to move forward. They invited us to run a workshop during Australian Government Design Week, and we decided to look for moves in analogous contexts. What move can we apply to learn more about how this challenge was solved in another context?

We explored how airline pilots handle novel situations and emergencies by having an interview with one, because flying planes and

Using Moves

managing a pandemic both require structured decision-making in unpredictable circumstances.

Participants walked away with powerful insights:

- Some noticed that pilots use structured frameworks to make decisions in novel situations and realized they could adopt similar frameworks for their department.

- Others saw how pilots quickly prioritize actions in emergencies, rapidly processing relevant information in line with predetermined priorities. This inspired them to develop clearer prioritization structures.

- Many were struck by the culture of continuous learning in aviation, with pilots frequently debriefing in real-time. This led some teams to experiment with daily learning stand-ups to evaluate their decisions and adjust accordingly.

A good analogy must go beyond simple outward similarities and delve into the deeper structure of the situation. It's easy to fall for surface resemblances, such as "X context looks like Y." The essential element is to find structural features in your analogous situation that match the core elements of your challenge.

Analogies for the problem: Government leadership in the COVID-19 pandemic

Core Feature of Problem	Analogous Context	Shared Deep Structure
No Direct Historical Precedent	Airline Pilots Handling Novel Emergencies	Both require structured decisions in unpredictable novel environments.
High-Stakes, Fast-Paced Coordination	Formula One Pit Crews	Both require precise teamwork and rapid communication under tight time pressure.

Innovation-ish

Core Feature of Problem	Analogous Context	Shared Deep Structure
Need for Real-Time Adaptation	Disaster Response Teams	Both must respond immediately to evolving conditions.
High Public Visibility and Trust Issues	Public Relations Crisis Management	Both deal with skeptical or anxious audiences looking for guidance.
Diverse Stakeholders, Complex Decision Flows	Navy SEAL Teams	Both coordinate specialized units under high stakes, requiring clear roles and mission alignment.

We often tell our students to list the key elements of their problem, and then to ask themselves to come up with analogous contexts for each element of the problem. Then we suggest asking if the two contexts share a similar deep structure and parallel? The key here is to slow down and find a mindful analogy rather than a hasty one.

Once you do that, then you can determine what move you want to apply in that context.

Exploring Example Moves

The following are examples of moves, the mindsets they are commonly associated with, and related resources. As you'll see, there are no single definitions for them, only variations you can adapt to craft a version that suits your needs. You can be highly effective and perfectly *Innovation-ish* without ever using these specific moves.

Each one lists:

- The mindset it's commonly associated with.

- Additional mindsets where it can be applied.

- Resources where you can explore variations.

Move: Empathy Map

Move

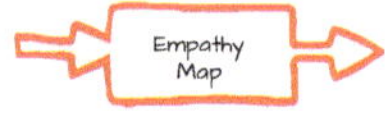

Description: A tool to visualize what users say, think, do, and feel, revealing deeper motivations and emotions.

Purpose: Enhance understanding of users' mindsets and contexts, build empathy, and guide user-centric decisions.

Methodology: Collect qualitative data, sort into quadrants (say, think, do, feel), and refine collaboratively.

Benefits: Creates a shared understanding, highlights emotional drivers, and aligns team decisions with user needs.

Practical Tips: Use direct quotes, compare "say" vs. "do," and combine with personas for richer user profiles.

Mindsets

Interactions: Share your filled-in or blank map with an interview subject for them to help fill in.

Iterations: Use the map as an observation tool during testing on early prototypes.

Inspirations: Use empathy maps to distill key elements in a story to inspire others.

Insights: Use to analyze qualitative data and infer thoughts and feelings as insights.

Innovation-ish

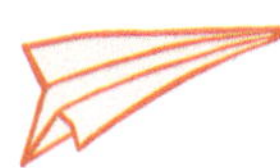

Innovation Dynamics

Convergence (Lift): Collecting inferred insights, prioritization, clustering.

Divergence (Gravity): Populating think/do, generating inferences.

Executive Function (Thrust): Cataloging insights, organizing qualitative data.

Move Definition

Defineable: Create one map for each person you interact with in a time period or set of collected data.

Shareable: The map itself can be shared and used in a team conversation or meeting to create group understanding.

Reusable: Can be used with any qualitative data (survey, interview, conversation, observation).

Actionable: No special tools are required; you can process any information you have with physical or digital tools.

Useful Resources

Miro Empathy Map Template
https://miro.com/templates/empathy-map
Accenture Empathy Map Guide
https://www.accenture.com/us-en/
blogs/software-engineering-blog/
what-is-an-empathy-map
Academic paper on Empathy Maps
https://ksiresearchorg.ipage.com/seke/
seke15paper/seke15paper_152.pdf

Using Moves

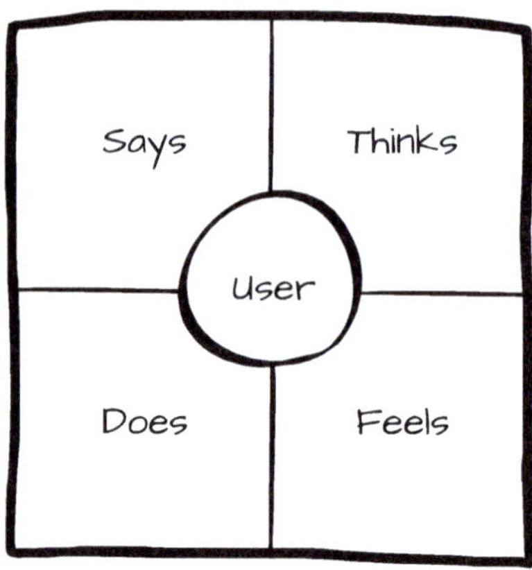

An Empathy Map records observations (Says, Does) and inferences (Thinks, Feels).

Move: How Might We

Move

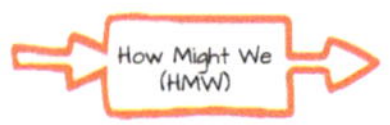

Description: A technique that turns challenges and insights into open-ended, generative questions starting with "How might we…?" We call those HMW questions.

Purpose: Encourage creative thinking, transform insights into opportunities, and foster a solution-oriented mindset.

Methodology: Analyze insights or problems, reframe them as HMW questions, and ensure they're broad enough to invite multiple ideas but narrow enough to provide focus.

Benefits: Stimulates ideation, ensures user-centricity and creates positive constraints that spark innovation.

Practical Tips: Generate multiple HMW questions from each insight, keep them short and user-focused, and select the most promising ones for further ideation.

Innovation-ish

Mindsets

Insights: A good way to ensure you are solving the right problem is to discuss and debate with the team the language used in framing the problem while making the problem statement concrete.

Iterations: Generating variations of the original idea can produce different outcomes and iterations to try.

Implications: Changing from How Might We. . . to After We Have. . . as a way to think about what happens if you are successful in solving the challenge defined in your How Might We. . .

Innovation Dynamics

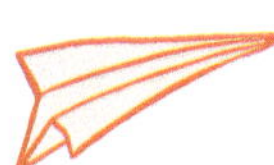

Convergence (Lift): Clarifying wording, prioritizing, finalizing few or one to use.

Divergence (Gravity): Generating a variety of options, finding alternatives and opposites, choosing different aspects of the problem.

Executive Function (Thrust): Documenting, clustering, capturing.

Move Definition

Definable: Generate a main How Might We. . . for your problem, then come up with a number of variations and generate solutions for each.

Shareable: HMW statements convey the problem being solved, who has it, and make it concrete so others can understand, examine, and question the problem.

Reusable: You can describe any problem as an HMW statement and use it to iterate on the same problem.

Actionable: Alone or in a group, you can generate or review HMW statements physically using a whiteboard or paper as easily as you can digitally in a tool or document.

(continued)

(continued)

Resources 	**Stanford d.school guide to How Might We. . . questions** https://dschool.stanford.edu/resources/ how-might-we-questions **Design Kit Methods How Might We. . .** https://www.designkit.org/methods/how-might- we.html **Service Design Doing How Might We. . . guide** https://www.thisisservicedesigndoing.com/ methods/how-might-we-questions-from- insights-and-user-stories

A good How Might We (HMW) statement is:

Generative	*You can imagine generating more than 100 ideas.*
Specific	*The user and why the problem is specific to them*
A problem	*The real and pressing need the user has*
Not a solution	*Starts with an active verbs, not a noun*

A How Might We includes the user, the problem, and why it specifically impacts them.

Innovation-ish

Move

Description: Explore how small actions or design decisions can lead to unexpected "butterfly effect" changes in systems design imagining future scenarios to understand long-term impacts.

Purpose: Anticipate downstream effects, encourage holistic thinking, and ensure more responsible innovation by considering consequences.

Methodology: Map potential cause-and-effect relationships, use scenarios or speculative artifacts to visualize future states.

Benefits: Awareness of interconnected systems, reduces harmful unintended consequences, and informs ethical design strategies.

Practical Tips: Start with a known change and trace its ripples; use worksheets or frameworks to identify possible outcomes; engage stakeholders in scenario planning to validate assumptions.

Mindsets

Implications: Anticipate the potential systemic impact of implementing an idea for unintended harm.

Interactions: Lead users through the exercise to gain information about their roles, needs, and potential stakeholders.

Insights: Test problem statements to ask the question, should we solve this problem before spending time on how to solve it.

Inspiration: Use an impact cascade to generate ideas for telling the urgency or benefits of solving a problem by both the story of intended and unintended consequences.

(continued)

191

Using Moves

Innovation Dynamics 	**Convergence (Lift):** Categorizing impacts. **Divergence (Gravity):** Enumeration impacts, PESTEL analysis, stakeholder map. **Executive Function (Thrust):** Collecting output, categories of analysis.
Move Definition 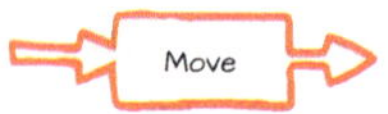	**Definable:** Consider a single outcome and capture it physically or digitally with a specified set of people (your team, your users, on each for a set of user types). **Shareable:** The results are a network map of relationships and outcomes, which is helpful in sharing with others. **Reusable:** You can reuse the work on other potential outcomes. Also, you can take any of the several outcomes listed in the exercise and use that to create another impact cascade from that perspective. **Actionable:** There is no preparation required; you can start today by yourself or schedule others to meet and work collaboratively.
Resources 	**Tessa's Article on Impact Cascades** https://medium.com/people-rocket/impact-cascades-speculative-design-efabfb34742 **The story of trophic cascades (what impact cascades are based on) in Yellowstone National Park** https://www.yellowstonepark.com/things-to-do/wildlife/wolf-reintroduction-changes-ecosystem

Innovation-ish

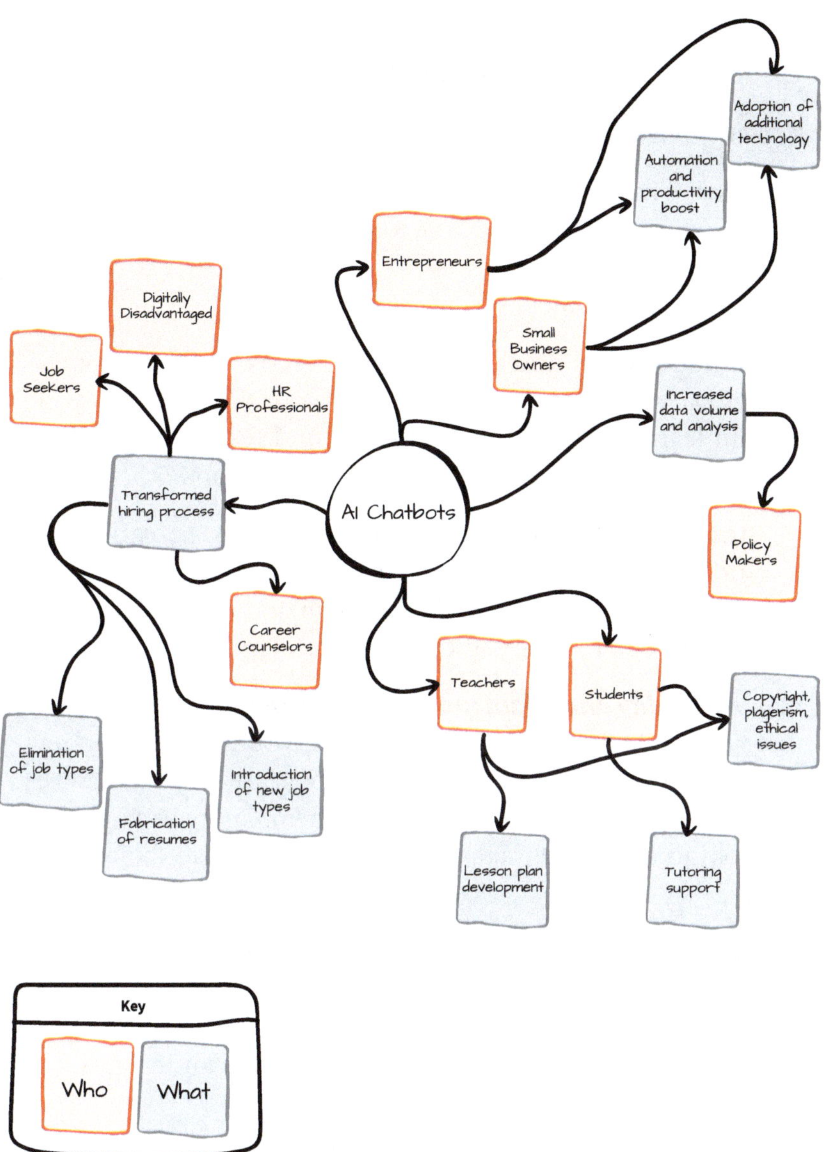

An Impact Cascade explores the future impacts on people and the system around them.

Key Takeaways

Moves come from:

Your own knowledge and experience. Innovation is about using what you already know and learning from those around you. Any skill, insight, or past experience can become a move to solve new problems.

Collaborators and external resources. Each collaborator on your team has their own historical moves that you can learn and adapt. You can also find resources on creativity, innovation, or other disciplines to adopt.

Analogous fields with parallel structures. Look beyond surface level structures to find more connections. These offer new ways to frame the problem and moves that were used in other fields you can customize and adopt.

You can modify and adapt moves to make them your own.
Just like modifying gear on a long hike, you can tweak innovation techniques, frameworks, and tools to fit your needs. You aren't bound by how others use them, and you have the freedom to adapt them creatively no matter where they come from.

A single move can work across multiple mindsets.
Moves like storytelling or user journey mapping aren't tied to just one way of thinking. They can support different phases of problem-solving helping you generate ideas, gain insights, or refine solutions.

Innovation-ish

Part IV

Metacognition

Chapter 13

Thinking About Moves

You have a big toolkit of moves from your experience, and you can adapt moves from others to fit your needs. You understand the mindsets and how they relate to the moves. And, we bet you still have questions?.

Where do you start?

What move should you make next?

Is it the "right" move?

What if it isn't?

Then what?

Knowing the mindsets and moves provides a foundation for your efforts, however activating innovation requires thoughtful decisions. There is no single "right" starting point. Every project has unique needs, resources, and people. They are also often already in progress when you start thinking about how to make it a little more Innovation-ish. This means the mindset you need to engage and the first move you choose will likely differ every time.

Choosing the right mindsets and moves takes time. The quality and speed of your progress depend on the choices you make. So, how can we make better choices instead of randomly trying things to see what works?

You might remember that in the moves chapters, we asked you to pick a real problem – one that is complex, challenging, and perhaps has been sitting unaddressed because you don't know how to start. Let's revisit that now. Pull up your answers and remind yourself of your thinking.

This moment of reflection is critical when taking on big, overwhelming problems. It allows you to break them into smaller, manageable steps. The problem feels smaller because it has been deconstructed into a series of small actions you can take.

The next step is challenging in a different way: you have to take action! As Nike's long-time ad campaign says, "Just Do It."

Each action shouldn't be difficult on its own. Most of the time, the individual steps are well within your capabilities. Just remember that initiating all those small actions, building on previous steps, adjusting as needed, and living with ambiguity requires hard work.

Mapping Your Moves

When your project can split into countless directions, a Move Map provides a structured way to determine which route will move you forward. A Move Map encourages deliberate practice, self-reflection, and the application of cognitive strategies to help you consistently advance toward solving a problem. It serves as a self-created roadmap, replacing the need for a rigid creative problem solving process with a set of adaptable steps to follow.

Every Move Map begins with a key question: *What's the most important thing I need to know right now to make progress?*

This is your core design question. The one you must answer to move forward based on where you are in your project and what your goals are. While you may have several pressing issues, your core question is the one whose answer will directly determine your next step.

For instance, you might need to understand the environment, customer values, or daily routines. Or perhaps you need to determine whether people will actually enroll in your offering. If your team has already identified a solution and begun implementation, your most important question might shift to "How much will customers pay for our offering?" or "What features of the offering do our leaders buy into the most?"

Making sure your core question is crystal clear is essential. A project can easily stray into side issues, so keep this question front and center whenever you choose your next step.

We run an intensive class for professional working graduate students. As accomplished professionals, their breadth of knowledge and experience was impressive. One year a team chose to focus on a challenge around safety in shared spaces on campus.

Their first core question: *What are students' actual experiences with safety on campus?*

They weren't just looking for statistics; they wanted to understand the lived reality. Through quick conversations, they uncovered a major concern that students frequently worried about leaving personal items unattended while stepping away from their desks. They didn't want to lose their spot in the library, and they also didn't want their belongings stolen.

After several rounds of discussion and exploration, the team came up with an idea: a special library desk featuring a locking compartment beneath the tabletop and a light indicator to show if the desk was occupied. The concept looked promising until they tested it with a diverse group of potential users, and a new problem emerged.

Students kept bumping their knees against the lockbox underneath the desk.

At this point, their core question shifted: *"What is the best placement for the lockbox?"*

Recognizing they were in an iterative phase, the team switched to an Iterations Mindset. They brainstormed all possible moves to help answer their new question. Then, they selected a single move, prototyping a physical version of the lockbox in different positions, to test.

When selecting a specific move, it's important to document:

- Your expectations about the outcome.
- What do you hope to learn from the action?

This step serves two key purposes:

- It provides a preliminary review, helping you determine if a move won't yield the insights you need, so you can pivot before investing too many resources.
- It helps identify existing biases, ensuring you don't just see evidence that supports your assumptions.

Creating a Move Map

Move Maps empower you to learn, adapt, and iterate your way to a solution and are central to the Innovation-ish approach. Unlike rigid design frameworks, Move Maps require reflection, prompting you to slow down, evaluate your reasoning, and consider your options, rather than following a one-size-fits-all process that may not align with your unique context.

Predefined processes often dictate a rigid sequence of actions, regardless of results. If those steps fail to answer your core question, you can end up stuck. In contrast, a Move Map puts you in control, as it allows you to tap into your own experiences, systematically build on them, and make your thinking visible so you and your team can reflect and adapt in real-time.

Move Maps are not meant to be completed in one sitting; they evolve as you make progress. They also involve two different modes of thinking:

Activity Questions focus on the tangible actions you've taken and the real-world outcomes you observe.

Awareness Questions prompt you to pause, process insights, and learn from your experiences.

Switching between these two modes can be challenging, so give yourself space and time. Think of your Move Map like an orienteering chart: it shows you where you've been and helps you plan your next step with your compass in hand.

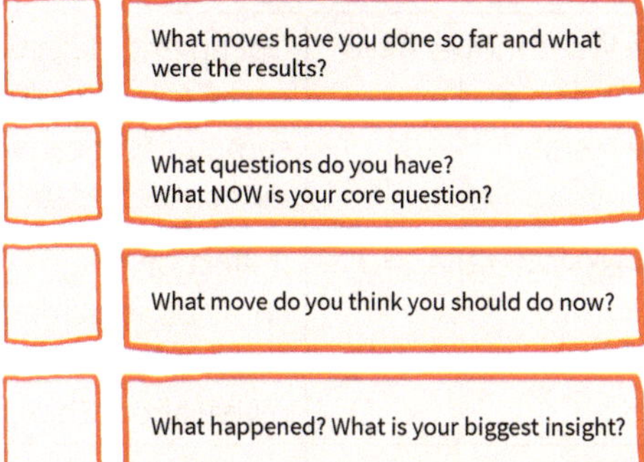

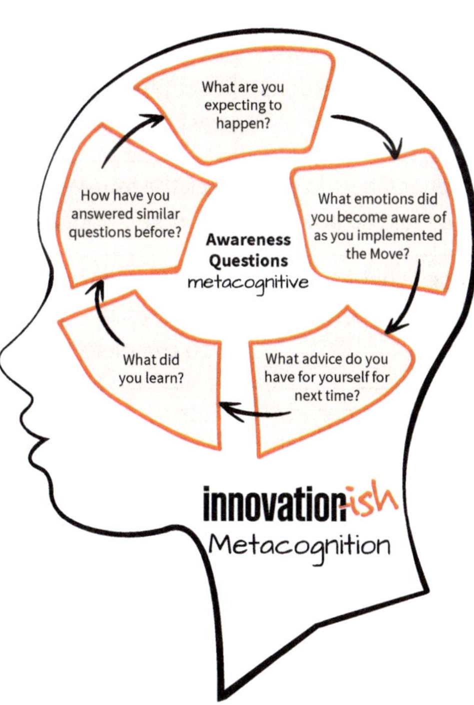

To answer the Activity Questions well, you need to answer the Awareness Questions also.

201

Thinking About Moves

Move Map questions

	Activity: What moves have you done so far and what were the results?	Document the actions or experiments you've taken and summarize the immediate outcomes or data you gathered.
	Awareness: What did you learn?	Reflect on the insights and knowledge gained from those actions, focusing on what they reveal about the problem.
	Activity: What questions do you have? What NOW is your core question?	Identify all the questions you have about your problem that you need to answer to move forward. Pick what is the single most important question about the problem that you need to answer.
	Awareness: How have you answered similar questions before?	Recall and summarize the methods or approaches you've used in the past to tackle similar problems.
	Activity: What move do you think you should do now?	Pick the move you plan to take next to address your core question.
	Awareness: What are you expecting to happen?	Describe your anticipated results or outcomes that you will achieve once you complete the move.
	Activity: What happened? What is your biggest insight?	Record the actual results of your move.
	Awareness: What emotions did you become aware of as you implemented the Move?	Reflect on your emotional responses during the process, noting any feelings that might have influenced your move.
	Awareness: What advice do you have for yourself for next time?	Provide you future self with actionable advice, based on your experiences and emotional responses, to guide future moves.

Imagine you're on a team researching how your packaging is recycled. As you fill out your Move Map (see Move Map example #1), you begin by documenting the moves you've already taken, such as interviews or observations, and noting their results. Then, you reflect on what you learned from those actions and define your current core question.

Next, you recall how you've tackled similar questions in the past and decide on your next move, specifying what you expect to happen. After implementing that move, you record what actually happened and capture your biggest insight, along with the emotions you experienced during the process. Finally, you note any advice for yourself for the next time.

That's the magic of a Move Map: it organizes your thinking in a clear, iterative structure, helping you refine your approach with each step.

Move Map example #1

	Activity What moves have you done so far and what were the results?	I had informal chats with retail staff about buyer behavior.
	Awareness What did you learn?	Retail staff indicated that they thought customers got very confused and overwhelmed by instructions on food packaging and therefore gave up on trying to recycle it.
	Activity What questions do you have? What NOW is your core question?	What might go through a customer's mind when buying, eating, and disposing of RetailCo? Core Question: What does the customer care about in disposing of RetailCo packaging?

(continued)

Thinking About Moves

(continued)

	Awareness How have you answered similar questions before?	POV, interviews, observations, focus group.
	Activity What move do you think you should do now?	One-hour observation of customers discarding RetailCo wrappers in a busy food court.
	Awareness What are you expecting to happen?	I expect to see confusion or frustration about packaging disposal from the customers in the food court.
	Activity What happened? What is your biggest insight?	Some customers carried the wrapper around, looking for a labeled recycling bin rather than tossing it. Several customers kept the wrapper, and when asked shared that they were taking it home, believing it was safer to recycle there. Insight: The biggest barrier looks like it might be bin signage, not unclear wrappers or a lack of customer knowledge.
	Awareness What emotions did you become aware of as you implemented the Move?	I felt more curious than expected. Observing real behavior was eye-opening. I was surprised that I had empathy for customers who felt unsure where to put their trash.
	Awareness What advice do you have for yourself for next time?	I'd note specific questions in advance and also try observations in multiple locations or at different times.

After completing your first Move Map, you step back to review your observations. You notice that customers often seem confused about where to dispose of their packaging, leading you to wonder if unclear bin signage is the main issue. This realization is eye-opening and takes a moment to accept since it isn't what you expected. You recognize that feeling and turn it into curiosity.

With this in mind, you update your Move Map with a new core question: *Is unclear signage the main barrier?* This insight guides your next move: a prototype test to determine whether revising the signage improves disposal behavior.

Move Map example #2

	Activity What moves have you done so far and what were the results?	I observed that many customers appeared confused about where to dispose of RetailCo packaging, suggesting that the messaging might be unclear.
	Awareness What did you learn?	I learned that customer confusion could stem from inconsistent or ambiguous recycling instructions rather than issues with the packaging itself.
	Activity What questions do you have? What NOW is your core question?	Is the biggest barrier to proper packaging disposal truly unclear bin signage, rather than ambiguous wrappers or a lack of customer knowledge?
	Awareness How have you answered similar questions before?	I've previously relied on direct observations and follow-up interviews to pinpoint the root causes of customer confusion. I've also used testing and prototypes before to check behavior since it's a better indicator sometimes than just what a customer says.

(continued)

Thinking About Moves

(continued)

	Activity What move do you think you should do now?	Prototype tests by installing revised signage at one location while keeping another as a control, then monitoring the rate of correct disposal.
	Awareness What are you expecting to happen?	I expect that if unclear signage is the main issue, the site with the revised signage will show a significant improvement in the proper disposal rate.
	Activity What happened? What is your biggest insight?	The prototype test resulted in a 35 percent increase in correct disposal at the site with revised signage. Quick interviews revealed that customers found the new visuals clearer and more engaging. Insight: Unclear bin signage is a primary barrier to proper packaging disposal.
	Awareness What emotions did you become aware of as you implemented the Move?	I felt both relief and excitement as the data validated my hypothesis and confirmed that a simple change in signage could have an impact.
	Awareness What advice do you have for yourself for next time?	Next time, I'll try testing several signage options at once and take a few more detailed notes on customer reactions to really pinpoint which elements make a difference.

Ultimately, a well-documented Move Map makes your thinking visible, allowing you and your team to adapt and advance your project without relying on a predefined process. It helps you develop the skill of identifying what your project needs next to move toward a solution with clarity and purpose.

Key Takeaways

Move Maps help guide your innovation journey.
Instead of following a rigid process, you don't start in the same place every time. Begin wherever you are in your project.

The core question drives your progress.
Move Maps allow you to define your core question, document your steps, and adapt based on real insights, ensuring you always take the most relevant next step.

Iteration, feedback, and emotional awareness guide you.
The move is the most visible part of your journey, but not the only part. Capturing results, reflecting on your learning and emotional responses are critical to informing the next tactical step.

Chapter 14

Being Metacognitive

The Move Map is a structured way to force yourself to think about your actions, emotions, motivation, knowledge, ideas, strategies, and context. It prompts you to reflect by asking key questions, such as:

- What did you learn?

- How have you answered similar questions before?

- What are you expecting to happen?

- What emotions did you become aware of as you implemented the move?

- What advice do you have for yourself next time?

This process is essential to all creative and innovative work. It is known as metacognition.

Meta: Being self-aware and self-referential.

Cognition: Thinking and feeling.

Metacognition is generally considered as thinking about thinking and feeling.

Being metacognitive involves mental habits that help you plan, monitor, and adjust how you learn or solve problems. When you build this self-awareness into your work, you can catch biases early, adapt strategies, and improve continuously.

In one of her highly sought-after classes at Harvard University, Dr. Tina Grotzer, Principal Research Scientist and Faculty Director of the Next Level Lab, shows students a video. As they watch, she prompts them to observe what's happening and how they think and feel about it. Students often get frustrated trying to do both of the tasks in a short amount of time. And that's the point.

As Tina and collaborator Dr. Megan Cuzzolino suggest, metacognition and cognition should not compete for attention. Purposeful pauses for metacognitive reflection, rather than attempting multitasking both (which is impossible since it is really just rapid serial processing), lead to better outcomes.

As you complete your Move Map, give yourself the time and space to be both cognitive and metacognitive when needed. Don't rush to fill it in all at once. Engaging in metacognition requires cognitive effort. Trying to think about your thinking constantly is exhausting and unproductive. Strategic pauses for reflection are key to using metacognition effectively.

It doesn't have to look exactly like our Move Map, or any Move Map for that matter. You just need to be aware of and understand your thought processes, recognize patterns, and be mindful of the factors influencing your decisions. The Move Map is simply a tool to create space for this essential work.

It takes practice and isn't always easy, but the payoff is significant. Research shows that in comparison to lower-performing designers, high-performing designers engage in more metacognitive activities such as planning, monitoring, and evaluating. Other studies link metacognition to stronger creative skills, including ideation, development, problem-solving, and better self-regulation and adaptability.

We can all develop this skill. People who use metacognition well tend to learn more deeply, solve problems more effectively, and perform better over time. It is not because they're more intelligent. It is because they're more aware of their thinking and feeling.

This isn't always easy. It can be incredibly challenging to reflect on your thinking processes when they lead you down a path influenced by bias or fail to produce the results you expected.

But do you know what's even worse? Spending time and money on innovative solutions that don't work because you didn't take the time to reflect.

Mapping your moves is about applying metacognitive skills to your Innovation-ish practice to help you determine your next steps.

Innovation-ish

It is the opposite of thoughtlessly following a process. Instead, it is a flexible approach that allows anyone to be Innovation-ish.

Reflecting to Choose Your Strategy

As we discussed, metacognition is thinking about thinking and feeling. However it's not only about thinking about it. In creative problem-solving, a good metacognitive approach functions less like a mirror and more like a control panel. It helps you monitor, evaluate, and adjust your cognitive approach as the problem unfolds.

To turn metacognition into a strategy, we need to use metacognitive thinking to guide action. This means focusing on:

Awareness: Noticing what you are thinking and feeling.

Evaluation: Considering the evidence and determining whether it is working for you.

Control: Using your evaluations to adjust your plan, switch tactics, or try something new.

In class, we call this Active Metacognition. Active Metacognition means using awareness of your thinking to actively shape your next move.

The key here is to notice patterns, make sense of what's happening, and use that insight to keep learning and moving forward in your Innovation-ish journey.

How passive reflection differs from active metacognition during creative work

Passive Reflection	Active Metacognition
That team brainstorm was really hard.	That brainstorm was hard. I was trying to evaluate ideas too early. Next time, I'll focus on just generating ideas, and hold critique until later.

(continued)

Being Metacognitive

(continued)

Passive Reflection	Active Metacognition
I don't want to go interview people.	I'm resisting interviews because I'm worried I'll ask bad questions. I'll write a rough guide and do a low-stakes pretend interview with my family to build confidence.
I can't decide which idea to prototype first.	I think I'm stuck choosing because I haven't defined what I want to learn. I'll rank the ideas by how quickly they'll give me useful feedback, then start there.
This idea is great. I don't think it has any unintended consequences.	I'm excited about this idea which might mean I'm overlooking blind spots. I'll run a quick pre-mortem to imagine what could go wrong before I move ahead.
My story landed so well.	The story landed because I focused on one clear message and used a personal example. That combination seemed to make it more relatable. I'll use that approach again when I want to connect emotionally.

All of this matters because Innovation-ish work is cognitively demanding, especially when problems are uncertain or poorly defined. Metacognition helps you allocate your mental resources (and your time) more effectively, ensuring you're solving the right problems in the right ways.

How do we practically make active metacognition happen? How do we actually build habits around noticing, evaluating, and adjusting our thinking? One of the most powerful ways is by regularly asking ourselves strategic metacognitive questions.

Asking Metacognitive Questions

A good metacognitive question goes a long way. Over the years, we have noticed that students and clients often get stuck pushing from a cognitive question to a metacognitive one. For example:

We will often see them ask this **cognitive question:** *What is the answer to this problem?*

As opposed to this **metacognitive version:** *What do I think the answer is right now? Why do I think that?*

Cognitive questions typically focus on the task at hand, dealing with specific content, contexts, and direct problem-solving. In your Move Map, these are your Activity Questions.

Metacognitive questions focus on how you are thinking, prompting you to reflect on your reasoning and approach. They target your processes, not just the final result. They might ask, why am I thinking this? Or what influences my assumptions? In your Move Map, these are your Awareness Questions.

Types of Awareness Questions

Cognitive Questions	Metacognitive Questions
Activity: What moves have you done so far and what were the results?	Awareness: What did you learn?
Activity: What questions do you have? What NOW is your core question?	Awareness: How have you answered similar questions before?
Activity: What move do you think you should do now?	Awareness: What are you expecting to happen?
Activity: What happened? What is your biggest insight?	Awareness: What emotions did you become aware of as you implemented the move?
	Awareness: What advice do you have for yourself for next time?

Our move map is just an example of what we have found works over the years. However, you are welcome to create your own

Being Metacognitive

Move Map. We caution that while Activity Questions can be quite simple to formulate, Awareness Questions take practice to refine.

Good metacognitive questions should help you do one of six things:

Notice what's going on in your mind. Research shows that good questions prompt learners to observe their thinking in real-time. For instance, what are they noticing, confused about, having clarity on, or making assumptions about? Example questions that do this are:

- What's going through my mind right now?
- What am I assuming without checking?
- Is anything feeling unclear or surprising to me?

Debate what you're good at and what you struggle with. Thinking about your declarative and conditional knowledge helps you recognize patterns in your cognition, strengths, and blind spots. Example questions that do this are:

- Which parts of this come easily to me? Why?
- Where do I usually get stuck? What tends to trip me up?
- What strategies have (or haven't) worked for me before?

Evaluate your confidence. Here, you want to practice noticing how sure you are, checking for overconfidence or uncertainty, and questioning the soundness of your reasoning.

- How confident am I in this answer? Why?
- What might I be missing?
- Could I be wrong? and what would make me notice that?

Interrogate how your emotions are impacting your thinking. Emotions and motivation can distort focus or shape effort. Good questions can help you step back and see how your mental state is influencing your thinking.

Innovation-ish

- How am I feeling about this task? And is this pushing me to avoid the task or overcomplicate it?

- Is my mood influencing what I'm focusing on or ignoring?

- What emotion do I notice most right now? and what's it telling me about how I'm thinking?

Use what you've learned in new situations. Good questions encourage you to see connections between your existing knowledge and new contexts and help you to apply your knowledge flexibly.

- Where have I seen a problem like this before?

- How can I adapt what I already know to this new situation?

- What does this remind me of? and how is it different or the same?

Determine an actionable and appropriate next step. This is the essence of metacognitive regulation, a type of metacognition focused on planning and evaluating strategies to move forward. Good questions should help lead you to try a new tactic, revise an idea, or refine an approach.

- What's one thing I could try differently next time?

- What would a better strategy look like?

- What's the very next step I need to take?

Metacognitive questions take practice. The six types outlined above can help you stay focused, reflect more clearly, and get to Active Metacognition.

Choose the ones that fit your work. Use them regularly. Over time, they'll help you understand how you think and feel and how that is influencing your Innovation-ish work.

We have provided a library of questions we've collected over the years, organized by mindset. While this is not an exhaustive list, it can serve as a starting point for developing your own metacognitive practice.

Example metacognitive questions for each Innovation-ish mindset

Mindset	Five Example Metacognitive Questions
Interactions	• In what ways am I adapting my approach based on the feedback and insights gained from these interactions? • What am I learning from interactions and how is it influencing my work? • Am I making assumptions about the people I am interacting with, and how can I verify these assumptions? • How am I ensuring that human needs and perspectives are central to my process? • What biases might I be bringing into these interactions, and how can I mitigate them?
Insights	• What criteria am I using to interpret this data? • How might my personal experiences or beliefs influence my interpretation? • Am I considering multiple viewpoints in my analysis? • How am I validating the insights I've gained to ensure they are robust and actionable? • What alternative explanations or conclusions might exist?
Ideas	• Have I allowed enough space for truly 'out there' thinking before introducing constraints? • How am I generating ideas, and are there other methods I could try? • Am I separating idea generation from idea evaluation? • Where might I find inspiration outside my usual domains or comfort zone? • When do I notice myself shutting down ideas prematurely, and what strategies can I use to stay open-minded longer?

Innovation-ish

Mindset	Five Example Metacognitive Questions
Iterations	• How am I preparing myself to let go of ideas that are not working? • In what ways am I learning from each iteration to improve subsequent versions? • How am I balancing the need for iteration with the need to progress toward a final solution? • What strategies am I using to ensure that each iteration is informed by the previous one? • How am I ensuring that the iteration process is constructive and not just critical?
Inspirations	• How am I communicating the essence and value of my idea to different stakeholders? • What strategies am I using to gain support and buy-in for my idea? • In what ways am I adapting my story or pitch based on the audience and their feedback? • How am I measuring the effectiveness of my efforts to inspire and enroll others in my idea? • How am I responding to feedback or different viewpoints?
Implications	• How am I critically assessing the feasibility and ethical considerations of implementing my idea? • What methods am I using to evaluate the potential positive and negative impacts of my idea on various stakeholders? • How am I ensuring that the idea is sustainable and responsible? • In what ways am I considering the long-term consequences and cascading effects of my idea? • How am I planning and preparing for the challenges of scaling and fully implementing my idea?

Being Metacognitive

Key Takeaways

Metacognition means thinking about thinking and feeling

It is the practice of reflecting on your own cognitive and emotional processes. Metacognition looks at why we think or feel what we do. It informs what next steps we take and how we learn and perform them.

Active metacognition

Metacognition shouldn't just be reflective, it should be strategic. Typically it includes:

- **Awareness:** Noticing what you are thinking and feeling.

- **Evaluation:** Considering the evidence and determining whether it is working for you.

- **Control:** Using your evaluations to adjust your plan, switch tactics, or try something new.

Cognitive and metacognitive questions work together

Cognitive questions focus on the task (e.g., "What did I learn?"), while metacognitive questions encourage reflection (e.g., "Why did I think that?"). Both are crucial for meaningful progress.

Activating Innovation

Fueling Innovation

By now, we've seen that *anyone* can create breakthrough solutions to real problems in the real-world with an Innovation-ish approach. We've shown how the Innovation-ish Compass can help you navigate beyond your Innovation Hesitation.

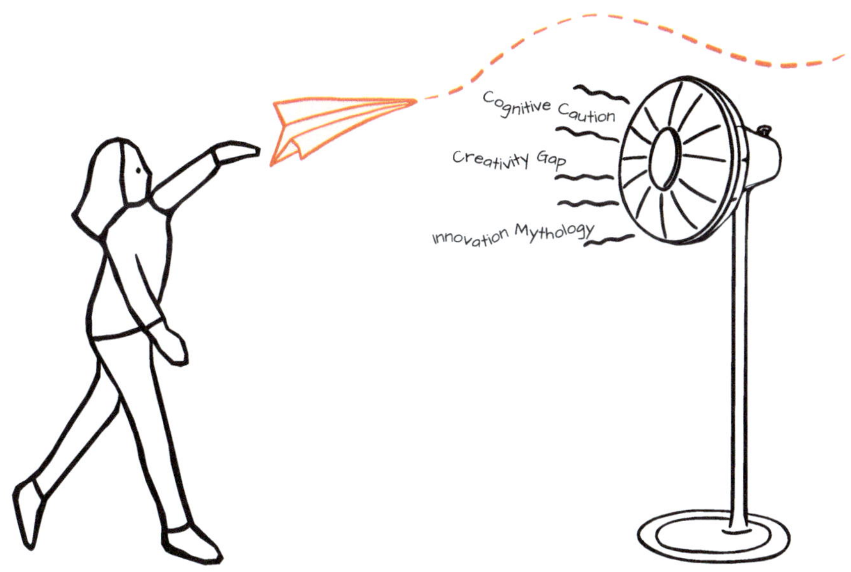

To activate innovation, you need two surprising sources of fuel – ones that most people try to avoid. To reach your innovation potential, you need to be able to:

- Harness Ambiguity, and
- Embrace Failure.

Creating breakthrough solutions is about inventing the future. That journey is inevitably filled with ambiguity and failure. It's natural to see these as sources of Innovation Hesitation, even triggers of Cognitive Caution. And they can be.

Both ambiguity and failure can spark apprehension or even fear. But you can turn that fear into fuel to accelerate your innovation.

In this chapter, we'll break down what it really means to lean into ambiguity and learn from failure.

Harness Ambiguity

Being Innovation-ish means you are creating something new, whether it's new to your situation or new to your organization. When you set out to be innovative, what you *don't* know can sometimes feel much larger than what you *do* know.

How big is the problem?
Is there a problem, and what is it?
Is the cost of solving it larger than living with it today?
Is there a second problem behind the first one?
Do you have the experience to tackle this?

These are just a few of the questions that may emerge, and it can be overwhelming to hold so many unknowns at once. The level of ambiguity alone can make you hesitate, shut down, or push the problem aside until you gain some clarity.

In fact, that is a completely reasonable human response.

Let's talk about how the amygdala, a part of the brain involved in emotional processing, responds to ambiguity.

When I (Tessa) was talking to my daughter about her brain and what is happening when she has a meltdown, we named her amygdala "The Warrior" after a character in her book by the same name. One of the amygdala's main jobs is to scan the environment for anything that might be a threat, like a grizzly bear approaching your campsite, and keep you safe, just like a warrior would.

When we face ambiguous situations, our amygdala – and other parts of our limbic system – tend to overreact and interpret the situation as "There might be a grizzly bear!" They sound the alarm before we've even had a chance to think things through. It's a great survival mechanism if we're about to bump into real danger (like a grizzly bear!). Yet in everyday life, it often treats normal uncertainty as a crisis.

This happens so quickly, that the prefrontal cortex and analytic networks don't have time to assess the situation and decide that, no, that's not a grizzly bear. It's just a massive rock with a bush that kind of looks like one.

Because ambiguity doesn't feel good, our instinct is often to avoid it. We might:

- Stay fixed in place, hesitating to step into the unknown.
- Cling to the safety of certainty, refusing to engage with the ambiguity at all.
- Rush through it, grabbing onto the first concrete answer just to escape the discomfort.

In our classes, we've seen students react very differently to uncertainty. Some lean into it, excited by the unknown. Others resist, blaming the problem, the process, or even their teammates. The same patterns emerge in the corporate world. Some people say, "We don't know the answer, but we're going to figure it out!" Others insist, "I already know what's best. We don't need more input."

Why do we react so differently to it?

It all comes down to our tolerance for ambiguity. Researchers have even developed scales to measure how comfortable people are with uncertainty.

People with a high tolerance for ambiguity are comfortable with change, open to multiple perspectives, and willing to delay decisions until they gather enough information – even when aware of potential threats, like that grizzly bear.

On the other end, people with a low tolerance for ambiguity prefer clear structure, predictable outcomes, and well-defined steps. They tend to seek certainty and may resist situations where the next step isn't obvious. While this mindset is beneficial in high-stakes, safety-critical environments, it can sometimes limit innovation. Constantly on alert for potential threats, like that grizzly bear, they make concrete plans and quick decisions to keep things safe.

Neither a high nor low tolerance for ambiguity is inherently better. We need both. We probably don't want an airline pilot who embraces unresolved ambiguity too much, yet we do want an innovator who can sit comfortably with uncertainty.

In the world of Innovation-ish, ambiguity is never a grizzly bear waiting to eat you and your family. Instead, ambiguity is where the magic happens. Avoiding it might mean missing an opportunity.

Fortunately, your tolerance for uncertainty isn't a fixed thing. The key is recognizing that you can shift tolerance with dedication, practice, and self-awareness. Even in the short term, you can adjust your approach by consciously engaging with ambiguity rather than resisting it.

To build this self-awareness, take time to explore your relationship with ambiguity and humility. Remember there are no right answers, and it's important you build this self-awareness.

Think about the most recent time you faced an ambiguous situation. Maybe you were given unclear instructions by a supervisor, navigating cultural or language differences with friends, troubleshooting a new smart device, or grocery shopping in a foreign city. Recall the actions you took and how you felt. Did you embrace the uncertainty, or did you feel frustrated and rush to find an immediate answer? Would you describe yourself as someone with a high tolerance for ambiguity, a low tolerance, or somewhere in between?

Once you recognize your natural response, you gain insight into how you approach uncertainty. Do you lean into ambiguity with curiosity and humility, or do you resist it? Do you find yourself rushing through it, just trying to get past the discomfort? The moment you become aware of your reaction, you gain the ability to change it.

No matter your current level of comfort with ambiguity, remember that everyone experiences moments of hesitation when their amygdala signals potential danger. The key is recognizing when that instinct kicks in and choosing how to respond. Instead of resisting:

- **Acknowledge it.** Pause and notice your reaction.
- **Reframe it.** Remind yourself, "This isn't a threat. This is an opportunity."
- **Engage with it.** Instead of avoiding ambiguity, ask, "What can I learn from this uncertainty?"

The more you practice, the more natural it becomes. Ambiguity isn't a roadblock, it's an invitation to explore, discover, and create something new. The next time uncertainty arises, try saying: "Hello, ambiguity! It's good to see you here."

The more you practice, the more natural it becomes, and slowly you are able to embrace it.

For the first two weeks of my (Rich) five months hiking the wonderful Pacific Crest Trail, I would wake up and pore over maps and data books to help me navigate the day's journey – fighting against any kind of ambiguity. One day, I began hiking with a small group of fellow adventurers, and my planning routine turned into a group conversation, while I sometimes disagreed with the consensus plans that the group arrived at, the goal was still the same – to eliminate the ambiguity for the day ahead. And then I finally realized that our very thoughtful and specific intentions rarely matched what actually happened each day.

Having all the data, conversations, and experiences from our discussions was insufficient for preparing an accurate hiking agenda. Our planning did not include, for instance, the amount of shade we would encounter, the temperature, the availability of water along the trail, or the beauty of the landscape. Each of these factors were ambiguous to us at the start of the day and they ultimately influenced the decisions we made throughout the day, such as when to pause for breaks, have lunch, or stop for the day to camp.

Fueling Innovation

After I noticed this, I decided to lean into just being comfortable with the ambiguity. I stopped participating in the morning planning conversations, choosing instead to listen and agree with the proposals, knowing that their decisions at sunrise would likely change by late morning or midafternoon.

Preparing a broad daily goal and then making lots of small decisions allowed more flexibility in how my hike went each day. The decisions I made along the way were informed by what I was experiencing, and they allowed me to adjust as needed and ultimately made the hike better. I was comfortable with the ambiguity behind the daily plan.

Being open to the ambiguity of the day ahead and learning to harness it as powerful meant that I was able to be present in and the surroundings and let me change my focus from "using data to plan the day and achieve my mileage goals" to "having an enjoyable, mindful experience that embraced beauty, comfort, and adventure."

Solving problems using an Innovation-ish approach means embracing this process of learning as you go. You experience ambiguity because you don't know what you will learn from others using an Interactions Mindset. You don't know in advance the outcomes of engaging in an Insights Mindset. You will learn the quality of ideas with moves, such as prototyping, in an iteration mindset. These and other aspects of being Innovation-ish mean that you will likely be in a state of creative ambiguity for significant portions of your work. This act of harnessing the ambiguity – is one of three core values of activating Innovation.

Embrace Failure

Most people have a reaction to the word failure. Perhaps even reading the title of this section made you pause to consider if you wanted to continue. Congratulations on being brave. If you had the opposite reaction and read on with anticipation, then we hope to provide some new insights for you as well.

We are conditioned to fear failure, minimize it, and push it away. It's easy to see failure as a lack of our own abilities. Often, it's the feelings associated with failure we avoid more than the impacts of the failure itself. According to prospect theory, humans tend to feel losses or failures more heavily than successes. The sociometer theory suggests that our self-esteem is a guide to our perception of acceptance and our place in the social hierarchy.

There are many pithy quotes about failure, especially in relation to innovation and entrepreneurship, to help address some of these social dynamics:

- "Fail early to succeed faster."

- "Fail fast, fail early to fail forward."

- "Celebrate failure."

- "Mistakes are gifts."

- "Keep failing until you don't."

These sharp insights are commonly heard in innovation, startups, and elementary schools. They can inspire and encourage people during challenging times. They can also be interpreted in unhelpful ways at times.

Let's start with the fact that with innovation, nobody is *trying to fail*. They are trying to stretch beyond what they know, attempting things that have not been done before, and struggling with ideas that may seem impossible. With humility, it becomes clear that you won't always succeed, especially when you are stretching your capabilities and trying something new.

There are two kinds of failure. The first is the *failure of execution*, where failure comes from not preparing. This could be dedicating too little time or treating it with less care than it deserves. For example, making frequent mistakes in scheduling your calendar or skipping a vital checklist procedure. These are familiar tasks that, without the proper attention, can fail. This is the type of failure to correct, not to embrace.

227

Fueling Innovation

The second is the *failure in stretching*, where failure comes from trying something new. You are stretching your abilities in spite of risk and uncertainty. And you are reaching beyond your experience to make discoveries. It's nearly impossible to do something perfectly the first time, but the benefits of trying outweigh the risks. This is the kind of risk-taking to embrace in an Innovation-ish approach.

We're not saying you must always take risks. You may decide to make risk-averse choices, lowering the chance of failure significantly. There are many situations where that might be the right choice.

For example:

- If you are stretching in several areas already, it might be the right choice to avoid a new one.
- If you have significant uncertainty in your work or in your life, perhaps you want to avoid new stretches.

What most of those quotes are driving at is that we will at times fail; it is how we react to it that matters most. When it inevitably happens, do you: (1) Push it away and deny it? (2) Give up and stop trying? or (3) Learn from the attempt and try again?

It's a natural reaction to avoid failure, but we do so at a cost. Any risk you take has the potential for failure, which means that our instincts are to avoid taking risks. To harness ambiguity, we need to manage our response to uncertainty.

If you are going to embrace good, stretching failure, you need to find a way past your natural tendency to avoid it.

To prevent our feelings of failure, we often turn to denying them instead of addressing them. This prevents us from making decisions that let us avoid the failures in the first place. Most people don't deny them outright calling a failure a success, they have a much more elegant way to do it.

Bernard Roth, a colleague, one of the founders of the d.school at Stanford University and Author of *The Achievement Habit*, tells a story from his own life. He was a board member and attended regular board meetings, but found he was often late. Each time, he

Innovation-ish

had a good excuse. The meeting was several miles away, often with significant traffic and construction delays. He was also busy with many responsibilities and calls to make. For a long time, these reasons helped him believe it wasn't his fault, until one day he realized it was.

It dawned on him that while blaming the traffic for his tardiness, in reality, he was the problem. He knew the traffic could be bad and could have planned for it. It didn't matter how good his excuses were. His late appearances impacted the other board members and the meeting. Ultimately, he was failing at the commitment he had made.

That moment led him to a provocative idea that he describes as: "All reasons are bullshit."

"A 'reason,'" he shares, "is just a story we tell to justify failures and make ourselves feel better. The better the story, the easier it is to accept, yet the impact remains the same." Once you have this insight, you may start to notice it in your daily communication. We see and hear reasons from ourselves and others. These reasons mask the failure and make them more socially acceptable.

One day, in a meeting, Bernie shared his insight with us. As an exercise, he had us pair up and share a time we failed to deliver something on time. Then, our partner had to respond, with sarcasm, "Oh, THAT's a good reason." We had to come up with another excuse. Again, "Oh, THAT's a good reason." Laughter filled the room, and so did self-reflection.

The lesson was clear: we are responsible for our actions, no matter how good our reasons sound. We avoid that responsibility because we want to avoid failure.

This technique is intended for self-reflection, not used against others you want to act more responsibly. If you're tempted to use this on others "to teach them responsibility," we hope you'll catch yourself and think, "Oh, THAT's a good reason!"

Once you stop avoiding failure, what remains is how you respond to it. In each case, if you learn, adjust, and keep going you are not failing. Only when you stop trying to move forward does the result become fixed.

Reframing failure guides your response and keeps you moving forward. The bright side of "embracing failure" is that there are often results that you can learn from.

In my (Rich) home, there is always another skill or another level to reach. Whether it's gymnastics, catching a football, or learning math, we use a powerful word when our kids are confronted with something they don't know how to do:

"Yet!"

I've come to love that word. We often hear them get frustrated when trying something new. Then they stop, look up, and say, usually quite dramatically, "I can't do this. . . yet." At first, we had to coach them to embrace that "Yet!" – but the pause gets shorter and shorter all the time.

"Yet" reframes failure as a step in learning. Just one word implies that it's not the end. The reaction asks for more practice and different approaches to learn more.

Science provides another way to reframe failure. Science is the practice of finding answers to unknown questions. It takes a great deal of experimentation to learn in science. When a scientist runs an experiment, no matter what the results are, they call it data. Many of the most interesting learnings from science are the unexpected results. Repeating experiments with known and predictable outcomes might feel safer, but it doesn't afford much learning.

Yet, as Next Level Lab researcher, Dr. Megan Cuzzolino observed in her work on awe and scientific inquiry, we are often trained to do safe experiments from our own experiences in school. Many science classrooms prioritize safe, known experiments as the pedagogical tools for teaching science. Thereby inadvertently training students to avoid genuine exploration because of the risk of failure and diminishing their capacity for awe – an emotion that helps fuel creativity and innovation.

The thing is, data is neutral, it's not success or failure. It is simply the results or observations to interpret. When testing an idea or trying a new move, you can consider the results data. You can collect data on the results of your prototype or a Move you try. As with real life professional scientists, it is often the unexpected and surprising results that give you the best insights.

Another way to reframe failure is to consider it part of the process of risk-taking. It's usually pretty easy to avoid failure if you only do small things that you know you can do with a high degree of certainty. This will limit what you can do, and it's not likely to produce many new ideas.

This attitude was expressed nicely by Gordon Moore, a founder of Intel: "If everything you try works, you aren't trying hard enough."

Being Innovation-ish involves taking risks. For several years at the d.school, we co-taught a class where we explored different kinds of risk. We ran a Failure Fair in the class. We set up stations where students could experience different kinds of risk. This meant playing a type of poker for financial risk, singing karaoke in front of their classmates as social risk, attempting different levels of logic puzzles for intellectual risk, etc. Students also had the option of not participating so they could assess their risk tolerance.

Much of the acceptance, even celebration of failure, is actually better described as celebrating the risk-taking itself. Making bold leaps and developing bold new ideas involves the risk that each new idea will actually turn out to be a way "not to do" it. Trying, collecting data, learning, and trying again means engaging with a series of risks.

Exploring your tolerance for different types of risks and failures, practicing celebrating risk-taking, and seeing failure as a necessary learning experience are helpful steps towards embracing failure.

Key Takeaways

Innovation is fueled by ambiguity and failure

Ambiguity and failure are surprising sources of fuel for innovation that many people experience as a source of hesitation. Most problem-solving prioritize certainty and structure. Not knowing the answers and exploring the unknown are powerful tools.

Ambiguity isn't dangerous; it's necessary

The discomfort of uncertainty is natural, but becoming comfortable with ambiguity creates space for innovation. You can increase your tolerance for ambiguity with practice.

Failure isn't personal; it's practical

Avoiding failure overlooks the potential learning opportunity in failure. Reframing failure by separating execution from stretching failure, viewing results as data make it easier to embrace. Owning failure without excuses allows you to learn and move forward effectively.

Chapter 16

Take Small Steps

Starting a new practice can be daunting. The first time you pick up a musical instrument or walk into a gym, you may feel nervous. What you know about the practice is often vastly outweighed by what you do not yet understand. Remember, everyone starts in the same place. Even Serena Williams once struggled with her first tennis serve, and Gordon Ramsay wasn't always a master in the kitchen; they were both once beginners.

Each of us has the capacity to improve. Your progress depends on the time you devote to learning and the level of mastery you aim for. Of course, preparing for a concert performance requires more time than for a sing-along around a campfire. Similarly, improving your health and wellness doesn't mean you need to become an ultramarathon runner. Perhaps you have set a more modest fitness goal focused on health and well-being.

You can start small by going for a walk, taking a yoga class, or going for a swim. Working out once a week for 60 minutes is a reasonable first step. You may not even notice the changes in your well-being, but you will have already overcome any internal resistance. You will also likely have changed how you see yourself. You are now a person who works out regularly.

The next step is to expand on that idea and increase your practice, perhaps to two days a week and then three. As you progress, the time you dedicate increases, and you may achieve your goal. If you set a new goal of a five-mile race or even the ultra-marathon, you will develop your practice the same way.

On my (Rich) Pacific Crest Trail Hike, my goal was to hike 20 miles per day. The night I began my training, I took a 30-minute walk around my neighborhood. Each week, I added 30 minutes to my daily walks, eventually reaching six hours a day before starting the hike at the Mexican border. It all began with a small step.

Just like physical fitness and our soccer example in Chapter 2, an innovation practice requires consistent effort. The more you practice, the more natural it becomes. Whether you're a beginner or advanced, doing something is better than nothing. The more you do, the more impact it has. And, the longer you engage in your practice, the easier it gets and the greater the improvements. Remember, progress is built one small step at a time.

Increasing Innovation-ish-ness

You can go from a novice achieving roof-shots to an expert refining their ability to innovate by developing your Innovation-ish practice. Think of the elite designers in famous companies and brands as Olympic athletes – they are adept. The difference between them and you isn't some special X factor. It's the amount of time and practice they put into achieving their own personal level of excellence.

Just like workouts, start small. Consider using a project you have already started. You can incorporate one move from one mindset to add a little bit of innovation. If that is all you do, your project is a little bit better. If that is all you have the capacity for, we applaud your success in getting past the starting point. Well done! In the next project, it will be that much easier to repeat a similar move.

We call this increasing your Innovation-ish-ness.

Your next step might be adding a second move in the same mindset or trying a different move in another mindset. Either way, you will be adding a bit more innovation to the project and you're better off for it.

Innovation-ish

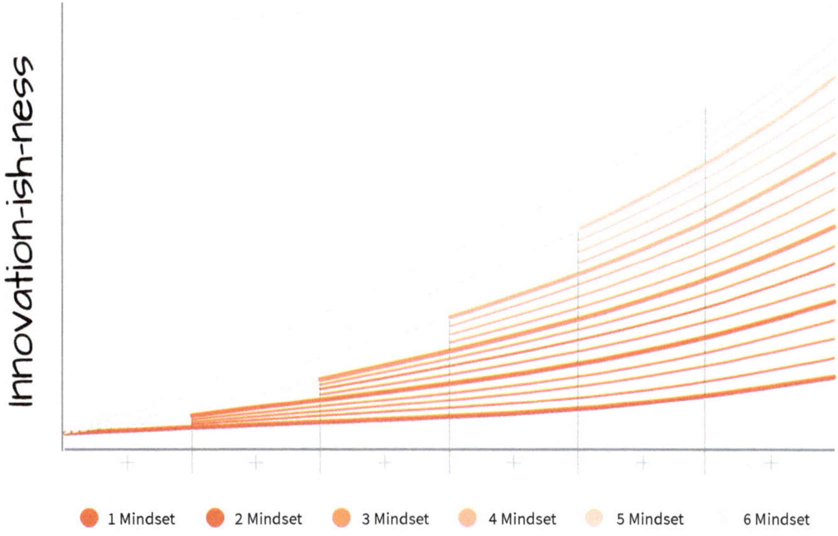

It's okay to start with only one move. Each one you add increases your Innovation-ish-ness.

Remember, doing one move increases your Innovation-ish-ness. Doing a second increases it a bit more. You get stronger and faster in your Innovation-ish practice. And as you move to daily practice, doing more and more moves, you will be heading toward your goal of being more innovative.

As with exercise, each person has their own goal. It's the same with innovation. You have to decide how much Innovation-ish-ness you need for a given project. Your deadlines, colleagues, leadership, and goals will influence your Innovation-ish-ness goal.

Innovation-ish-ness is about adding moves and mindsets to your work – when you can, as much as you can.

Now that you know you can start small, all that is left is to decide to do it. You need to give yourself permission to start.

Giving Yourself Permission

My (Rich) daughter recently took her first "real" art class in first grade. The class covered shapes, outlines, and shading – the basic

Take Small Steps

building blocks of sketching and drawing. After the lesson, my daughter excitedly told me she had broken the kindergarten rule! She was taught to color outside the lines, which gave the giraffe's fur a more realistic look. I had never thought of the "kindergarten rule" as a rule. Mastering fine motor skills in kindergarten subtly became a barrier to her creativity. From a very young age, children receive signals about what is allowed and what is not. Sometimes those lessons are not what we intend to teach.

That moment wasn't just about art; it was a life lesson written in giraffe fur about realizing she had the power to challenge assumptions. Whether in childhood or in the workplace, we often wait for permission to innovate. However, true creativity begins when we recognize that we can give ourselves permission.

Our university students display similar evidence of the layers of rules they learned. The junior high rules, the social rules, the high school rules, the sports team rules, the first job rules, etc. At the beginning of the class, they are full of questions. They ask about the class details and what we, the teachers, are looking for so they can figure out how to succeed. They want clear rubrics and example past projects. In essence, they want to know the boundaries – where the lines are so they can color inside them – and how to prepare. It's similar to starting a new job, a new project, or thinking about adding a new skill to your toolkit. How will I navigate this situation?

During the class, we always get similar questions. Each time, it's slightly different, although it always comes back to *"Can we"* questions. "Can we change the tool we are using?" "Can we talk to different people than we did last week?"

The reason they ask is simple. They are trying to shift the risk of making a choice onto us rather than taking a different path themselves. We approved the plan, said yes, and gave them permission to proceed. As a result, they feel protected from mistakes, failure, and accountability. In truth, they have not made a choice, we have.

Innovation-ish

Once they start giving themselves permission, they shift to "How do we?" questions.

- When they choose to interview a new kind of stakeholder in our challenge, they ask, "How do we adjust the interview guide?"
- When they choose to build a prototype, they ask, "How do we ensure we don't bias the outcome?"
- When they analyze the data and see a pattern, they ask, "How do we make sure we aren't just confirming what we already know?"

This pattern isn't unique to students; it appears in businesses and organizations of every kind. Most of us have the rules we learned growing up and a few more with each job we have as adults. No one is going to invite you to practice Innovation-ish.

So eventually, you are going to have to give yourself permission. Once you stop waiting for permission, the next challenge is taking action. Just as individuals need permission to innovate, organizations must foster a culture that grants this permission at scale.

Practicing Permission Activity

Think back to the problem you identified in the Start Somewhere section. Now, try these steps:

1. Write down the most important Move you listed.
2. Note whose permission do you think you need to make that Move.
3. Now, ask yourself: What would actually happen if you didn't ask and just made the Move anyway?
   If you still feel like you need permission, write an email asking for it. (And if it helps, you can tell them that we said it was okay.)

Once you stop waiting for permission, the next challenge is taking action. Just as individuals need permission to innovate, organizations must foster a culture that grants this permission at scale.

Take Small Steps

You Have What You Need to Start

We wrote this book to make that approachable innovation more accessible to others. While we love teaching and working with clients, we know many more can benefit and create breakthrough solutions.

Over the course of this book, you've built a foundation for practicing Innovation-ish:

In **Part I**, you realized that navigating past Innovation Hesitation comes from the Innovation-ish Compass and learned how Innovation-ish Dynamics shape your thinking.

In **Part II**, you explored the power of mindsets, intentionally changing your view of the world to approach your problem in new ways.

In **Part III**, you discovered the power of moves. The discrete actions that drive your work. You already have many, can adopt them from collaborators, and adapt them from other sources making them your own.

In **Part IV**, you experienced the power that metacognition has on charting the course of your work and improving the quality of the results.

In **Part V**, you learned how creating an Innovation-ish culture and developing an Innovation-ish Practice starts with small steps and giving yourself permission to break the rules.

Now that you've explored the mindsets, moves, and approaches of Innovation-ish, you're ready to bring them into your work. You can start by sharing these ideas with others, applying them to small projects, or simply giving yourself permission to experiment. As we always say, "Innovation is not hard, it's hard work!"

If any lingering Innovation Hesitation remains, reflect on how your thinking has shifted and what new possibilities you now see?

We've seen Innovation-ish adopted by students from kindergarten to post-graduate levels and in organizations across government, corporate, and not-for-profit sectors. They solved problems ranging from jump-shot to moon-shot level impact.

- We've seen students take on nebulous problems and create innovations for circular economies, reducing waste's impact on marine wildlife.

- We helped hundreds of small business owners devastated by the COVID-19 pandemic explore new ways to pivot their businesses to adapt to the conditions.

- We led teams at Fortune 200 companies to redefine their approach to supply chain management, and dozens of not-for-profit organizations designed a new future with their strategic plan.

We started with the idea that Innovation-ish was "Innovation for Everyone." Now, after a decade of learning from students and clients, through moments of discovery, experimentation, and iteration. and witnessing its impact on so many people, we believe:

Anyone can create breakthrough solutions to real problems in the real world.

Key Takeaways

Innovation starts small, like anything we learn

Developing your skills in yoga, coding, or innovation through practice is a lifelong process. Wherever you are in your innovation journey, you can continue to build you ability one step at a time. Starting your Innovation-ish Practice changes your identity to be an innovator.

Give yourself permission

Many rules are unspoken and self-imposed. Instead of waiting for approval, take ownership of your creative process. Give yourself permission to experiment.

Small steps build Innovation-ish-ness

Adding one Innovation-ish action (Move) on a project, gets one moves worth of benefit and increases your Innovation-ish-ness. Each deliberate, modest move you take builds momentum over time, transforming everyday actions into breakthrough solutions.

You already have everything you need to start

Innovation-ish is accessible. You already have the creative ability, the historical moves, the ability to change mindsets. Take the time to let metacognitive reflection guide you. Increase your Innovation-ish-ness with one small step today.

Innovation-ish

Get Move-ing

Tear, fold, and have a safe flight

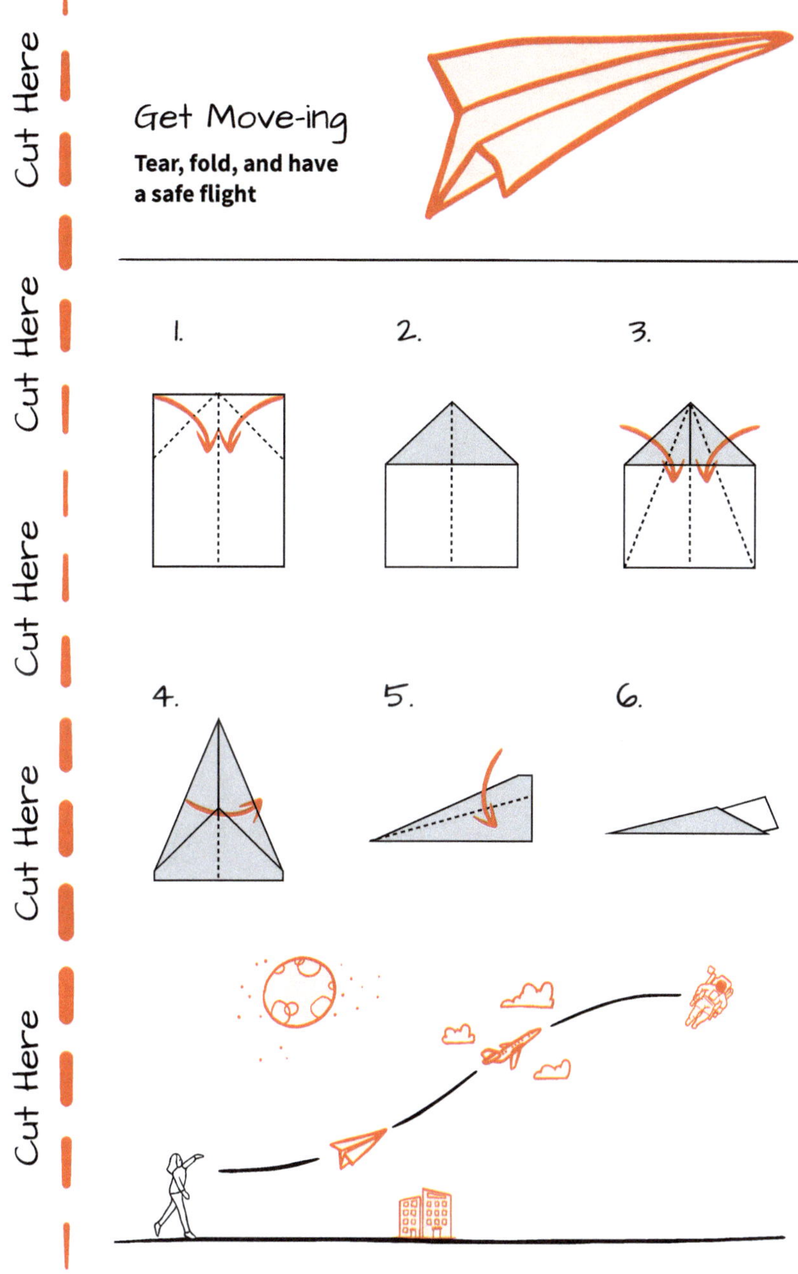

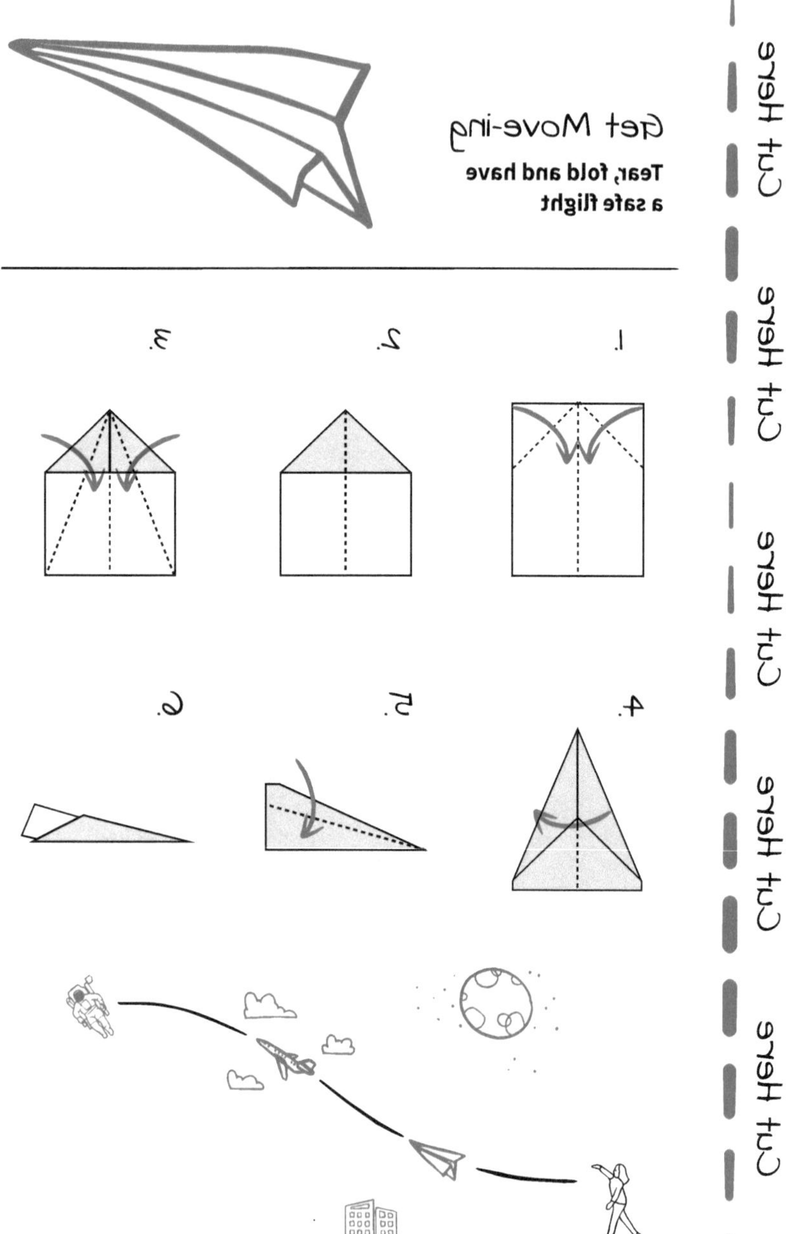

get Move-ing
Tear, fold and have a safe flight
1.
2.
3.
4.
5.
6.
Cut Here
Cut Here
Cut Here
Cut Here
Cut Here
Cut Here

The concept of Innovation-ish has emerged from a decade of our experiences as educators and consulting practitioners. We have seen that the neat boundaries of class projects do not reflect the complexities of real-world problem-solving. Our job as educators is to prepare students to apply these methods when they enter the world. And as consultants, to focus on driving toward the right outcome, not the right next step.

Separately, we both rejected the notion of innovation as a rigid process or a prescribed formula, recognizing it as mastery coming from practice and adaptation rather than simply following instructions. That shared perspective sparked an ongoing conversation, one that ultimately led to the creation of this book.

A little over ten years ago, while using design thinking as a strategy consultant, I (Tessa) started to notice that successful design projects never followed a rigid process, even though it was sold to clients that way and partitioners were trained at length in "the process." Progress was always about taking the next step that moved the team closer to a solution, regardless of methodology. The concepts and tools were valuable, but the approach had to remain dynamic.

Around the same time, I (Rich) was exploring similar ideas as a design educator at Stanford University and with clients as a consultant. In 2014 I introduced the sprint map during an Executive Education Program at the Stanford University Graduate School of Business. This framework empowered corporate managers and directors to select the next necessary "process phase" in any order. By documenting each sprint with a date, time, and ownership, teams could maintain forward momentum while adapting to the realities of problem-solving. Together, these experiences reinforced the idea that effective innovation is about navigating complexity with flexibility and intent.

We changed how we introduced the concept of innovation to both students and clients. When we removed the structured process, we made a key discovery: the process itself provided more than just steps and tools. It created a sense of safety. Removing that safety opened the door to uncertainty making the students more hesitant.

Building on Tessa's expertise in Cognitive and Learning Science and my (Rich's) improvizational approach to teaching improv acting, we both adopted a constructivist teaching methodology; one that we later discovered NASA calls "explore before explain." Students do guided activities, exercises, and project work before we explain and discuss the concepts to them. This is the opposite of the teach, then test approach so commonly found in education and training. If it was good enough for NASA, it was good enough for us!

"Explore before explain" produced longer-lasting learning but introduced its own uncertainty and ambiguity. Students, used to traditional teaching methods, struggled with this ambiguity. This approach required them to take responsibility for guiding their own work. We didn't teach or tell them the next step; we taught them how to choose it themselves. When we combined this with the ambiguity already present from the lack of a rigid innovation process, we could feel the hesitation build.

But, we know from great science and research on learning that learning needs to be slightly effortful for it to happen, and by putting learners in the (heavily scaffolded) drivers seat we were making them engage in effortful learning in an agentive way. After all, our job as educators was to ensure that learners could apply what we taught them outside of the classroom, not make the class easy.

Unsurprisingly, clients we worked with have had even less tolerance for ambiguity thanks to our students due to the business environment, pace, and deadlines – something we later understood as Cognitive Caution. We directly addressed the sources of this caution in our classes, discussing how they might embrace ambiguity and

Epilogue

asking our students to reflect on their thoughts and feelings about the work. Over time we saw them move from hesitation to action to navigate beyond the barrier of their caution.

Cognitive Caution was not the only type of hesitation we noticed. We saw many small ways that students would disengage when facing activities that pushed the edge of their creativity, like sketching, sharing ideas while brainstorming, even creating stories to present their work. It also came up in hundreds of small moments of coaching and questions during and after class. It was clear that the students didn't have confidence in their creative abilities. We could no longer ignore The Creativity Gap.

It's not a novel idea that some people don't consider themselves creative. The prevalence of it in our innovation classes and workshops was holding students and clients back from what we believed was their potential as designers. So we started to reframe creativity and helped them develop their creative skills, allowing them to experience increasing moments of creative flow.

We also encountered a great deal of "Innovation Mythology" in discussions with clients and students. They would enthusiastically talk about the secret sauce of Silicon Valley and its ecosystem Despite the fact that the experienced innovators we know in Silicon Valley patiently explain that there is no secret, just hard work and resilience in the face of failure, somehow the mythology was enduring. While running workshops, we would repeatedly hear the same myths and questions – questions about Eureka! moments, iconic lone geniuses, and the supposed necessity of learning from these special innovation spaces and places. Soon, it became clear that Innovation Mythology was a third source of hesitation.

We realized that all along we had been fighting this force of Innovation Hesitation, fueled by The Creativity Gap, Cognitive Caution, and Innovation Mythology. Directly addressing these forces became core to how we introduced the concepts of innovation. When we did, we saw relief washing over our students. Naming it and dispelling it created a pathway for them to engage with the material and develop their practice.

But now we also had to develop a better approach than the process. Over the years, we have experienced dozens of design and innovation processes in academia and consulting. Students would ask questions about articles they had read or frameworks they had explored. Professionals we taught had experience in their own company or with other training programs. We had taught and implemented many different processes ourselves.

We noticed that each one of these methods was trying to communicate the same set of ideas. Over time, we looked more critically at 10 of the most common design and innovation processes and started to see a pattern. We tested a few more and saw six mindsets held without changing them. Thinking we were on track, we sourced as many frameworks as we could – including design, innovation, and creativity methods. In total we have thematically coded over 80 frameworks in the development of the Innovation-ish Mindsets.

Reviewing those six ideas on a whiteboard in a maker space after hosting a prototyping session, we realized they were actually mindsets, and ones that could be adopted and navigated fluidly. This aligned with our process-less ideas, and we brainstormed the six mindsets outlined in this book, with one exception – Implementation instead of Implications. We realized that the implications included implementation in addition to being responsible for the impact of the work, and two weeks later Implications replaced Implementation as the sixth mindset.

Navigating through the mindsets could occur in any order by defining a short sprint of work. The goal was to solve the problem. In each sprint you evaluate your progress and choose your next step. This means that instead of a process, the path to solving is different for every problem. This is similar to many strategy games like chess – the goal is to capture the other players' pieces. The moves you make are different each game, even with the same goal. And so, the sprints became moves, and the sprint map the Move Map.

Documenting their work with the Move Map allowed us to see our students thinking more clearly. We noticed that when we coached students, they often experienced emotional responses and questioned their own choices. Teams improved when they reflected on how the moves worked and what they could do better. Their feelings also informed their work, giving them new insights that produced better results. We saw the impact that metacognitive reflection had on the quality of their work.

Over the course of a decade, these ideas evolved into the approach of the Awareness and Activity Questions within the Move Map. Blending mindsets, moves, and metacognition, this framework became the Innovation-ish Compass.

Overcoming Innovation Hesitation with The Innovation Compass made it easier for people to enter this world of design and innovation. Our students' project work was better than before; we could see the results. While they came into our class thinking they were not creative, they left with the established beginning of an innovation practice. We continued to work with clients to activate innovation in their organizations – guiding large teams on projects with tight deadlines and higher expectations for results. We soon saw our clients, new to innovation, teaching others and sharing their own practice and stories.

For students and clients, the Innovation Compass helped them navigate past Innovation Hesitation. Some had been hesitant to see themselves as innovators. Others had tried other methods and found them intimidating or producing somewhat disappointing results. Both groups reported that this approach was less intimidating and more approachable. And many were surprised by the breakthrough solutions they had created.

The solution was to make innovation more accessible. More approachable. More, well Innovation-*ish*.

Term	Definition
Innovation-ish	A practical, iterative approach to innovation rooted in collaboration, real-world problem-solving, and human-centered design. Emphasizes adaptability and learning over perfection and inclusive of other methodologies.
Design Thinking	An iterative, human-centered process that combines empathy, prototyping, and testing to solve complex problems.
Creative Problem Solving	A flexible yet structured process for developing solutions that are both original and effective.
Human Centered Design	A problem-solving philosophy that begins with human needs and ends with tailored, empathetic solutions.
Systems Thinking	A problem-solving approach that considers the larger network of interconnected elements and the ripple effects of small changes.
Innovation Hesitation	The tendency to delay or resist innovation due to fear, doubt, or process rigidity. Includes related patterns like The Creativity Gap, Innovation Mythology, and Cognitive Caution.

The Creativity Gap	A form of Innovation Hesitation stemming from the belief that innovation is reserved for a select few that is filled with self-doubt and imposter syndrome.
Innovation Mythology	A form of Innovation Hesitation that comes from belief in a false and idealized picture of innovation from commonly told stories making it feel unreachable.
Cognitive Caution	A form of Innovation Hesitation driven by natural, biological fear of risk, ambiguity, or uncertainty. It reflects our instinct to stick to safety and resist unfamiliar ideas.
Innovation Dynamics	A framework using flight dynamics (Lift, Weight, Thrust, Drag) to describe the cognitive forces at play in innovation and creative problem-solving.
Divergent Thinking (Lift)	Expansive thinking that opens up new possibilities and directions for exploration.
Convergent Thinking (Weight)	Focused, analytical thinking used to evaluate and narrow ideas into workable solutions.
Executive Function (Thrust)	The planning and organizational drive that pushes ideas forward into action.
Innovation Hesitation (Drag)	The mental or environmental resistance that slows innovation, often due to fear, ambiguity, or doubt.
Innovation Spectrum	A range of innovation types from small, incremental improvements (jump-shots, roof-shots, cloud-shots) to larger, system-changing breakthroughs (orbit-shots and moon-shots).
Jump-shot	Simple improvements in construction techniques and materials.

Glossary

Roof-shot	Developing more efficient solar panels or water systems.
Cloud-shot	Smart infrastructure networks or advanced energy management systems.
Orbit-shot	Revolutionary breakthroughs in urban sustainability and AI integration.
Moon-shot	An audacious, paradigm-shifting idea.
Innovation Compass	The antidote to Innovation Hesitation that helps navigate. A practical framework to decide on the next step forward in creating breakthrough solutions to problems. The compass includes Mindsets, Moves, and Metacognition.
Mindset	Any set of beliefs, attitudes, or mental shortcuts that shape how we perceive, interpret, and respond to the world.
Interaction Mindset	A mindset that prioritizes dialogue, collaboration, and mutual influence in the innovation process.
Insights Mindset	A mindset that emphasizes gathering qualitative data, recognizing patterns, and reframing problems based on new insights.
Ideas Mindset	A mindset focused on generating a wide range of creative, diverse ideas without seeking immediate solutions.
Iterations Mindset	A mindset that values learning through repeated cycles of prototyping, feedback, and refinement.
Inspirations Mindset	A mindset that uses compelling stories to build emotional connection and inspire others to take action.

| **Implications Mindset** | A mindset that evaluates how decisions and innovations impact people, environments, industries, and institutions in the broader system. |

Move — A concrete action that fosters innovation while remaining contextually grounded and feasible.

Historical Move — An innovation move drawn from personal experience, education, or past skills that have been effective before.

Translatable Move — A familiar move from one context that is intentionally adapted to a new mindset or situation.

Customized Move — A move uniquely designed for a specific audience, need, or challenge that is tailored rather than reused directly.

Analogous Move — A move borrowed from another domain or discipline that shares deep structural similarities and applied creatively to the current challenge

Metacognition — Thinking about thinking and feeling. The process of being self-aware and self-referential about your cognitive and emotional states.

Passive Reflection — Looking back on experiences without analyzing or applying lessons to improve future approaches.

Active Metacognition — The deliberate use of metacognitive reflection to guide decisions and next steps, actively shaping thinking rather than just observing it.

Glossary

Innovation-ish-ness	The degree to which innovation mindsets and moves are applied in practice. It increases with each intentional action toward innovation.
Innovation-ish Practice	The consistent application of innovation tools, habits, and behaviors within real-world work settings. Building mastery in innovation as a lifelong pursuit.

Endnotes

Chapter 1 – Innovation Hesitation
THE "CREATIVITY GAP"

Beghetto, R. A., & Kaufman, J. C. (2013). Fundamentals of creativity. *Educational Psychology Review, 25*(3), 285–294.

Kelley, T., & Kelley, D. (2013). *Creative Confidence: Unleashing the creative potential within us all.* Crown Business.

Sternberg, R. J., & Lubart, T. I. (1996). Investing in creativity. *American Psychologist, 51*(7), 677–688.

Tierney, P., & Farmer, S. M. (2002). Creative self-efficacy: Its potential antecedents and relationship to creative performance. *Academy of Management Journal, 45*(6), 1137–1148.

INNOVATION MYTHOLOGY

Csikszentmihalyi, M. (1996). *Creativity: Flow and the Psychology of Discovery and Invention.* Harper Perennial.

Hargadon, A. B. (2003). *How Breakthroughs Happen: The Surprising Truth About How Companies Innovate.* Harvard Business Review Press.

Paulus, P. B., & Nijstad, B. A. (2003). *Group Creativity: Innovation Through Collaboration.* Oxford University Press.

Sawyer, R. K. (2012). *Explaining Creativity: The Science of Human Innovation.* Oxford University Press.

COGNITIVE CAUTION

Baumeister, R. F., & Leary, M. R. (1995). The need to belong: Desire for interpersonal attachments as a fundamental human motivation. *Psychological Bulletin*, 117(3), 497–529.

Camerer, C., & Weber, M. (1992). Recent developments in modeling preferences: Uncertainty and ambiguity. *Journal of Risk and Uncertainty*, 5(4), 325–370.

Kahneman, D., & Tversky, A. (1979). Prospect theory: An analysis of decision under risk. *Econometrica*, 47(2), 263–292.

Tversky, A., & Kahneman, D. (1974). Judgment under uncertainty: Heuristics and biases. *Science*, 185(4157), 1124–1131.

CREATIVITY, WELL-BEING, AND EMPATHY

Davis, M. (1996). *Empathy: A social psychological approach*. Westview Press.

Singer, T., & Lamm, C. (2009). The social neuroscience of empathy. *Annals of the New York Academy of Sciences*, 1156(1), 81–96.

Forgeard, M. J. C., & Eichner, K. V. (2014). Creativity as a target and tool for positive interventions. In A. C. Parks & S. M. Schueller (Eds.), *The Wiley Blackwell Handbook of Positive Psychological Interventions* (pp. 137–154). Wiley Blackwell.

Singer, T., Lamm, C., Miller, M., & Kingstone, A. (2009). The social neuroscience of empathy. *Annals of the New York Academy of Sciences*, 1156(1), 81–96.

SURVEY STATISTICS

We conducted two surveys to inform our understanding of some of the prevalence of innovation mythology in adults in the United States. The first of these surveys included 300 participants sourced via the platform Prolific. Participants were a general population representative sample of United States adults. Then to verify our findings among specifically working adults, we conducted another survey via the same platform, but this time it included 200 participants who were working adults in the United States. The findings between these two studies were consistent.

STORIES AND QUOTES

Anthony, S. D. (2016, July 15). Kodak's downfall wasn't about technology. Harvard Business Review.

Mui, C. (2012, January 18). How Kodak failed. Forbes.

World Economic Forum. (2025, January 7). Future of Jobs Report 2025: 78 million new job opportunities by 2030 but urgent upskilling needed to prepare workforces.

Chapter 2 – Innovation-ish Dynamics

PROCESS VS. PEOPLE IN CREATIVITY

Brown, T. (2008). Design thinking. *Harvard Business Review*, 86(6), 84–92.

Carter, C. (2016, October 6). Let's stop talking about THE design process. Stanford d.school. Medium. Retrieved from https://medium.com/stanford-d-school/lets-stop-talking-about-the-design-process-7446e52c13e8 (accessed 21 May 2025)

Norman, D., & Verganti, R. (2014). Incremental and radical innovation: Design research vs. technology and meaning change. *Design Issues*, 30(1), 78–96.

CREATIVITY ACROSS THE LIFESPAN

Abra J. (1989). Changes in creativity with age: Data, explanations, and further predictions. *The International Journal of Aging and Human Development*, 28(2)

Barbot, B., & Rogh, W. (2020). Developmental trends in creative abilities and potentials. In M. Runco & S. Pritzker (Eds.), *Encyclopedia of Creativity* 3 (pp. 323–326). Academic Press.

Runco, M. A. (2014). *Creativity: Theories and Themes: Research, Development, and Practice*. Academic Press.

Russ, S. W., Hoffmann, J. D., & Kaufman, J. C. (Eds.). (2021). *The Cambridge Handbook of Lifespan Development of Creativity*. Cambridge University Press.

Torrance, E. P. (1974). *Torrance Tests of Creative Thinking*. Personnel Press.

The Left-Brain/Right-Brain Neuro-Myth

Gazzaniga, M. S. (2014). *Tales from Both Sides of the Brain: A Life in Neuroscience*. Ecco/HarperCollins.

Nielsen, J. A., Zielinski, B. A., Ferguson, M. A., Lainhart, J. E., & Anderson, J. S. (2013). An evaluation of the left-brain vs. right-brain hypothesis with resting state functional connectivity MRI. *PLoS ONE*, 8(8), e71275.

Novotney, A. (2013, November 1). No such thing as 'right-brained' or 'left-brained,' new research finds. *Monitor on Psychology*, 44(10). https://www.apa.org/monitor/2013/11/right-brained (accessed 23 April 2025).

Convergent Thinking, Divergent Thinking, and Executive Function

Cropley, A. (2006). In praise of convergent thinking. *Creativity Research Journal*, 18(3), 391–404.

Diamond, A. (2013). Executive functions. *Annual Review of Psychology*, 64, 135–168.

Finke, R. A., Ward, T. B., & Smith, S. M. (1992). *Creative Cognition: Theory, Research, and Applications*. The MIT Press.

Guilford, J. P. (1967). *The Nature of Human Intelligence*. McGraw-Hill.

Miyake, A., Friedman, N. P., Emerson, M. J., Witzki, A. H., & Howerter, A. (2000). The unity and diversity of executive functions and their contributions to complex "frontal lobe" tasks. *Cognitive Psychology*, 41(1), 49–100.

Runco, M. A. (2014). *Creativity: Theories and Themes: Research, Development, and Practice* 2 Academic Press.

Smeekens, B. A., & Kane, M. J. (2016). Working memory capacity, mind wandering, and creative cognition: An individual-differences investigation into the benefits of controlled versus spontaneous thought. *Psychology of Aesthetics, Creativity, and the Arts*, 10(4), 389–415.

DEFAULT MODE AND EXECUTIVE NETWORKS

Bartoli, E., Devara, E., Dang, H. Q., Rabinovich, R., Mathura, R. K., Anand, A., Pascuzzi, B. R., Adkinson, J., Kenett, Y. N., Bijanki, K. R., Sheth, S. A., & Shofty, B. (2024). Default mode network electrophysiological dynamics and causal role in creative thinking. *Brain: A Journal of Neurology*, 147(10), 3409–3425.

Beaty, R. E., Benedek, M., Wilkins, R. W., Jauk, E., Fink, A., Silvia, P. J., Hodges, D. A., Koschutnig, K., & Neubauer, A. C. (2014). Creativity and the default network: A functional connectivity analysis of the creative brain at rest. *Neuropsychologia*, 64, 92–98.

Beaty, R. E., Benedek, M., Kaufman, S. B., & Silvia, P. J. (2015). Default and executive network coupling supports creative idea production. *Scientific Reports*, 5, 10964.

Beaty, R. E., Benedek, M., Kaufman, S. B., & Silvia, P. J. (2018). Default and executive network coupling supports creative idea production. *Scientific Reports*, 8(1), 1–12.

Lazar, L. (2018). The cognitive neuroscience of design creativity. *Journal of Experimental Neuroscience*, 12: 1179069518809664.

Raichle, M. E. (2015). The brain's default mode network. *Annual Review of Neuroscience*, 38, 433–447.

Raichle, M. E. (2019). Creativity and the brain's default mode network. In S. Nalbantian and P. M. Matthews (Eds.), *Secrets of Creativity*. Oxford University Press.

Creativity as a Learned (and Social) Skill

Amabile, T. M. (1996). *Creativity in Context*. Westview Press.

Paulus, P. B., & Nijstad, B. A. (2003). *Group Creativity: Innovation Through Collaboration*. Oxford University Press.

Sawyer, R. K. (2012). *Group Genius: The Creative Power of Collaboration*. Basic Books.

Tierney, P., & Farmer, S. M. (2002). Creative self-efficacy: Its potential antecedents and relationship to creative performance. *Academy of Management Journal*, 45(6), 1137–1148.

Vygotsky, L. S. (1978). *Mind in Society: The Development of Higher Psychological Processes*. Harvard University Press.

On Human-Centered Design and the History of Creative Problem Solving

Brown, T. (2008). Design thinking. *Harvard Business Review*, 86(6), 84–92.

Dorst, K. (2011). The core of "design thinking" and its application. *Design Studies*, 32(6), 521–532.

IDEO. (2015). *The Field Guide to Human-Centered Design*. IDEO.org.

Isaksen, S. G., & Treffinger, D. J. (2004). Celebrating 50 years of reflective practice: Versions of creative problem solving. *The Journal of Creative Behavior*, 38(2), 75–101.

Kolko, J. (2015). Design thinking comes of age. *Harvard Business Review*, 93(9), 66–71.

Lebeck, P., Lee, T., & O'Mahony, L. (2023). Creative problem-solving. In *Creativity and Innovation* (pp. 117–147). Palgrave Macmillan.

Navaneethakrishnan, D. (2021). Human problem-solving: Standing on the shoulders of the giants. *Computational Economics*, 57(3), 857–868.

Norman, D., & Verganti, R. (2014). Incremental and radical innovation: Design research vs. technology and meaning change. *Design Issues*, 30(1), 78–96.

Design Council. (2025). The Double Diamond: A universally accepted depiction of the design process. https://www.designcouncil.org.uk/our-resources/the-double-diamond (accessed 21 May 2025)

Stories and Quotes

CNN Staff. (2012, October 4). Some of Steve Jobs' best quotes. CNN. https://www.cnn.com/2012/10/04/tech/innovation/steve-jobs-quotes/index.html (accessed 23 April 2025).

IDEO. (n.d.). Apple mouse. IDEO. Retrieved from https://www.ideo.com/works/creating-the-first-usable-mouse (accessed 21 May 2025).

Isaacson, W. (2011). *Steve Jobs*. Simon & Schuster.

Kelley, T., & Littman, J. (2001). *The Art of Innovation: Lessons in Creativity From IDEO, America's Leading Design Firm*. Currency/Doubleday.

National Inventors Hall of Fame. (2020, June 5). The invention of the Post-it® Note. Retrieved from https://www.invent.org/blog/trends-stem/who-invented-post-it-notes (accessed 21 May 2025).

Reiter-Palmon, R., & Illies, J. J. (2004). Leadership and creativity: Understanding leadership from a creative problem-solving perspective. *The Leadership Quarterly*, 15(1), 55–77.

Skonord, C. (2021, February 19). Post-it Notes: An employee idea that was originally a mistake. Ideawake. Retrieved from https://ideawake.com/post-it-notes-employee-idea-that-was-originally-mistake (accessed 23 April 2025).

Portis, A. (2011). *Not A Box* (Board book ed.). HarperCollins.

Chapter 3 – The Innovation-ish Compass

Moon-shots vs. Roof-shots

Christensen, C. M., Raynor, M. E., & McDonald, R. (2015). What is disruptive innovation? *Harvard Business Review*, 93(12), 44–53

Hargadon, A. B. (2003). *How Breakthroughs Happen: The Surprising Truth About How Companies Innovate*. Harvard Business Press.

Norman, D., & Verganti, R. (2014). Incremental and radical innovation: Design research vs. technology and meaning change. *Design Issues*, 30(1), 78–96.

Tushman, M. L., & O'Reilly, C. A. (1996). Ambidextrous organizations. *California Management Review*, 38(4), 8–30.

THE INNOVATION COMPASS INTRODUCTION

Dweck, C. S. (2006). *Mindset: The New Psychology of Success.* Random House.

Flavell, J. H. (1979). Metacognition and cognitive monitoring: A new area of cognitive–developmental inquiry. *American Psychologist,* 34(10), 906–911.

Gollwitzer, P. M. (1999). Implementation intentions. *American Psychologist,* 54(7), 493–503.

OVERCOMING INNOVATION HESITATION BY BEING INNOVATION-ISH

Bandura, A. (1997). *Self-Efficacy: The Exercise of Control.* W.H. Freeman.

Sternberg, Robert J., 'The psychology of creativity', in S. Nalbantian and P. M. Matthews (Eds.), *Secrets of Creativity: What Neuroscience, the Arts, and Our Minds Reveal.* Oxford Academic.

Tierney, P., & Farmer, S. M. (2002). Creative self-efficacy: Its potential antecedents and relationship to creative performance. *Academy of Management Journal,* 45(6), 1137–1148.

STORIES

NEOM. (n.d.). Changing the future of design & construction. https://www.neom.com/en-us/our-business/sectors/design-and-construction (accessed 23 April 2025).

Chapter 4 – Your Mindset Matters

MINDSETS AS COGNITIVE FRAMEWORKS (PLUS SCHEMAS, MENTAL MODELS, PATTERN RECOGNITION)

Bartlett, F. C. (1932). *Remembering: A Study in Experimental and Social Psychology.* Cambridge University Press.

Beckmann, J., & Gollwitzer, P. M. (1987). Deliberative vs. implemental states of mind. *Social Cognition*, 5(3), 259–279.

Crum, A. J., & Langer, E. J. (2007). Mind-set matters: Exercise and the placebo effect. *Psychological Science*, 18(2), 165–171.

Crum, A. J., Corbin, W. R., Brownell, K. D., & Salovey, P. (2011). Mind over milkshakes: Mindsets, not just nutrients, determine ghrelin response. *Health Psychology*, 30(4), 424–429.

Crum, A. J., Salovey, P., & Achor, S. (2013). Rethinking stress: The role of mindsets in determining the stress response. *Journal of Personality and Social Psychology*, 104(4), 716–733.

Damon, W. (2008). *The Path to Purpose: How Young People Find Their Calling in Life*. Free Press.

Dweck, C. S., & Leggett, E. L. (1988). A social-cognitive approach to motivation and personality. *Psychological Review*, 95(2), 256–273.

Dweck, C. S. (2006). *Mindset: The New Psychology of Success*. Random House.

Flavell, J. H. (1979). Metacognition and cognitive monitoring. *American Psychologist*, 34(10), 906–911.

Piaget, J. (1926). *The Language and Thought of the Child*. Harcourt, Brace.

Perkins, D. N. (1995). *Outsmarting IQ: The Emerging Science of Learnable Intelligence*. Free Press.

Senge, P. M. (1990). *The Fifth Discipline: The Art & Practice of the Learning Organization*. Currency Doubleday.

Taylor, S. E., & Gollwitzer, P. M. (1995). Effects of mindset on positive illusions. *Journal of Personality and Social Psychology*, 69(2), 213–226.

Kennedy, F., Carroll, B., & Francoeur, J. (2013). Mindset not skill set: Evaluating in new paradigms of leadership development. *Advances in Developing Human Resources*, 15(1), 10–26.

MINDSET SHIFTING, SELF-AWARENESS, AND MINDSET CONTAGION

Bandura, A. (1977). Self-efficacy: Toward a unifying theory of behavioral change. *Psychological Review*, 84(2), 191–215.

Beck, A. T. (1976). *Cognitive Therapy and the Emotional Disorders*. Penguin.

Beckmann, J., & Gollwitzer, P. M. (1987). Deliberative vs. implemental states of mind: The issue of impartiality in predecisional and postdecisional information processing. *Social Cognition*, 5(3), 259–279.

Brandstätter, V., & Frank, E. (2002). Effects of deliberative and implemental mindsets on persistence in goal-directed behavior. *Personality & Social Psychology Bulletin*, 28(10), 1366–1378.

Cialdini, R. B. (2009). *Influence: Science and Practice*. Pearson

Crum, A. J., Salovey, P., & Achor, S. (2013). Rethinking stress: The role of mindsets in determining the stress response. *Journal of Personality and Social Psychology*, 104(4), 716–733.

Flavell, J. H. (1979). Metacognition and cognitive monitoring: A new area of cognitive–developmental inquiry. *American Psychologist*, 34(10), 906–911.

Hatfield, E., Cacioppo, J. T., & Rapson, R. L. (1994). *Emotional Contagion*. Cambridge University Press.

Heslin, P. A., & Keating, L. A. (2017). In learning mode? The role of mindsets in derailing and enabling experiential leadership development. *The Leadership Quarterly*, 28(3), 367–384.

John, D. R., & Park, J. K. (2016). Mindsets matter: Implications for branding research and practice. *Journal of Consumer Psychology*, 26(1), 153–160.

Murphy, M. C., & Dweck, C. S. (2016). Mindsets shape consumer behavior. *Journal of Consumer Psychology*, 26(1), 127–136.

Zühlsdorff, K., Dalley, J. W., Robbins, T. W., & Morein-Zamir, S. (2023). Cognitive flexibility: Neurobehavioral correlates of changing one's mind. *Cerebral Cortex*, 33(9), 5436–5446.

ACTIVE INGREDIENTS

Jones, S., Bailey, R., Brush, K., & Kahn, J. (2017, December 8). Kernels of practice for SEL: Low-cost, low-burden strategies. EASEL Lab, Harvard Graduate School of Education. Commissioned by the Wallace Foundation.

We conducted a systematic review of more than 80 of the most popular Innovation Frameworks, Design Thinking Frameworks, and Creative Problem-Solving Frameworks. Most were from organizations like IDEO, McKinsey, Accenture, Frog, Lumina, Google, Institute for the Future, and NESTA. Others were from Academic Institutions that teach this kind of work, such as the Stanford d.school, Harvard University Innovation Labs, Princeton University, and University of Colorado. A few were from academic researchers who have proposed frameworks. All of them were thoughtful, well considered, nuanced, and offered a lot to learn and consider. After examining each of these frameworks in great detail, we started to notice that, at their core, they were trying to teach very similar ways of viewing the world and approaching creative problem-solving. They just had different names or terms and proposed different activities or sequences. At first, we distilled the common elements, the active ingredients, and we walked back to the first principles each framework was teaching. But knowing what we know about Mindsets, we also asked of each framework, "What Mindsets are you trying to get your users to engage with?"

Chapter 5 – The Interactions Mindset

BEGINNERS EYES

Suzuki, S. (2011). *Zen Mind, Beginner's Mind: Informal Talks on Zen Meditation and Practice* (T. Dixon, Ed.; H. Smith, Pref.). Shambhala.

Ottati, V., Price, E., Wilson, C., & Sumaktoyo, N. (2015). When self-perceptions of expertise increase closed-minded cognition. *Journal of Experimental Social Psychology*, 61, 131–138.

EMPATHY

Davis, M. H. (1983). Measuring individual differences in empathy: Evidence for a multidimensional approach. *Journal of Personality and Social Psychology*, 44(1), 113–126.

Davis, M. (1996). *Empathy: A Social Psychological Approach*. Westview Press.

Singer, T., & Lamm, C. (2009). The social neuroscience of empathy. *Annals of the New York Academy of Sciences*, 1156(1), 81–96.

CONFIRMATION BIAS

Klayman, J., & Ha, Y. W. (1987). Confirmation, disconfirmation, and information in hypothesis testing. *Psychological Review*, 94(2), 211–228.

Nickerson, R. S. (1998). Confirmation bias: A ubiquitous phenomenon in many guises. *Review of General Psychology*, 2(2), 175–220.

QUALITATIVE VS. QUANTITATIVE DATA

Creswell, J. W. (2013). *Qualitative Inquiry & Research Design: Choosing Among Five Approaches*. SAGE.

Johnson, R. (1997). Examining the validity structure of qualitative research. *Education*, Winter(2), 282–292.

Merriam, S. B. (2002). *Qualitative Research in Practice: Examples for Discussion and Analysis*. Jossey-Bass.

Merriam, S. B., & Tisdell, E. J. (2015). *Qualitative Research: A Guide to Design and Implementation* (4th ed.). Jossey-Bass.

Saldaña, J. (2015). *The Coding Manual for Qualitative Researchers*. SAGE.

Shaffer, D. W. (2017). *Quantitative Ethnography*. Cathcart Press.

Timmermans, S., & Tavory, I. (2012). Theory construction in qualitative research: From grounded theory to abductive analysis. *Sociological Theory*, 30(3), 167–186.

Weiss, R. (1994). Interviewing. In Learning from Strangers: The Art and Method of Qualitative Interview Studies. Free Press.

REFLEXIVITY AND SELF-AWARENESS IN RESEARCH

Finlay, L. (2002). Negotiating the swamp: The opportunity and challenge of reflexivity in research practice. *Qualitative Research*, 2(2), 209–230.

Schön, D. A. (1983). *The Reflective Practitioner: How Professionals Think in Action*. Basic Books.

SOCIAL AND CULTURAL SENSITIVITY IN RESEARCH

Hook, J. N., Davis, D. E., Owen, J., Worthington, E. L., & Utsey, S. O. (2013). Cultural humility: Measuring openness to culturally diverse clients. *Journal of Counseling Psychology*, 60(3), 353–366.

Merriam, S. B., & Tisdell, E. J. (2015). *Qualitative Research: A Guide to Design and Implementation* (4th ed.). Jossey-Bass.

Merriam, S. B. (2002). *Qualitative Research in Practice: Examples for Discussion and Analysis*. Jossey-Bass.

SITUATED COGNITION

Brown, J. S., Collins, A., & Duguid, P. (1989). Situated cognition and the culture of learning. *Educational Researcher*, 18(1), 32–42.

Chapter 6 – The Insights Mindset

COGNITIVE LOAD

Cooper, G. (1990). Cognitive load theory as an aid for instructional design. *Australasian Journal of Educational Technology*, 6(2).

Paas, F. G. W. C., Renkl, A., & Sweller, J. (2004). Cognitive load theory: Instructional implications. *Educational Psychology*, 38(1), 1–4.

Sweller, J. (1988). Cognitive load during problem solving: Effects on learning. *Cognitive Science*, 12(2), 257–285.

COGNITIVE BIASES

Nickerson, R. S. (1998). Confirmation bias: A ubiquitous phenomenon in many guises. *Review of General Psychology*, 2(2), 175–220.

Pronin, E., Lin, D. Y., & Ross, L. (2002). The bias blind spot: Perceptions of bias in self versus others. *Personality and Social Psychology Bulletin*, 28(3), 369–381.

Tversky, A., & Kahneman, D. (1974). Judgment under uncertainty: Heuristics and biases. *Science*, 185(4157), 1124–1131.

THEMATIC SATURATION

Guest, G., Bunce, A., & Johnson, L. (2006). How many interviews are enough? An experiment with data saturation and variability. *Field Methods*, 18(1), 59–82.

Saunders, B., et al. (2018). Saturation in qualitative research: Exploring its conceptualization and operationalization. *Quality & Quantity*, 52(4), 1893–1907.

DEDUCTIVE, INDUCTIVE, AND ABDUCTIVE REASONING

Douven, I. (2021). Abduction. In E. N. Zalta (Ed.), *The Stanford Encyclopedia of Philosophy* (Summer 2021 Edition). Stanford University.

Elo, S., & Kyngäs, H. (2008). The qualitative content analysis process. *Journal of Advanced Nursing*, 62(1), 107–115.

Fife, S. T., & Gossner, J. D. (2024). Deductive qualitative analysis: Evaluating, expanding, and refining theory. *International Journal of Qualitative Methods*, 23.

Hawthorne, J. (2025). Inductive logic. In E. N. Zalta (Ed.), *The Stanford Encyclopedia of Philosophy* (Spring 2025 Edition). Stanford University.

Lipton, P. (2004). *Inference to the Best Explanation* (2nd ed.). Routledge.

Peirce, C. S. (1931–1935). *Collected Papers of Charles Sanders Peirce* (C. Hartshorne & P. Weiss, (Eds.). Harvard University Press.

Shin, S.-J. (2022). Peirce's deductive logic. In E. N. Zalta (Ed.), *The Stanford Encyclopedia of Philosophy* (Spring 2022 Edition). Stanford University.

Timmermans, S., & Tavory, I. (2012). Theory construction in qualitative research: From grounded theory to abductive analysis. *Sociological Theory*, 30(3), 167–186.

SYNTHESIS

Gardner, H. (2006). *Five Minds for the Future*. Harvard Business Review Press.

Gardner, H. (2020). *A Synthesizing Mind : A Memoir From the Creator of Multiple Intelligences Theory*. The MIT Press.

Gell-Mann, M. (1995). *The Quark and the Jaguar: Adventures in the Simple and the Complex*. St. Martin's Griffin.

Problem Framing and the Framing Effect

Dorst, K., & Cross, N. (2001). Creativity in the design process: Co-evolution of problem–solution. *Design Studies*, 22(5), 425–437.

Entman, R. M. (1993). Framing: Toward clarification of a fractured paradigm. *Journal of Communication*, 43(4), 51–58.

Meinel, M., Eismann, T. T., Fixson, S. K., & Voigt, K.-I. (2023). The weakest link: The importance of problem framing in design thinking. In K. Straker & C. Wrigley (Eds.), *Research Handbook on Design Thinking* (pp. 232–245). Edward Elgar Publishing.

Seelig, T. (2012). *inGenius: A Crash Course on Creativity*. HarperOne.

Seelig, T. (2015). *Insight Out: Get Ideas Out of Your Head and Into the World*. HarperOne.

Tversky, A., & Kahneman, D. (1981). The framing of decisions and the psychology of choice. *Science*, 211(4481), 453–458.

Learning Transfer

Forshaw, T., & Longmire, M. (2024). Emerging findings on learning transfer between novel roles for working learners and learning workers. In R. Lindgren, T. I. Asino, E. A. Kyza, C. K. Looi, D. T. Keifert, & E. Suárez (Eds.), *Proceedings of the 18th International Conference of the Learning Sciences – ICLS 2024* (pp. 2269–2270). International Society of the Learning Sciences.

Forshaw, T. (2025). Learning Transfer During Role Transitions at Work. In 2025 *American Educational Research Association Annual Meeting Proceedings* (Forthcoming).

Forshaw, T. (forthcoming). *Transfer by Design: Learning in the Flow of Work During Complex and Changing Times*. President and Fellows of Harvard College, Cambridge, MA.

Stories and Quotes

Boulton, G. (2016). Turning children's medical scans into adventures. *Milwaukee Journal Sentinel*. https://www.twincities.com/2016/02/20/turning-childrens-medical-scans-into-adventures (accessed 23 April 2025).

Brown, T. (2008). Design thinking. *Harvard Business Review*, 86(6), 84–92.

GM Investor. (2020, March 27). Ventec Life Systems and GM partner to mass produce critical care ventilators in response to COVID-19 pandemic [Press release]. PR Newswire https://www.prnewswire.com/news-releases/ventec-life-systems-and-gm-partner-to-mass-produce-critical-care-ventilators-in-response-to-covid-19-pandemic-301031046.html (accessed 23 April 2025).

Kelley, T., & Kelley, D. (2012). Fighting the fears that block creativity. *Harvard Business Review*, https://hbr.org/2012/11/fighting-the-fears-that-b (accessed 23 April 2025).

Kelley, T., & Kelley, D. (2013). Kids were terrified of getting MRIs. Then one man figured out a better way. Slate. https://slate.com/human-interest/2013/10/creative-confidence-a-new-book-from-ideo-s-tom-and-david-kelley.html (accessed 23 April 2025).

Liedtka, J. (2014). Innovative ways companies are using design thinking. *Strategy & Leadership*, 42(2), 40–45.

Marquand, R. (Director). (1983). Star Wars: Episode VI – Return of the Jedi [Film]. Lucasfilm Ltd.

University of Pittsburgh Department of Radiology. (n.d.). Pediatric Radiology Division. UPMC.

Ventec Life Systems. (2020, March 27). Ventec Life Systems and GM partner to mass produce critical care ventilators in response to COVID-19 pandemic. https://www.venteclife.com/news/ventec-life-systems-and-gm-partner-to-mass-produce-critical-care-ventilators-in-response-to-covid19-pandemic (accessed 21 May 2025).

Chapter 7 – The Ideas Mindset

JUDGMENT SUSPENSION

Edmondson, A. (1999). Psychological safety and learning behavior in work teams. *Administrative Science Quarterly*, 44(2), 350–383.

Osborn, Alex (1953). *Applied Imagination: Principles and Procedures of Creative Problem Solving*. Charles Scribner's Sons.

West, M. A., Richter, A. W., Shalley, C. E., & Zhou, J. (2008). Climates and cultures for innovation and creativity at work. In *Handbook of Organizational Creativity* 1 (pp. 211–236). Routledge.

"Yes, And" and Improvisational Techniques

Johnstone, K. (1981). *Impro: Improvisation and the Theatre.* Routledge.

Leonard, K., & Yorton, T. (2015). *Yes, And: How Improvisation Reverses "No, But" Thinking and Improves Creativity and Collaboration—Lessons from the Second City.* HarperBusiness.

Sawyer, R. K. (2012). *Group Genius: The Creative Power of Collaboration.* Basic Books.

Collective Intelligence and Diverse Perspectives

Hong, L., & Page, S. E. (2004). Groups of diverse problem solvers can outperform groups of high-ability problem solvers. *Proceedings of the National Academy of Sciences*, 101(46), 16385–16389.

Jehn, K. A., Northcraft, G. B., & Neale, M. A. (1999). Why differences make a difference: A field study of diversity, conflict and performance in workgroups. *Administrative Science Quarterly*, 44(4), 741–763.

Page, S. E. (2007). *The Difference: How the Power of Diversity Creates Better Groups, Firms, Schools, and Societies.* Princeton University Press.

Phillips, K. W., Liljenquist, K. A., & Neale, M. A. (2009). Is the pain worth the gain? The advantages and liabilities of agreeing with socially distinct newcomers. *Personality and Social Psychology Bulletin*, 35(3), 336–350.

van Knippenberg, D., De Dreu, C. K. W., & Homan, A. C. (2004). Work group diversity and group performance: An integrative model and research agenda. *Journal of Applied Psychology*, 89(6), 1008–1022.

Woolley, A. W., Chabris, C. F., Pentland, A., Hashmi, N., & Malone, T. W. (2010). Evidence for a collective intelligence factor in the performance of human groups. *Science*, 330(6004), 686–688.

COGNITION OF BRAINSTORMING

Beaty, R. E., Kenett, Y. N., Hass, R. W., & Schacter, D. L. (2023). Semantic memory and creativity: The costs and benefits of semantic memory structure in generating original ideas. *Thinking & Reasoning*, 29(2), 305–339.

Diehl, M., & Stroebe, W. (1987). Productivity loss in brainstorming groups: Toward the solution of a riddle. *Journal of Personality and Social Psychology*, 53(3), 497–509.

FLOW STATE IN CREATIVITY

Csikszentmihalyi, M. (1990). *Flow: The Psychology of Optimal Experience*. Harper & Row.

Rosen, D., Oh, Y., Chesebrough, C., Zhang, F. (Zoe), & Kounios, J. (2024). Creative flow as optimized processing: Evidence from brain oscillations during jazz improvisations by expert and non-expert musicians. *Neuropsychologia*, 196, 108824.

Sawyer, R. K. (2012). *Explaining Creativity*. Oxford University Press.

WILD IDEAS AND GOING FOR VOLUME

Chan, J., & Schunn, C. D. (2015). The importance of iteration in creative conceptual combination. *Cognition*, 145, 104–115.

Chesbrough, H. (2003). *Open Innovation: The New Imperative for Creating and Profiting From Technology*. Harvard Business Press.

Girotra, K., Terwiesch, C., & Ulrich, K. T. (2009). Idea generation and the quality of the best idea (INSEAD Business School Research Paper No. 2009/65/TOM). SSRN.

Tushman, M. L., & O'Reilly, C. A. (1996). Ambidextrous organizations: Managing evolutionary and revolutionary change. *California Management Review*, 38(4), 8–29.

Brainstorming Levers and Conceptual Expansion

Smith, S. M., Ward, T. B., & Finke, R. A. (1995). *The Creative Cognition Approach*. MIT Press.

Ward, T. B. (1994). Structured imagination: The role of category structure in exemplar generation. *Cognitive Psychology*, 27(1), 1–40.

Cognitive Load, Externalizing Ideas, and "Sticky Notes"

Kirsh, D. (2010). Thinking with external representations. *AI & Society*, 25(4), 441–454.

Sweller, J. (1988). Cognitive load during problem solving: Effects on learning. *Cognitive Science*, 12, 257–285.

Zhang, J. (1997). The nature of external representations in problem solving. *Cognitive Science*, 21(2), 179–217.

Tyranny of the Pen and Social Dynamics in Idea Recording

Chen, Y., Yu, C., Yuan, Y., Lu, F., & Shen, W. (2021). The influence of trust on creativity: A review. *Frontiers in Psychology*, 12, article 706234.

Connolly, T., Routhieaux, R. L., & Schneider, S. K. (1993). On the effectiveness of group brainstorming: Test of one underlying cognitive mechanism. *Small Group Research*, 24(4), 490–503.

Jetten, J., Spears, R., & Manstead, A. S. R. (1997). Distinctiveness threat and prototypicality: Combined effects on intergroup discrimination and collective self-esteem. *European Journal of Social Psychology*, 27(6), 635–657.

Paulus, P. B., & Yang, H. C. (2000). Idea generation in groups: A basis for creativity in organizations. *Organizational Behavior and Human Decision Processes*, 82(1), 76–87.

Decision-Making Trap

Putman, V. L., & Paulus, P. B. (2011). Brainstorming, brainstorming rules and decision making. *The Journal of Creative Behavior*, 43(1), 29–40.

Stories

Crouch, T. D. (2002). *First Flight: The Wright Brothers and the Invention of the Airplane*. National Geographic Society.

Ford, H., & Crowther, S. (2005). *My Life and Work*. Project Gutenberg.

Gilbert, L., & Moore, G. (1981). *Particular Passions: Grace Murray Hopper*. Lynn Gilbert.

McCullough, D. (2015). *The Wright Brothers*. Simon & Schuster.

Utley, J., & Klebahn, P. (2022). *Ideaflow: The Only Business Metric That Matters*. Portfolio.

Yale University. (2025). *Grace Murray Hopper*. Yale University Department of Computer Science.

Chapter 8 – The Iterations Mindset

Prototyping, Rapid Testing, and Feedback Loops

Dow, S. P., Heddleston, K., & Klemmer, S. R. (2009). The efficacy of prototyping under time constraints. *Proceedings of the 27th International Conference on Human Factors in Computing Systems (CHI '09)*, 1337–1340.

Schrage, M. (1999). *Serious Play: How the World's Best Companies Simulate to Innovate*. Harvard Business School Press.

Failing Fast

Cannon, M. D., & Edmondson, A. C. (2005). Failing to learn and learning to fail. *Long Range Planning*, 38(3), 299–319.

Sharp, J., & Macklin, C. (2019). *Iterate: Ten Lessons in Design and Failure*. The MIT Press.

Thomke, S. (2001). Enlightened experimentation: The new imperative for innovation. *Harvard Business Review*, 79(2), 66–75.

Sunk-Cost Fallacy

Arkes, H. R., & Blumer, C. (1985). The psychology of sunk cost. *Organizational Behavior and Human Decision Processes*, 35(1), 124–140.

Thaler, R. (1999). Mental accounting matters. *Journal of Behavioral Decision Making*, 12(3), 183–206.

Design Fixation

Condoor, S., & LaVoie, D. (2007). Design fixation: A cognitive model. In *DS 42: Proceedings of ICED 2007, the 16th International Conference on Engineering Design*, Paris, France, 28.-31.07. 2007.

Jansson, D. G., & Smith, S. M. (1991). Design fixation. *Design Studies*, 12(1), 3–11.

Kim, D. (2016). The barriers to design creativity. *Archives of Design Research*, 29(3), 77–95.

Leahy, K., Daly, S. R., McKilligan, S., & Seifert, C. M. (2020). Design fixation from initial examples: Provided versus self-generated ideas. *Journal of Mechanical Design*, 142(10).

Comparative Feedback: Multiple Prototypes vs. Single Concept

Dow, S. P., Fortuna, J., Schwartz, D., Altringer, B., Schwartz, D. L., & Klemmer, S. R. (2012). Prototyping dynamics: Sharing multiple designs improves exploration, group rapport, and results. *Proceedings of the SIGCHI Conference on Human Factors in Computing Systems (CHI '12)*, 2803–2812.

Gerber, E. (2009). Using improvisation to enhance the effectiveness of brainstorming. *Creativity and Innovation Management*, 18(1), 60–69.

Embodied Cognition

Constant, A., Friston, K. J., & Clark, A. (2024). Cultivating creativity: Predictive brains and the enlightened room problem. *Philosophical Transactions of the Royal Society B*, 379.

Glenberg, A. M. (2015). Few believe the world is flat: How embodiment is changing the scientific understanding of cognition. *Canadian Journal of Experimental Psychology*, 69(2), 165–171.

Malinin, L. H. (2016). Creative practices embodied, embedded, and enacted in architectural settings: Toward an ecological model of creativity. *Frontiers in Psychology*, 6, Article 1978.

Evidence-Based Decision-Making vs. Opinion

Bertrand, M., & Duflo, E. (2017). Field experiments on discrimination. In A. V. Banerjee & E. Duflo (Eds.), *Handbook of Economic Field Experiments* (Vol. 1, pp. 309–393). North-Holland.

Morwitz, V. G., & Fitzsimons, G. J. (2004). The mere-measurement effect: Why does measuring intentions change actual behavior? *Journal of Consumer Psychology*, 14(1–2), 64–74.

The Risk of Biased Testing

Nederhof, A. J. (1985). Methods of coping with social desirability bias: A review. *European Journal of Social Psychology*, 15(3), 263–280.

Rosenthal, R., & Rosnow, R. L. (1975). *The Volunteer Subject*. John Wiley & Sons.

Stories and Quotes

Bohn, D. (2015, January 15). *Google Glass is Dead; Long Live Google Glass*. The Verge.

ClearlyAgile. (2022, March 6). Nordstrom Innovation Lab – Sunglass iPad App Case Study [Video]. YouTube. https://www.youtube.com/watch?v=GFImT1_bBDw (accessed 23 April 2025).

Crouch, T. D. (2002). *First Flight: The Wright Brothers and the Invention of the Airplane*. National Geographic Society.

Israel, P. (1998). *Edison: A Life of Invention*. Wiley.

Jonnes, J. (2003). *Empires of Light: Edison, Tesla, Westinghouse, and The Race to Electrify the World*. Random House.

Killed by Google. (n.d.). Killed by Google. https://killedbygoogle.com (accessed 23 April 2025).

McCullough, D. (2015). *The Wright Brothers*. Simon & Schuster.

Restauri, D. (2014, November 18). A personal story: How low-cost technology is saving babies' lives. *Forbes*.

Ries, E. (2011). *The Lean Startup: How Today's Entrepreneurs use Continuous Innovation to Create Radically Successful Businesses*. Crown Business.

Savoia, A. (2019). *The Right It: Why So Many Ideas Fail and How to Make Sure Yours Succeed*. Harper Business.

Stross, R. E. (2007). *The Wizard of Menlo Park: How Thomas Alva Edison Invented the Modern World*. Crown Publishing Group.

Chapter 9 – The Inspirations Mindset

EMOTIONAL CONTAGION

Barsade, S. G. (2002). The ripple effect: Emotional contagion in groups. *Administrative Science Quarterly*, 47(4), 644–675.

Hatfield, E., Cacioppo, J. T., & Rapson, R. L. (1994). *Emotional Contagion*. Cambridge University Press.

COGNITIVE AND AFFECTIVE EMPATHY

Brewer, W. F., & Lichtenstein, E. H. (1982). Stories are to entertain: A structural-affect theory of stories. *Journal of Pragmatics*, 6(5–6), 473–486.

Busselle, R., & Bilandzic, H. (2008). Fictionality and perceived realism in experiencing stories: A model of narrative comprehension and engagement. *Communication Theory*, 18(2), 255–280.

Davis, M. H. (1983). Measuring individual differences in empathy: Evidence for a multidimensional approach. *Journal of Personality and Social Psychology*, 44(1), 113–126.

Feinberg (Eds.). *Patient-Based Approaches to Cognitive Neuroscience* (pp. 195–208). MIT Press.

Singer, T. (2006). The Neuronal Basis and Ontogeny of Empathy and Mind Reading: review of literature and implications for future research. *Neuroscience and Biobehavioral Reviews* 30(6), 855–863.

Recency Effect

Glanzer, M., & Cunitz, A. R. (1966). Two storage mechanisms in free recall. *Journal of Verbal Learning and Verbal Behavior*, 5(4), 351–360.

Murdock, B. B. (1962). The serial position effect of free recall. *Journal of Experimental Psychology*, 64(5), 482–488.

Narrative Persuasion

Aaker, J. (1997). Dimensions of brand personality. *Journal of Marketing Research*, 34(3), 347–356.

Green, M. C., & Brock, T. C. (2000). The role of transportation in the persuasiveness of narratives. *Journal of Personality and Social Psychology*, 79(5), 701–721.

Heath, C., & Heath, D. (2007). *Made to Stick: Why Some Ideas Survive and Others Die*. Random House.

Stanford Graduate School of Business. (2013). Jennifer Aaker: Harnessing the power of stories [Video]. YouTube. https://www.youtube.com/watch?v=9X0weDMh9C4 (accessed 23 April 2025).

van Laer, T., Ruyter, K. D., Visconti, L. M., & Wetzels, M. (2014). The extended transportation-imagery model: A meta-analysis of the antecedents and consequences of consumers' narrative transportation. *Journal of Consumer Research*, 40(5), 797–817.

Elephant and Rider

Haidt, J. (2006). *The Happiness Hypothesis: Finding Modern Truth in Ancient Wisdom*. Basic Books.

Heath, C., & Heath, D. (2010). *Switch: How to Change Things When Change is Hard*. Crown Business.

Story Spine/Pixar Pitch/Narrative Structures

Adams, K. (2007). *How to Improvise a Full-Length Play: The Art of Spontaneous Theater*. Allworth Press.

Gallo, C. (2014). *The Storyteller's Secret*. St. Martin's Press.

STORIES AND QUOTES

Jenni, K. E., & Loewenstein, G. (1997). Explaining the "identifiable victim effect." *Journal of Risk and Uncertainty*, 14(3), 235–257.

Neowin. (2009). Zune HD Commercial – "Portable Perfection" [Video]. YouTube. https://www.youtube.com/watch?v=W1hOkc2nx5A (accessed 23 April 2025).

Siri Pod. (2009). Apple iPhone 4 Ad – Meet Her [Video]. YouTube. https://www.youtube.com/watch?v=lrXc92TLbl0 (accessed 23 April 2025).

Small, D. A., Loewenstein, G., & Slovic, P. (2007). Sympathy and callousness: The impact of deliberative thought on donations to identifiable and statistical victims. *Organizational Behavior and Human Decision Processes*, 102(2), 143–153.

SussexSaferRoads. (2010). Embrace Life – always wear your seat belt [Video]. YouTube. https://www.youtube.com/watch?v=h-8PBx7isoM (accessed 23 April 2025).

Saujani, R. (2021, October 27). Fixing tech's gender gap [Video]. Stanford eCorner. https://ecorner.stanford.edu/videos/fixing-techs-gender-gap (accessed 23 April 2025).

Chapter 10 – The Implications Mindset

SYSTEMS THINKING

Holling, C. S. (1973). Resilience and stability of ecological systems. *Annual Review of Ecology and Systematics*, 4(1), 1–23.

Meadows, D. H. (2008). *Thinking in Systems: A Primer*. Chelsea Green Publishing.

DUAL PROCESSING THEORY

Kahneman, D. (2011). *Thinking, Fast and Slow*. Farrar, Straus and Giroux.

Stanovich, K. E., & West, R. F. (2000). Individual differences in reasoning. *Behavioral and Brain Sciences*, 23(5), 645–665.

OVERCONFIDENCE BIAS

Fischhoff, B., Slovic, P., & Lichtenstein, S. (1977). Knowing with certainty: The appropriateness of extreme confidence. *Journal of Experimental Psychology: Human Perception and Performance,* 3(4), 552–564.

Moore, D. A., & Healy, P. J. (2008). The trouble with overconfidence. *Psychological Review,* 115(2), 502–517.

COGNITIVE LOAD AND COMPLEXITY

Cooper, G. (1990). Cognitive load theory as an aid for instructional design. *Australasian Journal of Educational Technology,* 6(2).

Paas, F., & van Merriënboer, J. J. G. (1994). Variability of worked examples. *Cognition and Instruction,* 12(1), 35–57.

Sweller, J. (1988). Cognitive load during problem solving. *Cognitive Science,* 12(2), 257–285.

VALUE OF DIVERSE PERSPECTIVES FOR RISK REDUCTION

Page, S. E. (2007). *The Difference: How the Power of Diversity Creates Better Groups, Firms, Schools, and Societies.* Princeton University Press.

van Knippenberg, D., De Dreu, C. K., & Homan, A. C. (2004). Work group diversity and group performance. *Journal of Applied Psychology,* 89(6), 1008–1022.

UNINTENDED CONSEQUENCES

De Zwart, Frank. 2015. Unintended but not unanticipated consequences. Theory and Society 44(3), 283–297.

Parvin, N., & Pollock, A. (2020). *Unintended by Design: On the Political Uses of "Unintended Consequences."* Engaging Science, Technology, and Society.

Stories and Quotes

Apple Studios. (2022). *WeCrashed* [TV series]. Apple TV+.

Carreyrou, J. (2015, October 16). Hot startup Theranos has struggled with its blood-test technology. *The Wall Street Journal*.

Carreyrou, J. (2018). *Bad Blood: Secrets and Lies in a Silicon Valley Startup*. Knopf.

Duhigg, C. (2012). *The Power of Habit*. Random House.

Gibney, A. (Director). (2019). *The Inventor: Out for Blood in Silicon Valley* [Film]. HBO Documentary Films.

Grensing-Pophal, L. (2024, October 10). The double-edged sword of Easy Apply: Boon for applicants, bane for recruiters. *HR Daily Advisor*.

Hamblin, J. (2015, March 2). A brewing problem: What's the healthiest way to keep everyone caffeinated? *The Atlantic*.

Hanigan, M. (2015, February 4). *How LinkedIn Fundamentally Ruined Recruitment*. Entrepreneur.

Holmes, R., Jarvis, B., & ABC News (Producers). (2019). The dropout [Audio podcast]. ABC Audio. https://abcaudio.com/podcasts/the-dropout (accessed 21 May 2025).

Lowry Solutions. (n.d.). The Walmart RFID mandate: What you need to know. Retrieved February 28, 2025, from https://lowrysolutions.com/blog/the-walmart-rfid-mandate-what-you-need-to-know/ (accessed 23 April 2025).

Moore, G. A. (1991). *Crossing the Chasm: Marketing and Selling High-Tech Products to Mainstream Customers*. Harper Business.

New Profit, & People Rocket. (2024). Unlocking the 'black box' in philanthropy: Comprehensive report on pipeline development uncovering actionable insights for equitable philanthropy. New Profit.

Nowell, C. (2023, February 10). Are Coffee Pods Really Eco-Friendly? The Truth Behind the Surprising Findings. *The Guardian*.

Osterwalder, A., & Pigneur, Y. (2010). *Business Model Generation: A Handbook for Visionaries, Game Changers, and Challengers*. Wiley.

Randolph, M. (2019). *That Will Never Work: The Birth of Netflix and the Amazing Life of an Idea.* Little, Brown and Company.

Sherman, D. (2017, March 1). High Line Magazine: Creating a more equitable High Line. The High Line Blog. https://www.thehighline.org/blog/2017/03/01/high-line-magazine-creating-a-more-equitable-high-line/ (accessed 28 February 2025).

Smith, D. W., & Ferguson, G. (2005). *Decade of the Wolf: Returning the Wild to Yellowstone.* Lyons Press.

Smith, D. W., Stahler, D. R., & MacNulty, D. R. (Eds.). (2020). *Yellowstone Wolves: Science and Discovery in the World's First National Park.* University of Chicago Press.

The Dropout. (2022). [TV miniseries]. 20th Television, Elizabeth Meriwether Pictures, Searchlight Television.

Westlake, J. (2020, June 19). Should you use the "Easy Apply" Option on LinkedIn? The Muse.

Chapter 11 – Moves Are Actions

OVERCOMING ANALYSIS PARALYSIS WITH SMALL WINS

Amabile, T., & Kramer, S. (2011). "The power of small wins." *Harvard Business Review*, 89(5).

Duhigg, C. (2012). *The Power of Habit.* Random House, p. 109 ff.

Gollwitzer, P. M. (1999). Implementation intentions. *American Psychologist*, 54(7), 493–503.

Janis, I. L., & Mann, L. (1977). *Decision Making: A Psychological Analysis of Conflict, Choice, and Commitment.* Free Press.

Kuppens, P. et al. (2010, May 25). Emotional inertia and psychological maladjustment. *Psychological Science*, 21(7).

BREAKING BIG PROBLEMS INTO SMALLER PIECES

Cooper, G. (1990). Cognitive load theory as an aid for instructional design. *Australasian Journal of Educational Technology*, 6(2).

Custers, R. & Aarts, H. (2010). The unconscious will. *Science*, 329(5987), 47–50. (On how small cues can prompt goal-directed action.)

Sweller, J. (1988). Cognitive load during problem solving. *Cognitive Science*, 12(2), 257–285.

Chapter 12 – Using Moves

THE EINSTELLUNG EFFECT

Barlach, L., & Plonski, G. A. (2021). The Einstellung effect, mental rigidity and decision-making in startup accelerators. *Innovation & Management Review*, 18(3), 276–291.

Bilalić, M. et al. (2008). Inflexibility of expert-reality or myth? Quantifying the Einstellung effect in chess masters. *Cognitive Psychology*, 56(2), 73–102.

LEARNING TRANSFER

Detterman, D. K. (1993). The case for the prosecution: Transfer as an epiphenomenon. In D. K. Detterman & R. J. Sternberg (Eds.), *Transfer on Trial* (pp. 1–24). Ablex Publishing.

Forshaw, T. (forthcoming). *Transfer by Design: Learning in the Flow of Work During Complex and Changing Times*, President and Fellows of Harvard College, Cambridge MA.

Forshaw, T. & Longmire, M. (2024). Emerging findings on learning transfer between novel roles for working learners and learning workers. In R. Lindgren, T. I. Asino , E. A. Kyza, C. K. Looi, D. T. Keifert, & E. Suárez (Eds.), *Proceedings of the 18th International Conference of the Learning Sciences – ICLS 2024* (pp. 2269–2270). International Society of the Learning Sciences.

Forshaw, T. (2025). Learning Transfer During Role Transitions at Work, *2025 American Educational Research Association Annual Meeting Proceedings* (Forthcoming).

Forshaw, T., Capeci, I., & Longmire, M. (2024). *Transferring Existing Skills and Knowledge into New Roles At Work*. Next Level Lab, Harvard Graduate School of Education.

Perkins, D. N., & Salomon, G. (1992). Transfer of learning. *International Encyclopedia of Education* (2nd ed.), 2, 6452–6457.

THE POWER OF YET

Burnette, J. L., O'Boyle, H. E., VanEpps, E. M., Pollack, J. M. and Finkel, E. J. (2013). Mind-sets and self-regulation. *Personality and Social Psychology Review*, 17(2), 141–158.

Dweck, C. S. (2006). *Mindset: The New Psychology of Success*. Random House.

ANALOGICAL REASONING

Bassok, M. (2003). Analogical transfer in problem solving. In J. E. Davidson & R. J. Sternberg (Eds.), *The Psychology of Problem Solving* (pp. 343–370). Cambridge: Cambridge University Press.

Chan, J., & Schunn, C. (2014). The impact of analogies on creative concept generation: Lessons from an in vivo study in engineering design. *Cognitive Science*, 38(1), 1–30.

Dunbar, K. (1995). How scientists really reason. *The Nature of Insight*, 365–395.

Gentner, D. (1983). Structure-mapping: A theoretical framework for analogy. *Cognitive Science*, 7(2), 155–170.

Gentner, D., & Smith, L. (2012). Analogical reasoning. In V. S. Ramachandran (Ed.), *Encyclopedia of Human Behavior* (2nd ed., pp. 130–136). Elsevier.

Gentner, D., & Smith, L. A. (2018). Analogical learning and reasoning. In D. Reisberg (Ed.), *The Oxford Handbook of Cognitive Psychology*. Oxford University Press.

Self-Efficacy Theory

Bandura, A. (1997). *Self-Efficacy: The Exercise of Control*. W. H. Freeman.

Schunk, D. H. (1995). Self-efficacy, motivation, and performance. *Journal of Applied Sport Psychology*, 7(2), 112–137.

Stories

Department of Foreign Affairs and Trade. (2020, July 23). Executive masterclass: Innovation-ish tools for leading through ambiguity [Conference session]. Eventbrite.

Forshaw, T., & Braden, R. (2019, August 30). Helping the APS Get Innovation(ish). Department of Industry, Science and Resources.

Chapter 13 – Thinking About Moves

No sources

Chapter 14 – Being Metacognitive

Metacognition

Cuzzolino, M. P., & Grotzer, T. A. (2022). *The Icing on the Cake: How Metacognition Enhances Learning*. Next Level Lab, Harvard Graduate School of Education.

Efklides, A. (2006). Metacognition and affect: What can metacognitive experiences tell us about the learning process? *Educational Research Review*, 1(1), 3–14

Flavell, J. H. (1979). Metacognition and cognitive monitoring. *American Psychologist*, 34(10), 906–911.

Gross, J. J. (1998). The emerging field of emotion regulation. *Review of General Psychology*, 2(3), 271–299.

Grotzer, T. A. & Cuzzolino, M. (2023). *Reflecting on Your Learning in the Workplace.* Next Level Lab, Harvard Graduate School of Education.

Grotzer, T. A. (2024). *Becoming an Expert Learner (EDU H110L).* Harvard Graduate School of Education.

Grotzer, T. A. (2025). *Applying Cognitive Science To Learning And Teaching (EDU T543).* Harvard Graduate School of Education.

Sabaliauskas, S., Gražulis, D., Žilinskienė, N., & Kaukėnas, T. (2025). Metacognitive strategies improve self-regulation skills in expert sports coaches. *Scientific Reports*, 15(1), 3434.

Sadykova, A., Iskakova, M., Ismailova, G., Ishmukhametova, A., Sovetova, A., & Mukasheva, K. (2024). The impact of a metacognition-based course on school students' metacognitive skills and biology comprehension. *Frontiers in Education*, 9, article 1460496.

Salovey, P., & Mayer, J. D. (1990). Emotional intelligence. *Imagination, Cognition and Personality*, 9(3), 185–211.

Schraw, G., & Dennison, R. S. (1994). Assessing metacognitive awareness. *Contemporary Educational Psychology*, 19(4), 460–475.

Schraw, G., & Moshman, D. (1995). Metacognitive theories. *Educational Psychology Review*, 7(4),

Stanton, J. D., Sebesta, A. J., & Dunlosky, J. (2021). Fostering metacognition to support student learning and performance. *CBE Life Sciences Education*, 20(2), fe3.

Rivas, S. F., Saiz, C., & Ossa, C. (2022). Metacognitive strategies and development of critical thinking in higher education. *Frontiers in Psychology*, 13, article 913219.

Veenman, M. V. J., Van Hout-Wolters, B. H. A. M., & Afflerbach, P. (2006). Metacognition and learning: Conceptual and methodological considerations. *Metacognition and Learning*, 1(1), 3–14.

Zeitlhofer, I., Hörmann, S., Mann, B., Hallinger, K., & Zumbach, J. (2023). Effects of cognitive and metacognitive prompts on learning performance in digital learning environments. *Knowledge*, 3(2), 277–292.

Cognitive vs. Metacognitive Questions

Cuzzolino, M. P., & Grotzer, T. A. (2022). *The Icing on the Cake: How Metacognition Enhances Learning*. Next Level Lab, Harvard Graduate School of Education.

Cuzzolino, M.P., Sun, M., Xu, J., Becerra, J., Fields, E., & Grotzer, T. (2024). *Leveraging the Power of Metacognition and Contextualized Agency for Workplace Learning*. New England Educational Research

Hester, R. (2021, August 4). 20 metacognitive questions to engage your science learners. Cambridge University Press. https://www.cambridge.org/it/education/blog/2021/08/04/20-metacognitive-questions-to-engage-your-science-learners (accessed 21 May 2025) .

NEERO. Organization (NEERO) Conference. Portsmouth, NH. April 25, 2024.

Efklides, A. (2006). Metacognition and affect: What can metacognitive experiences tell us about the learning process? *Educational Research Review*, 1(1), 3–14.

Kahneman, D. (2011). *Thinking, Fast and Slow*. Farrar, Straus and Giroux.

Zimmerman, B. J. (2002). Becoming a self-regulated learner. *Theory into Practice*, 41(2), 64–70.

Metacognition and Creativity

Forshaw, T., McGivney, E., & Braden, R. C. (2024). *Metacognition in Design and Design Education*. The Next Level Lab, Harvard University.

González-Tobón, J., Tellez, F.A., and Tamayo, O.E. (2019). Metacognition in the wild: metacognitive studies in design education, in N. Börekçi, D. Koçyıldırım, F. Korkut and D. Jones (Eds.), *Insider Knowledge, DRS Learn X Design Conference 2019*, 9–12 July, Ankara, Turkey.

Jia X, Li W, Cao L. (2019, Oct 24). The role of metacognitive components in creative thinking. *Frontiers in Psychology*, 10, 2404.

Kavousi, Shabnam, Miller, A., & Alexander, Patricia. (2020). The role of metacognition in the first-year design lab. *Educational Technology Research and Development*, 68.

Chapter 15 – Fueling Innovation

The Role of the Amygdala

Grotzer, T. A. (2024). *Avoiding Amygdala Hijack: How It Hurts Learning and Performance and What Fast Fish Learners Can Do*. Next Level Lab, Harvard Graduate School of Education.

Grotzer, T. A. (2024). *How the Amygdala Hijack Hurts Vulnerable Workers: What Can We do to Support Them?* Next Level Lab, Harvard Graduate School of Education.

LeDoux, J. E. (1996). *The Emotional Brain: The mysterious Underpinnings of Emotional Life*. Simon & Schuster.

Ochsner, K. N., & Gross, J. J. (2005). The cognitive control of emotion. *Trends in Cognitive Sciences*, 9(5), 242–249. (On how prefrontal regions help regulate amygdala output.)

Phelps, E. A., & LeDoux, J. E. (2005). Contributions of the amygdala to emotion processing. *Annual Review of Neuroscience*, 27, 1–28.

Young, K. (2017). *Hey Warrior*. Little Steps Publishing.

Ambiguity

Balgiu, B. A. (2014). The tolerance for ambiguity, self-esteem and perception of family-of-origin in relation to entrepreneurship potential. *Procedia – Social and Behavioral Sciences*, 141, 75–79.

Budner, S. (1962). Intolerance of ambiguity as a personality variable. *Journal of Personality*, 30(1), 29–50.

Furnham, A., & Avison, M. (1997). The tolerance of ambiguity and job satisfaction. *Personality and Individual Differences*, 22(2), 235–245.

MacDonald, A. P. (1970). Revised scale for ambiguity tolerance: Reliability and validity. *Psychological Reports*, 26, 791–798.

McLain, D. (2009). Evidence of the properties of an ambiguity tolerance measure. *Psychological Reports*, 105(3), 975–988.

Young, D. G. (2020). *Irony and Outrage: The Polarized Landscape of Rage, Fear, and Laughter in the United States*. Oxford University Press.

Zenasni, F., Besançon, M., & Lubart, T. (2008). Creativity and tolerance of ambiguity: An empirical study. *The Journal of Creative Behavior*, 42(1), 61–73.

FAILURE

Atkinson, J. W. (1957). Motivational determinants of risk-taking behavior. *Psychological Review*, 64(6), 359–372.

Conroy, D. E. (2001). Fear of failure: An exemplar for social development research in sport. *Quest*, 53(2), 165–183.

Cuzzolino, M. P. (2019). Experiences of transformative awe and the "small self" in scientific learning and discovery (Publication No. 28220627) [Doctoral dissertation, Harvard University]. ProQuest Dissertations & Theses Global.

Cuzzolino, M. P. (2021). "The awe is in the process": The nature and impact of professional scientists' experiences of awe. *Science Education*, 105(4), 681–706.

BEGINNERS EYES

Kross, E., & Grossmann, I. (2012). Boosting wisdom: Distance from the self. *Journal of Experimental Psychology: General*, 141(1), 43–48. (On self-distancing and humility in reasoning.)

Porter, T., & Schumann, K. (2018). Intellectual humility and openness to the opposing view. *Self and Identity*, 17(2), 139–162.

CURIOSITY AS A MOTIVATIONAL AND COGNITIVE DRIVER

Cuzzolino, M. P. (2021). "The Awe is In the Process": The nature and impact of professional scientists' experiences of awe. *Science Education*, 105, 681–706.

Kashdan, T. B. et al. (2009). The engine of well-being. *Current Directions in Psychological Science*, 18(4), 174–179.

Loewenstein, G. (1994). The psychology of curiosity. *Psychological Bulletin*, 116(1), 75–98.

Stories and Quotes

Computer History Museum. (n.d.). Gordon Moore (In Memoriam). Computer History Museum, from https://computerhistory.org/profile/gordon-moore/ (accessed 23 April 2025).

Jonson, B. (1598). Every Man in His Humor.

Roth, B. (2015). *The Achievement Habit: Stop Wishing, Start Doing, and Take Command of Your Life*. HarperBusiness.

Shakespeare, W. (1600). *Much ado about nothing*.

Chapter 16 – Take Small Steps

Examples and Stories

Stanford eCorner (2023). Entrepreneurial Thought Leaders Seminar Series. https://ecorner.stanford.edu (accessed 23 April 2025).

Epilogue

NASA eClips. (2020, April 17). NASA eClips Best Practices: The 5E Instructional Model [Video]. YouTube. https://nasaeclips.arc.nasa.gov/videosingular/bestpractices/nasa-eclips-best-practices-the-5e-instructional-model-video (accessed 21 May 2025).

Some Sources of Moves and Inspiration

Amabile, T. M. (1996). Creativity in context: Update to the social psychology of creativity. Westview Press.

Amabile, T. M., & Kramer, S. J. (2011). The progress principle: Using small wins to ignite joy, engagement, and creativity at work. Harvard Business Review Press

Answell, M. (2020). Mastering design thinking: The systematic approach to improve considerably your business success rate. Independently published.

Ashton, K. (2015). How to fly a horse: The secret history of creation, invention, and discovery. Doubleday.

Bland, D. J., & Osterwalder, A. (2019). Testing business ideas: A field guide for rapid experimentation. Wiley.

Britos Cavagnaro, L. (2023). Experiments in reflection: How to see the present, reconsider the past, and shape the future. Ten Speed Press.

Brown, T. (2009). Change by design: How design thinking transforms organizations and inspires innovation. HarperBusiness.

Brown, T. (2019). Change by design: How design thinking transforms organizations and inspires innovation (revised & updated). HarperBusiness.

Burgess-Auburn, C. (2022). You need a manifesto: How to craft your convictions and put them to work. Ten Speed Press.

Burnett, B., & Evans, D. (2016). Designing your life: How to build a well-lived, joyful life (Kindle edition). Knopf.

Campbell, E. (2013). A few minutes of design: 52 activities to spark your creativity [Cards]. Chronicle Books.

Catmull, E., & Wallace, A. (2014). Creativity, Inc.: Overcoming the unseen forces that stand in the way of true inspiration. Random House.

Chivukula, S. S., & Gray, C. (2023). Universal methods of ethical design: 100 ways to become more ethically aware, responsible, and active in your design work. Rockport Universal.

Connor, A., & Irizarry, A. (2015). Discussing design: Improving communication and collaboration through critique. New Riders.

Cross, N. (2011). Design thinking: Understanding how designers think and work. Berg Publishers.

Csikszentmihalyi, M. (1997). Creativity: Flow and the psychology of discovery and invention. Harper Perennial.

Curedale, R. (2019). Design thinking process & methods (5th ed.). Design Community College, Inc.

Dieffenbacher, S. F., & Hüttinger, C. (2022). How to create innovation: The ultimate guide to proven strategies and business models to drive innovation and digital transformation. Wiley.

Doorley, S., & Carter, C. (2022). Assembling tomorrow: A guide to designing a thriving future from the Stanford d.school. Ten Speed Press.

Goel, A. (2022). Drawing on courage: Risks worth taking and stands worth making. Ten Speed Press.

Hanington, B., & Martin, B. (2019). Universal methods of design, expanded and revised: 125 ways to research complex problems, develop innovative ideas, and design effective solutions. Rockport Universal.

Hazenberg, W., & Middendorp, D. (2010). 75 tools for creative thinking: A fun card deck for creative inspiration [Cards]. BIS Publishers.

Heath, C., & Heath, D. (2007). Made to stick: Why some ideas survive and others die. Random House.

IDEO. (2003). IDEO method cards: 51 ways to inspire design [Cards]. IDEO.

IDEO.org. (2015). The field guide to human-centered design. IDEO.org.

Kabayadondo, Z., & Goldman, S. (2017). Taking design thinking to school: How the technology of design can transform teachers, learners, and classrooms. Routledge.

Kalbach, J. (2016). Mapping experiences: A complete guide to customer alignment through journeys, blueprints, and diagrams. O'Reilly Media.

Some Sources of Moves and Inspiration

Keeley, L., Pikkel, R., Quinn, B., & Walters, H. (2013). Ten types of innovation: The discipline of building breakthroughs. Wiley.

Kelley, T., & Kelley, D. (2013). Creative confidence: Unleashing the creative potential within us all. Crown Business.

Kelley, T., & Littman, J. (2005). The ten faces of innovation: IDEO's strategies for beating the devil's advocate and driving creativity throughout your organization. Currency/Doubleday.

Kleon, A. (2015). The steal like an artist journal: A notebook for creative kleptomaniacs [Diary]. Workman Publishing.

Knapp, J., Zeratsky, J., & Kowitz, B. (2016). Sprint: How to solve big problems and test new ideas in just five days. Simon & Schuster.

Krogerus, M., & Tschäppeler, R. (2012). The decision book: Fifty models for strategic thinking. W. W. Norton and Company.

Kumar, V. (2012). 101 design methods: A structured approach for driving innovation in your organization. Wiley.

Lee, D. (2018). Design thinking in the classroom: Easy-to-use teaching tools to foster creativity, encourage innovation, and unleash potential in every student. Ulysses Press.

Lewrick, M. (2022). Design thinking for business growth: How to design and scale business models and business ecosystems. Wiley.

Lewrick, M., Link, P., & Leifer, L. (2018). The design thinking playbook: Mindful digital transformation of teams, products, services, businesses and ecosystems. Wiley.

Lewrick, M., Link, P., & Leifer, L. (2020). The design thinking toolbox: A guide to mastering the most popular and valuable innovation methods. Wiley.

Liedtka, J., & Ogilvie, T. (2011). Designing for growth: A design thinking tool kit for managers. Columbia Business School Publishing.

Liedtka, J., Salzman, R., & Azer, D. (2017). Design thinking for the greater good: Innovation in the social sector. Columbia Business School Publishing.

Lockwood, T. (2010). Design thinking: Integrating innovation, customer experience, and brand value. Allworth Press.

Some Sources of Moves and Inspiration

LUMA Institute. (2012). Innovating for people handbook of human-centered design methods [Spiral-bound]. LUMA Institute.

LUMA Institute. (2012). Innovating for people: Human-centered design planning cards [Cards]. LUMA Institute.

Martin, R. L. (2009). The design of business: Why design thinking is the next competitive advantage. Harvard Business Press.

Mastrogiacomo, S., & Osterwalder, A. (2021). High-impact tools for teams: 5 tools to align team members, build trust, and get results fast. Wiley.

McKercher, K. A. (2020). Beyond sticky notes: Co-design for real: Mindsets, methods and movements. Beyond Sticky Notes.

Meadows, D. H., & Wright, D. (2008). Thinking in systems: A primer. Chelsea Green Publishing.

Michalko, M. (2006). Thinkertoys: A handbook of creative-thinking techniques (2nd ed.). Ten Speed Press.

Muratovski, G. (2016). Research for designers: A guide to methods and practice. SAGE Publications.

Noel, L.-A. (2023). Design social change: Take action, work toward equity, and challenge the status quo. Ten Speed Press.

O'Donnell Wicklund Pigozzi and Peterson, & Mau, B. (2010). The third teacher: 79 ways you can use design to transform teaching & learning. Abrams.

Osterwalder, A., Pigneur, Y., Bernarda, G., & Smith, A. (2014). Value proposition design: How to create products and services customers want. Wiley.

Penin, L. (2018). An introduction to service design: Designing the invisible. Bloomsbury Visual Arts.

Resnick, M. (2017). Lifelong kindergarten: Cultivating creativity through projects, passion, peers, and play. MIT Press.

Sawyer, K. (2007). Group genius: The creative power of collaboration. Basic Books.

Sawyer, R. K. (2012). Explaining creativity: The science of human innovation (2nd ed.). Oxford University Press.

Seelig, T. (2012). inGenius: A crash course on creativity. HarperOne.

Some Sources of Moves and Inspiration

Seelig, T. (2017). Creativity rules: Get ideas out of your head and into the world. HarperOne.

Sherwin, D. (2010). Creative workshop: 80 challenges to sharpen your design skills. HOW Books.

Small, A., & Schmutte, K. (2022). Navigating ambiguity: Creating opportunity in a world of unknowns. Ten Speed Press.

Sobomehin, O., & Seidel, S. (2022). Creative hustle: Blaze your own path and make work that matters. Ten Speed Press.

Spencer, J., & Juliani, A. J. (2016). Launch: Using design thinking to boost creativity and bring out the maker in every student. Dave Burgess Consulting, Inc.

Stein Greenberg, S. (2021). Creative acts for curious people: How to think, create, and lead in unconventional ways. Ten Speed Press.

Sutton, R. I. (2002). Weird ideas that work: 11 1/2 practices for promoting, managing, and sustaining innovation. Free Press.

Tomitsch, M., & Borthwick, M. (2018). Design. Think. Make. Break. Repeat (Kindle edition). BIS Publishers.

Vullings, H., & Heleven, N. (2020). Cross-industry innovation: 77 cross-industry cases, a structured approach to action, key tools. BIS Publishers.

Wise, S. (2022). Design for belonging: How to build inclusion and collaboration in your communities. Ten Speed Press.

Witthoft, S. (2023). This is a prototype: The curious craft of exploring new ideas. Ten Speed Press.

Some Sources of Moves and Inspiration

Index

Page numbers followed by *f* and *t* refer to figures and tables, respectively.

Dropbox, 115
Dweck, Carol, 42

E

Eastman Kodak Company, 7
Edison, Thomas, 121
Emotional processing, 222–223
Empathy:
    engaging with, 53–54
    for human connection, 125
Empathy Map, 186*t*–187*t*, 188*f*
Evidence, trusting, 113–115
Executive Function (Thrust), 20, 21*f*, 24,
    24*t*, 250
Expert interviews, 63
"Explore before explain," 244

F

Failure:
    embracing, 226–231
    expecting, 111
    kinds of, 227–228
Fidelity, managing, 118–121, 119*f*, 120*f*
50 Wild Ideas, 98
Financial viability, 149–151, 150*f*
Focus:
    on idea generation, 89, 92–94
    on people, not steps, 15–17
Ford, Henry, 95
Framestorming, 84–85
Framing Effect, 83
Framing problems, 82–86
Fueling innovation, 221–232, 221*f*
    embracing failure, 226–231
    harnessing ambiguity, 222–226

G

Gardner, Howard, 71
Gardner, Phyllis, 153
GE Healthcare, 79–81

Gell-Mann, Murray, 71
General Motors, 68
Generating ideas, 88–94
    avoiding judgment, 89, 90
    broadening your perspectives, 89,
        91–92
    building on other ideas, 89–91
    focusing on generation, 89, 92–94
    ideas as moves, 158–161
Get Move-ing, 241*f*–242*f*
Girls Who Code, 123–124, 128, 133–134
Goals, navigation toward, 32–35, 33*f*
Grameen Bank, 14
Grotzer, Tina, 209–210
Growth Mindset, 42

H

Haidt, Jonathan, 127
Hastings, Reed, 153
Heath, Chip, 127
Heath, Dan, 127
The High Line, New York, 145–146
Hindsight bias, 72
Historical moves, 172–176, 173*t*, 252
Holmes, Elizabeth, 153
Hopper, Grace, 95
"How do we?," 237
How Might We?, 188*t*–190*t*
Human Centered Design, 16, 81, 249
Human connection, creating, 125
Humility, 55, 89, 224, 227

I

Ideas Mindset, 45*f*, 47, 87–105
    brainstorming, 97–104
    defined, 251
    embracing wild ideas, 94–98, 96*f*
    50 Wild Ideas activity, 98
    generating ideas, 88–94
    metacognitive questions for, 216*t*
    "Yes, And!" activity, 91